METHODISM IN RUSSIA
AND THE BALTIC STATES

D0862872

METHODISM IN RUSSIA AND THE BALTIC STATES
HISTORY AND RENEWAL

S T KIMBROUGH, JR.

EDITOR

Abingdon Press/Nashville

METHODISM IN RUSSIA AND THE BALTIC STATES
HISTORY AND RENEWAL

Library of Congress Cataloging-in-Publication Data

Kimbrough, S. T., 1936–
    Methodism in Russia and the Baltic states: history and renewal/
S.T. Kimbrough.
        p.   cm.
    Includes bibliographical references and index.
    ISBN 0-687-00600-7 (alk. paper)
        1. Methodist Church—Soviet Union—History.   2. Soviet Union—
    Church history.   3. Baltic Sea Region—Religion—20th century.
    4. Missions—Soviet Union.   5. Methodists—Missions—History.
    I. Title.
    BX8310.S65K55   1995
    287'.0947—dc20
                                                                                95-33101
                                                                                CIP

Chapter 1 is a translation of a chapter (10) from *Geschichte des Methodismus* by John L. Nuelsen, published by Anker-Verlag in 1929. Used by permission.

Chapters 2, 3, 4, and 8 are reprinted articles published in *Methodist History*. Used by permission.

The articles in chapter 7 "The Development of the Estonian Methodist Church and Related Annual Conferences" by Martin Prikask and "Historical Vignettes of Estonian Methodist Congregations" by Jaan Puskay are reprinted and translated from The Estonian Christian Advocate, *Kristlik Kaitsja*, 8/9 (1933): 120-123 and 127-132. Used by permission.

The article "Methodism in the Soviet Union Since World War II" appears in chapter 9 and is taken from *The Asbury Theological Journal* (Spring 1991). Used by permission.

95 96 97 98 99 00 01 02 03 04 — 10 9 8 7 6 5 4 3 2 1

MANUFACTURED IN THE UNITED STATES OF AMERICA

This book is dedicated to the faithful and forgotten members, clergy, and missionaries of the Methodist and Evangelical Churches of the Baltic region, Russia/Siberia, and Manchuria, who gave their lives in love and service for others, Christ, and the church, no matter the cost. Through the following words of one of the founders of Methodism may they be called to constant memory.

Come, let us join our friends above
That have obtained the prize,
And on the eagle wings of love
To joys celestial rise;
Let all the saints terrestrial sing
With those to glory gone,
For all the servants of our King
In earth and heaven are one.

Ten thousand to their endless home
This solemn moment fly;
And we are to the margin come,
And we expect to die;
Ev'n now by faith we join our hands
With those that went before,
And greet the blood-besprinkled bands
On the eternal shore.

Charles Wesley*

*Funeral Hymns (1759), originally five stanzas. The two stanzas printed here consist of original stanza 1 and a composite of original stanzas 3 (lines 1-4) and 4 (lines 5-8).

CONTENTS

FOREWORD

When in 1990 congregations registered as United Methodist churches in some places in Russia, a new chapter began in the story of *Methodism in Russia and the Baltic States*. Methodism already had a rich and diverse history in the countries that once belonged to the Russian Empire and the former Soviet Union. The warmth of a personal witness to Jesus Christ, the spirit of community and togetherness in the congregation, the social consciousness that could not forget about the neighbor's need, and the open heart to all true Christian sisters and brothers, regardless of their church affiliation—this all had made an impact on Russia and her nations. The Bolshevik Revolution in 1917 and the following Soviet regime had made this extinct, except for the Methodist Church in Estonia, although Methodism survived in Vladivostok until 1922, and in Saint Petersburg and Manchuria until 1927. As a result, Methodists and others forgot about this important part of the history of Christ's church.

This book brings to light once again the story of Methodism in the countries that once were a part of the Russian Empire. It witnesses to the authenticity of this story, because some of the authors write out of their personal involvement as contemporary eyewitnesses and as members and leaders of the church who assumed responsibility for its ministry and growth.

What is even more important, their spirit is alive despite suffering and *extinction*. They have provided the roots, they have cultivated the soil for the renewal of Methodism in Russia. It has returned to Russia in various ways during the last few years: in a prayer meeting among Korean Christians in Moscow; in the bridge-building witness of the Rev. Dwight Ramsey to the city of Ekaterinburg; in the medical and community service of United Methodist missionary Chris Hena. It is significant that the first witness of a renewed Methodist Church in Russia was part of the ministry of United Methodism in Estonia through a young Russian, Vladislav Spektorov.

It was 1983 when a strange figure dropped into the United Methodist Church in Tallinn, Estonia: a young man, tall, with long hair dyed green in parts—not your usual churchgoer. This high school student was living uneasily in the system as it existed in the Soviet Union. He was a protester, a

11

dissenter. He was also a seeker. He was looking for a "truth" that could sustain him, unlike the tired propaganda and sloganeering of the Communist Party.

The church congregation was surprised to see him in their midst, but he was treated warmly and invited to sit down. When the sermon began the young man listened attentively. This was a new language. Yes, it was in his native Russian, but the *message* was new. These new ideas not only informed his mind but also touched his heart. Later he confessed: "This hour changed my life." He did not find just another "truth"; he found the love of Christ.

The United Methodist Church in Tallinn became the young man's new home. He took every opportunity to come and learn more about Christ, despite the fact that his hometown of Samara was more than a thousand miles away. He became a member of the youth fellowship and enrolled in a preparatory course for the ministry.

By the time this young man reached college the authorities had learned of his conversion to Christianity, a dangerous step in a Communist society. He was alternately threatened with expulsion, if he continued as a believer and promised a career leading to a professorship, if he renounced his faith. Despite the risks, he persevered with his dream of publicly evangelizing the people of his home city.

In every Soviet city there was an organization called "Knowledge," whose main purpose was to oppose Christianity and defend scientific atheism. But when *glasnost* and *perestroika* broke out under the Gorbachev regime, "Knowledge" replaced its lectures on atheism with Bible studies. But the only professors available were atheists, whose stilted perspective disappointed the enthusiastic crowd that showed up for the first lecture.

This young man, Vladislav Spektorov, volunteered to teach Bible studies. The crowd came back. He shared his faith in Jesus Christ and invited his hearers to believe. As a result, they started a United Methodist Church.

Today Spektorov is an ordained deacon in The United Methodist Church. His congregation in Samara has about five hundred members. The church offers daily food for pensioners, teaches the gospel in schools, works in hospitals, and recently started a youth program that reaches out to high schools and colleges with the love and good news of Jesus Christ. Who knows how many other "Vladislavs," with dyed hair and discontent in their hearts, he can touch with the way offered him—the way of Jesus Christ.

Bishop Rüdiger R. Minor
Eurasia Area, The United Methodist Church

PREFACE

Fascinating, interesting, and challenging are words that describe the material in *Methodism in Russia*.

These same terms also describe the excitement with which churches have enthusiastically responded to the new possibility of Christian mission in Russia and Eastern Europe during the last decade of the twentieth century.

The coming down of the wall in Berlin announced to the world a new day in East/West relationships. Immediately following this world-changing event, many church groups wanted to explore what might be done in mission within the lands where church work had been limited by the prevailing antireligious atmosphere for many decades.

In January of 1991, before the breakup of the Soviet Union, Dr. Randolph Nugent, the general secretary of the General Board of Global Ministries of The United Methodist Church, and I, as president of the Board, went to Moscow to talk with government officials, Russian Orthodox Church leaders, and social service agencies. Our visit to the cold, snow-covered streets of Moscow was in response to a call from people who believed that The United Methodist Church could help the people of Russia during a time of rapidly changing conditions. It was as if a new Macedonian call had been received to come over and work together for a better future. The reception we experienced was very warm compared to the weather.

A window of opportunity had been opened and a need expressed. Representatives of the government of the Soviet Union and the social service agencies were eager for humanitarian aid such as high vitamin content foods and medicines. The Russian Orthodox Church was interested in exploring a mutually beneficial relationship.

In the three years since the first contact was made in early 1991, thousands of people have been helped through the humanitarian aid made available by United Methodist people, and The United Methodist Church has supported the Russian Orthodox Church in its effort to move forward under the opportunities it now has under the new social conditions. In addition, a number of United Methodist churches have been organized, and an official presence has been established under the leadership of a bishop in Moscow.

In this book Dr. Kimbrough has drawn together significant records about United Methodist involvement in the lands of the former USSR, which provide a background of information not well known, if at all, by most persons in The United Methodist Church and other churches. What an exciting story of mission this collection of documents presents. We are in Dr. Kimbrough's debt for making it available to us. Some of the documents are presented here in English for the first time.

In addition to presenting the documents, which trace a century of mission activity, the author adds an up-to-date account of present activity of The United Methodist Church in countries of the former Soviet Union. This contemporary story presents both a challenge and an opportunity.

The whole Christian world is pleased that a time of new opportunity for improved relationships between the East and West is a reality of the last years of the twentieth century. Peace, cooperation, and goodwill do not happen without effort. The window for new relationships that we discovered on our exploratory visit in 1991 offers to us a challenge for Christian mission, friendship, and sharing that might help to make a different world in the future.

Bishop J. Woodrow Hearn, president,
Council of Bishops,
The United Methodist Church

Acknowledgments

First of all, I express deep gratitude to Dr. R. Bruce Weaver, coordinator of New Mission Development in the Commonwealth of Independent States, for having first posed an interpretive question regarding the current Russia Initiative of The United Methodist Church, which launched me on this journey. The journey could not have been made, however, without the invaluable support and counsel of Dr. Randolph Nugent, general secretary of the General Board of Global Ministries (GBGM), whose vision has inspired the current Russia Initiative. That vision was also shared and shaped by Bishop J. Woodrow Hearn, to whom I express appreciation for his introductory statement.

I am also indebted to the Rev. Robert J. Harman, deputy general secretary of the World Division of GBGM, for the reminder to *remember the forgotten* Evangelical Church missionaries, pastors, and laity of Latvia, and to Bishop Rüdiger Minor of the Eurasia Area of The United Methodist Church for the insights of contemporary United Methodist history in Russia. I am particularly grateful to Dr. Weaver and the Rev. Harman for making available personal correspondence and official documents of GBGM having to do with the current Russia Initiative.

There are numerous others who have provided valuable inspiration, information, and counsel in the process of the research for this volume, to whom deep appreciation is also expressed: the Rev. Kostas Burbulys, a former Lithuanian Methodist pastor living in the United States; Bishop Walter Klaiber of the *Evangelisch-methodistische* Church of Germany; the Rev. Richard Lupp, a former Lithuanian Methodist pastor living in Germany; the Rev. Helmut Nausner, superintendent of the Methodist Church in Vienna, Austria, for the special gift of a copy of Bishop John L. Nuelsen's book, *Geschichte des Methodismus;* Mrs. Marilyn Oden, author of *Land of Sickles and Crosses;* the Rev. Heigo Ritsbek, Estonian United Methodist pastor now residing in the United States; Bishop Franz W. Schaeffer, retired United Methodist bishop living in Zurich, Switzerland; the Rev. Wilhelm Volskis, senior pastor of St. John's United Methodist Church, Staunton, Virginia; Dr. Michel Weyer, lecturer in Church History at the *Theologisches Seminary of the Evangelisch-methodistische* Church in Reutlingen, Germany; the following staff members of GBGM: Dr. Kenneth R. Lutgen, Jr., associate general secretary of the United Methodist Committee on Relief (UMCOR); Ms. Cathie Lyons, associate general secretary of the Health and Welfare Ministries program department; Mr. Kelly E. Miller, former assistant general secretary for administration of UMCOR; Ms. Joyce D. Sohl, deputy general secretary of the Women's Division; Ms. Betty Thompson, retired director of public relations; Dr. James White, executive secretary for Europe; Ms. Wendy Whiteside of UMCOR; Dr. Rena M. Yocom, associate general secretary of the Mission Education and Cultivation Department of GBGM; and Dr. Charles Yrigoyen, Jr., general secretary of the General Commission on Archives and History of The United Methodist Church.

I am particularly grateful to the following persons for checking the manuscript for correct transliterated spellings of Lithuanian, Latvian, Estonian, and Russian words, personal and place names: the Rev. Kostas Burbulys (Lithuanian); the Rev. Konstantin Witt and the Rev. Heigo Ritsbek (Estonian); Mr. Gene Matthews (Korean); the Rev. Wilhelm Volskis and the Rev. Kristaps Caune (Latvian); Mrs. Galena V. Roraback (Russian); and Bishop Ole E. Borgen (Scandinavian languages.) The assistance of Bishop Hans Växby and Mr. Håkan Ekholm with the details of Swedish and Finnish Methodism was indispensable.

Constant thanks must be given for those who sowed some of the first seeds of "Methodist" mission renewal in the former Soviet Union: the Rev. Vladislav Spektorov, Mr. Chang Son Kum, Mr. Young Cheul Kvon, the Rev. Young Cheul Cho, the Rev. Dea Hee Kim, and the Rev. Dwight Ramsey.

I am particularly indebted to the heritage that Bishop John L. Nuelsen has bequeathed us, namely, his commitment to a Wesleyan holistic vision of Christian mission and evangelism, which opened avenues of transformation for Methodist outreach in Russia and the Baltic states during the 1920s and 1930s. His commitment was coupled with an indefatigable pen, which has left innumerable published and unpublished documents that have made the writing of this volume much more manageable than it might have been; however, thorough research of Bishop Nuelsen's correspondence and papers has yet to be undertaken. Perhaps these pages will inspire a young student of church history and/or missiology to take up this task.

Acknowledgments

To the hosts of scribes who have recorded missionary history and those who have published it, especially during the trying times of the Bolshevik Revolution and Soviet domination and through times of war and occupation by foreign troops, present and future generations will offer thanks and praise.

S T Kimbrough, Jr.

Introduction

The story of Methodism in Finland, the Baltic states, and Russia, and of the *Evangelische Gemeinschaft*[1] (Evangelical Church) in Latvia, is one of holistic mission where education, prayer, the inner witness of the Spirit, praising God in song, sound preaching of the Word, sacramental life, and social outreach were and are mutual imperatives. In the pages that follow, one reads the testimony to the implementation of such imperatives by the faithful communities of those who stood and those who stand in the Wesleyan tradition.

Their fight against illiteracy through the building of schools and the establishment of Sunday schools, the building of hospitals and orphanages, the development of skills to enable employment in societies and cultures riddled with unemployment and few job opportunities, and the witness to the transforming power of God individually and corporately, testify to the implementation of a holistic Wesleyan outreach. It was not through failure that these missionary efforts were eventually discontinued. To the contrary, they were extremely effective in the areas reached. However, the antireligious posture resulting from the Bolshevik Revolution and the rise of Communism, clerical misunderstandings, the exercise of episcopal power, and institutional survival tactics brought an end to a formal missionary thrust in the countries of the former Russian Empire and Soviet Union. Even so, there were continued efforts to keep alive the work begun by missionaries, indigenous pastors, and laity. Some of these resulted in surviving Christian communities identified as "Methodist" in Estonia and Ukraine.

It should be noted that the church community initiated in Latvia by the *Evangelische Gemeinschaft* endured as a formal religious community longer than the Methodist communities in Russia and Manchuria, with the exception of Estonia and Ukraine. The Methodist congregations in Lithuania and Latvia survived into the 1940s, but finally the members and clergy were forced by the Soviets to flee or merge with other denominations, for example, Lutheran. Many, of course, did not survive and suffered persecution, imprisonment, and death. German Lithuanians were repatriated by Adolf Hitler. Most Lithuanian Methodists were of German origin.

For years one could but stand in awe, and still must do so, of those who in spite of oppression remained loyal to their faith, endured the hardest of times, and taught those of us who equate freedom of mobility with freedom itself that there is an inner freedom that surpasses all else, indeed transcends all human barriers.

I remember well the year 1978, when I taught biblical studies and Hebrew as a guest faculty member of the M. Flavius Illiricus Theological Faculty in Zagreb, Yugoslavia. Although Yugoslavia was certainly the most progressive of the Communist states at the time and provided mobility to its population in ways others did not, the government still had subtle ways of dealing with the religious community, which made life difficult. For example, this theological school, which had been newly founded by Lutherans, Methodists, and Baptists of Yugoslavia, essentially had no full-time local students. It was impossible to devote all of one's time to school, for employment was mandatory. Therefore, the study program covered seven years because one had to be employed full time, and those who wished to attend theological school had to do so outside their working hours. This was, of course, mild and subtle oppression compared to the open persecution of Christians and other religious groups in many countries of the then so-called "east block."

This volume brings together for the first time a collection of previously published articles, newly written chapters, and unpublished materials, that address the Methodist and Evangelical Churches in Finland, the Baltic states, and some of the countries of the now designated Commonwealth of Independent States (CIS), as well as part of Manchuria along the border with Siberia. Some of the material appears here in the author/editor's English translation for the first time. The insights to be gleaned from these pages are extremely important for church history and the history of missions, ecumenical theology/studies, political science, and the contemporary mission of the church. The subsequent chapters are filled with facts not widely known, with vision, inspiration, and self-criticism, which shall continue to renew those who seek to be faithful to Christ and the church in its outreach and witness wherever they are.

In the chapters that follow, one sees that the early Methodist and Evangelical Church work in northeastern Europe, which began in the late nineteenth century, moved with authentic witness into Finland, Lithuania, Latvia, Estonia, Russia proper, Siberia, and Manchuria. At times church leadership stood in the way of the missions by denying funding and inhibiting the work of local and indigenous leadership. On the whole, however, those involved in these missional activities held high the Wesleyan spirit of holistic outreach, which, in living out Christ's mandate of love, bypasses no human need. It is from this sense of Wesleyan spirituality that the church today may draw great strength.

Chapter 1 is a summary of the beginnings of Methodism in Finland, Russia, and the Baltic states, and is an English translation of a portion of chapter 10 from Bishop John L. Nuelsen's (et al.) *Geschichte des Methodismus* (1929). Through his years of involvement with Methodism in Central Europe and its work in Russia and the Baltic region, Nuelsen brings unique insight to the history and movements of governments, churches, and missions from the turn of the century to 1929. The translation is faithful to Nuelsen's record of many historical developments in the present tense, though clearly the reader will understand them in the past tense.

The next three chapters originally appeared in *Methodist History*. Chapter 2 focuses on the role of Dr. George A. Simons and the beginnings of Methodism in Russia. Donald Carl Malone provides an excellent treatment of the intriguing and complex story of Methodism's early relationships to the monarchal government, to the provisional government after the Bolshevik Revolution, and to the Russian Orthodox Church. Chapter 3 offers a glimpse into Methodism in Saint Petersburg, particularly through the records of the *Khristianski Pobornik*, a Russian *Christian Advocate*, launched by Dr. George A. Simons. Chapter 4 tells the story of the mission of the Methodist Episcopal Church, South, in Siberia and Manchuria, which was begun in 1920 and ended in 1927. At its height it had three flourishing departments: Korean, Chinese, and Russian.

Chapter 5 covers an important but often forgotten part of Methodism's story in the Baltics, namely, that of the missions of the Evangelical Church in Latvia. Very little serious research has been done on this significant outreach in the Baltic states, which originated primarily through the North Germany Conference of that denomination. Both German and American mission publications of the Evangelical Church have been examined for information regarding the Latvian mission, and the results are recorded here.

Chapter 6 addresses a neglected subject: the history and outreach of Methodism in Lithuania and Latvia. Some important corrections to previously written histories about the origin of Methodism in these countries is offered. One document that traces the origin of Methodism in Lithuania is published here for the first time. The Baltic and Slavic Mission Conference, itself a miracle of mission and evangelism, is examined as an inclusive mixture of Wesleyan and biblical traditions with strong interests in Christian unity and indigenous ministry.

There follow three chapters on Methodism in Estonia: its birth, its persecution, its transition to United Methodism, and its growth and survival to the present. Chapter 7 includes two articles originally published in a 1925 issue of the Estonian *Kristlik Kaitsja (Christian Advocate):* (1) "The Development of the Estonian Methodist Church and Related Annual Conferences," by Martin Prikask, who served for a number of years as the district superintendent of the Estonian District of the Baltic and Slavic Missionary Conference, and was later executed by the Soviets; and (2) "Historical Vignettes of Estonian Methodism," by Jaan Puskay, an Estonian Methodist pastor. The former discusses the beginnings of Methodism in Estonia and the relationships to the various annual and mission conferences of the region. The latter is a brief summary of the growth of Estonian Methodist congregations. Neither article is written as an exercise in historical science, but each provides valuable insight into the firsthand experience of the emerging congregations of Estonia, what was effective and ineffective in its mission. The English translation of the two articles is by Maarit Vaga.

Chapter 8, which first appeared in *Methodist History,* was written by Estonian United Methodist, the Rev. Heigo Ritsbek, who has devoted considerable study to Methodism's birth and continuing outreach in Estonia. The chapter tells the story of Estonian Methodism's persecution and survival during the Soviet occupation from 1940 to 1941. Chapter 9 originally appeared in the *Asbury Theological Journal* and is printed here in an abridged edition. It explores the work of Methodism in Estonia from World War II to the present.

In conclusion, chapter 10 reviews the early beginnings of the Methodist movement in countries of the former Soviet Union. It then turns to a chronicle of the outreach of United Methodism in the Baltic states and Russia since 1990. Also discussed in the chapter are issues related to United Methodist and Russian Orthodox cooperative ministries, the rebirth of Methodism in Latvia and Lithuania, and United Methodism's current work with hospitals in Kazakhstan. A brief statement regarding the missionary work of the Korean Methodist Church in countries of the Commonwealth of Independent States is also included. Finally, some observations are made about the future of United Methodist and Russian Orthodox dialogue and the future of mission and evangelism from a Wesleyan perspective.

Finally, it is important to remember in reading this volume that matters of national identity cannot clearly be defined in nineteenth and twentieth century European history merely by ethnic, linguistic, religious, political, and geographical boundaries. Political domination has fluctuated tremendously, and national borders have been constantly displaced by war and persecution.

Therefore, it is somewhat ambiguous and arbitrary to speak of *Methodism in Russia,* for Russia's boundaries have been fluid and its population, under the old domination, has been a patchwork of nations, peoples, languages, religions, and cultures. *Methodism in Russia* here, however, is intended to designate the work of The Methodist Episcopal Church, The Methodist Episcopal Church, South, The German Methodist Church, The Evangelical Church *(Evangelische Gemeinschaft)*, and The United Methodist Church among Russian-speaking people and among other nationalities who lived under the reign of the old Russian Empire and the former Soviet Union. The history reviewed in this volume awakens anew the hope of all who longed and still long to share the witness of the gospel in the spirit of the Wesleys with the people of Russia and of other republics of the former Soviet Union.

Note that opening and closing brackets around material in footnotes or texts of previously published articles indicate the editor's clarifications and occasional amplifications.

S T Kimbrough, Jr.
Executive Secretary of Mission Evangelism
General Board of Global Ministries
The United Methodist Church

Map of the Baltic states, regions of Russia, and China (Manchuria) in which Methodism was begun in the late nineteenth and early twentieth centuries.

★ **Contemporary capital cities** and locations of Methodist congregations before World War II, except Moscow. All currently have United Methodist congregations, except Vilnius. (St. Petersburg was the capital of Russia in the tsarist period.)

● **Cities in which Methodist work was located.** (Not all locations are shown.) All currently have United Methodist congregations except those in Lithuania.

O **Cities of geographical reference**

RUSSIA

CHINA (Manchuria)
●Harbin

Vladivostok

KOREA Sea of Japan

East China Sea

JAPAN

FINLAND
Vaasa
Gulf of Bothnia
Helsinki
St. Petersburg
Tallinn
ESTONIA
Baltic Sea
Riga ★ LATVIA
Liepaja
LITHUANIA
Kaunas Vilnius
Kybartai
Moscow ⊛
RUSSIA
BELARUS
Kiev
UKRAINE
Kaminica Uzhgorod
Odessa
Black Sea

CHAPTER 1

The Methodist Church in Finland, Russia, and the Baltic States[1] 1880–1928

John L. Nuelsen, Theophil Mann, J. J. Sommer
English translation: S T Kimbrough, Jr.

The Methodist Church in Northeastern Europe

Christianity, the Reformation, and Methodism came to the Baltic countries and Finland from the south and west, (i.e., from Germany and Sweden), and from these countries to Russia.

Finland

The Finnish tribes were led to Christianity in the twelfth and thirteenth centuries by the Roman Catholic Church of Sweden and the Greek Catholic Church of Russia. Both countries vied for the political domination of Finland. This resulted in the Swedes settling in the west and south of the country and the Russians in the east. At the time of Swedish domination the Reformation came to Finland, whose reformer was Michael Agricola, a student of Luther. The Lutheran Church became so deeply rooted in Finland that even Russia, which later dominated Finland, could not touch it, except at one point: The transfer of membership to the Greek Catholic Church was permitted. According to earlier law it was forbidden to leave the Lutheran Church. Finland achieved religious freedom only in the last third of the nineteenth century, in that from 1889 the transfer to Protestant religious communities by adults was permitted, and in 1909 general religious freedom was introduced. Finland had been affected by Pietism in the eighteenth century. However, significant religious movements first began in the nineteenth century and still have an impact: Pietism more in the east, the so-called new Lutheran direction in the southwest, and the followers of the great atonement preacher Laestadius in the north.

The appearance of Methodism in Finland, as well as in Germany and in other northern countries, is a result of the emigration of Finnish people to other countries, especially the United States.[2] In 1866 two brothers, Wilhelm and Gustav Bärnlund, arrived in Finland and settled in their home city of Kristinestad. They had been in America for many years and were converted through the work of Pastor Hedström on the Bethel ship *John Wesley* in New York. They felt the need to witness for Jesus in their homeland. As a result, many people were awakened and experienced their Savior. There followed a widespread awakening, in part because of the urgent cry of poor sinners for grace, and in part because of the storm of persecution that the enemies of godly matters created.

In 1870 and 1874, Gustav Bärnlund traveled to Sweden to request that the conference there send a pastor to Finland, because he wished to return to America. The rapid development and spreading of the work in Sweden, however, made it impossible to fulfill the request at the time. As two Swedish lay preachers, however, heard the Macedonian call from Finland and saw the burdened and sinful life of many in Finland, they left their homeland, inspired by love and compassion, and went to Finland without money and friends to proclaim the joyous message and salvation in Christ. One of the lay preachers was named Karl Lindborg. He went first to Vaasa in 1880 where a great awakening took place around the new year, 1881. Lindborg received the new converts and traveled much throughout the country. After traveling some 100 kilometers on foot, he arrived in Kristinestad, where he found the small group that Bärnlund had gathered. They had waited fifteen years for a preacher, and now their prayer had been heard and the messenger of God had arrived. Full of joy and gratitude, Lindborg prepared a building for a place of worship and gave it to the small congregation, which it dedicated in 1882 as the first chapel in Finland. This house of God became a holy place for many souls.

The other Swedish lay preacher was C. Martinsén from Stockholm, who arrived in Finland some years after Lindborg. He settled in Kotka, rented a hall there, and preached twice every Sunday to very attentive listeners.

Lindborg established a large district, which extended from Kristinestad in the south to Åbo, the Åland island, and in the north to Gamlakarleby, and covered some 420 kilometers; and he accepted an invitation to Saint Petersburg where some ten thousand Swedes lived at the time. In 1881 and 1882, Lindborg made two trips to Sweden to request additional help from the conference, but it was not until 1883 that the request could be fulfilled and preacher Wagnsson could be sent to Vaasa. At this time congregations were established in Gamlakarleby, Vaasa, and Kristinestad, with two Sunday schools and fifty students. In 1884, B. A. Carlson of Sweden was sent to Helsinki, the capital of Finland, and one year later Finland was made into a special district, whereas it had previously belonged to the Stockholm District. Carlson, the district superintendent, exercised a strong influence. Wherever he went people of all circumstances streamed to hear him. In 1885 the district had three preachers and 174 members. Of these sixty-five were in Helsingfors.

On November 7, 1884, a congregation was founded in Helsingfors. In 1907 a beautiful church with five hundred seats was built for the Swedish congregation. The work gradually expanded to the surrounding cities of Grankulla and Malm, and even farther into the countryside. Previously, in 1904, Pastor Karl Hurtig was assigned to Helsinki, and he served for more than twenty years[3] as a superb speaker and administrator of the congregation. Through his work the orphanage in Grankulla, housing seventy-two children, came into being. His importance is particularly strong since the civil war and liberation of 1918.

Larger congregations grew also in Vaasa (1881), Åbo (1886), Ekenäs (1886), Viborg (1892), and Borgå (1906)[4], and among the Swedish-speaking population in the urban and rural areas to Uleåborg in the north.

The work was also extended, however, to purely Finnish regions. In 1887, Karl Lindborg was sent to Björneborg, where primarily Finnish was spoken. Although he had to speak at first through a translator, the Lord brought the Word for the conversion of many souls. In the same year the mission received its first Finnish preacher, J. W. Häggman. The first preaching mission in Finland was held from November 16 to 18, 1886, in Vaasa. The work had spread widely, and everywhere the preaching was blessed with success. Nevertheless, very few joined the congregations, because many of the poor people could not give up the honor and advantages of membership in the state church.

The clergy and the state officials wanted to inhibit our work, and in 1885 Carlson was forbidden to deliver any religious speeches in Helsinki. However, the bishop in Borgå, Alopaeus, was a kind and truly Christian man who displayed much understanding for the new movement. On the whole, it should be noted that both the people and the officials demonstrated more and more understanding and goodwill toward our work.

In 1891 the church received the right of cooperation and was recognized by the government. At the beginning of 1923, a new law of religious freedom went into effect. According to the new law, people who did not belong to the state church did not have to pay tax for same and possessed full civil rights.

In 1892, Bishop Joyce organized the Finland and Saint Petersburg Mission. The work consisted of 9 preachers, 4 churches, 8 congregations, and 592 members. Preacher Roth served as superintendent, while Carlson returned to Sweden after seven years of effective work in Finland. After one year Roth was replaced by N. J. Rosén and the work was divided into three districts.

One of the greatest difficulties of the work was created by the two languages in Finland and the corresponding racial differences. The Swedes generally could not preach in Finnish, nor the Finns in Swedish. Hence, both Swedish and Finnish work developed. Nevertheless, in 1903 both were organized into a Mission Conference and divided into two districts: one Swedish and one Finnish. The conference had 14 preachers, 7 churches, 1,048 members, 21 Sunday schools, 67 teachers, and 1,386 Sunday school students. The first conference was held in 1904 in Hangö, and in 1911 the work was recognized as an annual conference. The practical difficulties, however, were so great that it appeared more effective to divide the conference. Hence, in 1923 the Finnish work was organized as Finland's Annual Conference and the Swedish as Finland's Swedish Mission Conference. The church in Finland was not completely divided in this way, for a common executive and a common pension fund were retained, and above all there remained much inner cooperation.

District Superintendent Häggman wrote:

> During the last year [1904] there have been many heroic acts of sacrifice. For example, one preacher and his wife had no bread, meat or fish to eat for two days. They lived from berries which they picked in the woods. They had spent their last penny for rental of the meeting hall and did not want to acquire any debt. Other preachers never have butter on the table; they have seldom more than dry rye bread to eat. The first congregation in Viborg dedicated its church on August 21, 1904. It has 300 seats and on the day of dedication it was completely filled.

One year later Häggman wrote:

> The possibilities for our work are marvelous. In St. Petersburg and environs we now have wide open doors for the gospel and we also have men who [can] preach. We only lack the money for the work. Today it would be possible to proclaim the gospel by the baptized in Russia's capital in Russian, Finnish and Swedish to salvation-hungry hearers, but we lack the means to do so. Seven students have completed their studies in our Preaching Seminar, a few of whom are gifted, powerful preachers. Everywhere they go an awakening follows. All seven worked for six months without receiving a penny of salary, and we do not know whether we can give them anything during the next year.

To understand these reports one must remember that the years 1904 and 1905 were the difficult war and revolution years in Russia. These events may have led to the aforementioned circumstances. On October 17, 1905, the tsar of Russia gave his country a constitution that guaranteed the people religious freedom.

In Hangö, a fresh air resort, a wealthy Russian woman donated a lovely chapel to the mission. People of the Greek Catholic Church live on the eastern border of Finland and their language is Finnish; however, their worship services are conducted in Russian, or more properly, in the Old Slavic Church language, which the Russians themselves do not understand. However, they have no schools for the language and no Bibles. The Russian priests do not allow them to read Finnish Bibles, and they cannot understand Russian. During the summer of 1907, the teacher of the theological seminary in Helsinki took a mission trip to these poor folk during his vacation. He found unbelievable ignorance but also a great desire for the Word of God among these mistreated people. As a reward for this sacrificial work, he had to spend a few days of his vacation in jail because he had preached the gospel. As he was led away, an elderly woman said to him with a choking voice, "Oh, if you could but come once a year!" This is the mission field of the Mission Conference in Finland, but an even greater one lies in the spacious land of Russia.

For a long time (since 1893) the Finnish work had its primary location in Tammerfors, where a lovely place of worship was dedicated in 1923. The spiritual movement in east Finland is very interesting. In 1921 District Superintendent K. F. Holmström wrote the following about it:

During the year a new congregation in the Andrea Parish in east Finland was organized and we have decided to give it the name The Methodist Congregation of Vuoksenlaakso [Vuoksen Valley]. Many parishes lie in this valley and the interest in our church is strong. Already nine years previously people from this area came with the request that we begin our work there and the district superintendent Häggman also made a trip there and preached. Due to the lack of preachers, however, we were not able to initiate work in Vuoksenlaakso. In the fall of the previous year they asked us once again for a visit and on December 27 Dr. Wirtanen of Viborg traveled to the valley and had the opportunity to preach in a number of villages before large crowds. On January 11 a group of four persons visited Helsinki, in order to request that we undertake regular activity in Vuoksenlaakso. Somewhat earlier I was informed through a report of a gathering there, that the believers yearned for a spiritual community and hence had turned to The Methodist Church with the request to be permitted to begin a Methodist congregation there; and, if this request should be granted, they wanted to build and pay for a church. The land for it was already promised gratis. With the visit of the group we decided in the name of the Lord to undertake regular work in Vuoksenlaakso.

I assigned Dr. Wirtanen, along with his responsibility for the congregation in Viborg, to visit Vuoksenlaakso at least once a month until the Annual Conference. He did so and I also made two visits and Brothers Häggmann, Rosén and Hyvärinen each made one.

The church, which is now being built, is located on a commanding hill and has over 500 seats. On January 21 the first members were received and to date 382 are probationary members and 173 have been received as members. Many have made the request to withdraw from the state church. At present we preach in five different villages; however, we have been invited to many other places and it will be possible to visit them as soon as we have a preacher specifically for this area.

The church was dedicated in 1922, and in the following year the last undivided Finnish Annual Conference was held there. The congregation at that time had 686 members and probationary members. Something similar to the events in Vuoksenlaakso took place during recent years in Säkkijärvi, but this work is still in the beginning stage. The Finnish work is now well organized. The foundational period is passed, and one looks with hope to the future. In 1926 there were 210 new probationary members. The total number of probationary members for 1926 was 736, and there were 1,518 members, 2,489 Sunday school students, 780 members of the youth organization and 416 youth departments, 30 preachers, and 14 lay preachers. Twelve churches have a value of 800,000 Finnish marks (ca. 80,000 German marks). The Swedish work during the same year reported 1,116 members and 105 probationary members, 12 preachers and 14 lay preachers, and 26 Sunday schools with 2,153 students. One must remember, however, that within a population of 2.5 million in Finland, only 300,000 are Swedish.[5]

The Swedish preachers are either educated originally for the work in Sweden or they are sent from Finland to the Swedish theological school and then return to work in their homeland. Only a few have received their education in Finland. For the work in Finland a school was founded in 1897 by J. W. Häggman, who studied theology at Boston University and until now has been the director of the school. Since the school's beginning, approximately sixty students have been taught there, at first in Tammerfors, and from 1907 onward in Helsinki.

To communicate information about his work, in 1881–82 R. J. Lindborg issued a publication called *Finska Evangelisten (The Finnish Evangelist)*. In 1886 B. A. Carlson began the publication *Nya Budbäraren (The New Messenger)*, which served the Swedish work as well. Beginning in September 1893, the Finnish *Rauhan Sanomia (The Message of Peace)* also was published, along with a children's paper, *Lasten Ystävä (The Children's Friend)*. At the same time the basis for a Finnish publishing house was laid, which brought out a Finnish edition of Wesley's sermons, a hymn book, the *Discipline* of the church, and various smaller publications.

A youth organization was established in 1893: now there are two, one Finnish and another Swedish. Along with the contribution to the general mission fund, the Tswikiro Mission Station in Rhodesia was designated "Finland's Lighthouse in Africa." In addition, a department of the Women's Missionary Society worked to educate women missionaries. Since 1881 a Seaman's mission has been opened in Kotka, and this work was turned over to our church some twenty-five years ago. There is also a small diaconal work, which has existed since 1907. Orphanages have been built, not only as requested in Helsinki, but also in Epilä, Viborg, Hangö, and Jakobstad. Also, a home for the elderly has been functioning in Åbo since 1922.

In this manner, the work of saving souls, nurturing spiritual growth, and expressing love has been going on in Finland for many years. One did not want to tear down anything that others had built, but instead to work with other Christians to fulfill the work of God, as one received the call of God. One did not wish to tear apart but to promote common effort.

Russia

In the eyes of western Europeans old Russia stands as a land of absolutism in both politics and the church, because for centuries it has banned to Siberia its political reformers and revolutionaries, as well as its evangelically minded and others who opposed the state church. Still, in the old Russian Empire there lived some ninety million Orthodox, ten million Roman Catholics, four million Lutherans *(Evangelisch)*, and more than five million Jews. In spite of the persecutions, or perhaps because of them, there were a large number of so-called sects from the *Starovjerzy* or Old Believers, who because of church/ritual reform had left the church and joined the more evangelically oriented Moravians, Baptists, or more exotic groups. The Methodists seem to be one of the last to begin missionary outreach in Russia, where, since the Edict of Toleration of Nicholas II in 1905, religious minorities received the right to exist. Methodism came from Finland directly to Saint Petersburg and from Germany to Lithuania and from there to the Baltic provinces when they were still a part of Russia. Now these countries are independent countries, and we distinguish the Baltic-Slavic Missionary Conference from the Russian Mission. It is to the latter that we now turn.

Pastor B. A. Carlson has made clear that his plan from the beginning was concerned more with Russia than with Finland. In April of 1888 he received a warm invitation to come to Saint Petersburg (Leningrad), but he could not go due to lack of time and money. He replied, "Now is the proper time to begin a mission here."

In May of 1889, however, we find Carlson in the Russian capital. He preached twice at the location of the Temperance Union and twice elsewhere with friends of that organization. From that time on he began a monthly evangelization trip to Saint Petersburg, and in August, during the time when Bishop C. H. Fowler was there, he rented a meeting hall and held gatherings, which were greatly blessed. In November a small Methodist congregation was organized with seven members. One of the members, H. K. Ridderström, became a local preacher and was assigned to the congregation in Carlson's absence. In 1890 there were eleven members in Saint Petersburg. Nevertheless, many obstacles made the work difficult. No announcements of the times of worship were permitted, and the sermons had to be translated. In 1893 one could report, however, that many souls had come to faith, especially among the Finnish-speaking population. During the next year the district superintendent reported again many converts: fourteen members were received, and some forty friends of the mission supported it. The difficulties, however, were not diminished. In 1924 there were twenty members. Gatherings were held in private homes under the direction of the local preacher, K. Strandroos, who reached out particularly to the Swedish-speaking foreigners.

In 1907 a large step forward was made in the Russian work when Bishop Burt assigned a young pastor, Dr. George A. Simons, to direct the work in Saint Petersburg and in the rest of Russia. On October 10 he arrived in Saint Petersburg and began the work with Strandroos and Pastor Hjalmar Salmi as an assistant. The latter could preach in Swedish, Finnish, and Russian, and the number of hearers became larger and larger. Police were often present and wrote down the sermons, but the authorities made no hindrances to the work. Invitation cards were distributed, and one could now announce meetings in the newspapers.

In a village near Saint Petersburg, an elderly religious man had prayed for fourteen years that the Lord would lead an evangelist to his and the neighboring village. One year after this man's death, H. Salmi arrived there and held the first gathering in the house of the man who had prayed so long. That man's two sons were the first who were converted, and afterwards they became ardent workers in the Sunday school and youth group, which Salmi founded. An awakening spread through the village and many were converted to God.

Also in southern Russia the Methodists have the possibility of a hopeful field of work. In October of 1908, Pastors Simons and Durdis visited the conference of *Molokanen* (milk drinkers). These are sincere Bible Christians, who are often called southern Russia's Methodists. Their president, S. D. Sacharoff, was a member of the Duma.

The first Sunday in November of 1908 will remain a significant day in the history of Russian Methodism, because on that day the Bethany Diaconal Home in Saint Petersburg was opened. Sister Anna Eklund, who received her education at the Bethany Society in Hamburg and Frankfurt am Main, is the director.

The energetic Bishop Burt was very concerned that preachers be educated for Russia. With the exception of a few preachers who were sent from Germany to Russia, there were candidates for the Russian work in Berea, Ohio (USA), in Uppsala (Sweden), and also in the Alliance Bible School of Dr. Jellinghaus in Berlin.

Beginning in January of 1908, Pastor Simons issued a quarterly newsletter in English about Methodism in Russia, in order to awaken interest throughout Europe and America for the work in Russia, and also to receive financial assistance. Seldom have the Methodists undertaken a mission with such energy and conviction as the work in Russia, and nowhere were the signs of hope greater than in this country.

In 1909 the church in Russia was legalized, and in 1911 the work there was organized as its own mission. Without question, the Revolution had changed much in this vast country, and also our work was initially hindered. Nevertheless, Sister Anna Eklund in Saint Petersburg could continue to work as a messenger of compassion. The following is the report of Pastor Oskar Poeld in Leningrad on the occasion of Eklund's sixtieth birthday. It is included here for the light it sheds on church life in Russia.

May 25, 1927 begins the sixtieth year of the Russian Methodist Church's diaconal heroine and leader, Sister Anna Eklund. The Christ's Church of the Methodists in Leningrad had extraordinary joy in sponsoring this celebration to honor its special member. The altar was richly decorated with flowers. In the evening there was a celebrative worship service with a church concert. Many telegrams and letters were received from all of the countries with which Sister Anna is in contact: primarily from America, Germany, Finland, Sweden and the Baltic countries.

Bishop J. L. Nuelsen congratulated Sister Anna by letter and telegram. Many leading persons and coworkers of our church from various countries, thanks to the great trust which Sister Anna enjoys with the Soviet government, have visited the United Soviet Republic of Russia and have evoked great interest in the work of evangelization in Russia during this period.

Our valued leader and dear Sister Anna can look back upon a rich and blessed life. Since her training at the Hospital of the Bethany Society in Frankfurt am Main, Sister Anna has now been active in diaconal work for thirty-five years. She served two years ago as the delegate from Russia of the middle European Central Conference of the Methodist Church, and was awarded the Jubilee Cross of the Bethany Society, an honor for twenty-five years of extraordinary service, at a beautiful ceremony in Frankfurt.

Sister Anna has been working in Russia for nineteen years and for the last nine years (1918-1927) without the usual, constant presence of a supervising American Superintendent. The first ten years (1908-1918) were under the leadership of our Superintendent Dr. G. A. Simons, who was constantly in Russia and is now directing the work of the Methodist Church in the Baltic States with rich blessings.

In spite of the complicated situation of the church today in Russia and the particularly difficult financial conditions of the Methodist Mission during the last three years, with the help of God Sister Anna has been able to maintain the work and the church and to bring the work forward: one can note that there are now forty preaching stations today in Russia. As representative of the Methodist Church in Russia, Sister Anna is a wise and dear mother for the young preachers and sisters, who effectively work in our congregations and among the Russian people and are all sons and daughters of this great Russia. At the same time under Sister Anna's leadership the blessed children's work was continued and in the course of these years one can note especially joyous successes.

During these years the old church [Orthodox] in Russia became very divided. One part, the "Living Church,"[6] wanted to come into a relationship with our church. For political reasons this could not be fulfilled. One can imagine, however, that through such movements, approaches to the free churches of western Europe, from the standpoint of the Russian Orthodox Church as well as from that of the younger offshoots, would be made somewhat easier. Also the Russian officials must abandon their aversion to Christian work. In this regard our bishops have certainly done much. It was primarily Bishop Nuelsen, who, through his untiring efforts, persuaded the Soviet government to permit the printing of an edition of the Bible, the so-called Peoples' Bible, in the government printing shop in Leningrad (1926).

The words of Bishop Burt at the annual conference in Tammerfors can still be an inspiration to Methodists and other Christians: "The greatest thing that we can do for world peace is to convert Russia to the true religion of Christ."[7]

Baltic States

For centuries the Baltic states have been riddled with political and religious battles. The land where the Finnish tribes lived was Christianized and colonized by the Germans. The Reformation came very early from Germany to this area, which Germans, Poles, Swedes, and Russians sought to dominate. Bound to this political struggle for domination were the struggles of the churches: Roman Catholic and Russian Orthodox against Lutheran. From the beginning of the eighteenth century to the end of the

World War, Russia ruled, and the Baltic states were the Russian Baltic Sea provinces. From the middle of the eighteenth century well into the nineteenth century, when nationalism was dominant in the Baltic churches, the Moravians had a very effective work there. Toward the middle of the nineteenth century their influence diminished greatly due to the new awakening in the life of the state church. It was at this time that the Baptists began to gain ground there.

The work of the Methodist Church in the Baltic states began at the turn of the century. It was brought into being through a circle of people of German origin who had transformed an awakening in the 1890s into a Christian community, and who sought a relationship to an active church community. At first they had business connections with the bookstore of the German Methodist Church in Bremen, but around 1900 they established a connection with the Methodist congregation in Königsberg and finally set up their own congregational district with the primary stations being Kaunas and Virbalis/Kybartai,[8] which belonged to the annual conference in northern Germany until 1907. Brave lay preachers such as Karl Pieper from Kaunas performed the major work during the first years until Pastor G. Durdis was assigned the leadership of the work in Kaunas and the surrounding area. The chapel in Virbalis/Kybartai, which was dedicated in 1909, was the first Methodist house of worship on the soil of the old Russian Empire. The church in Kaunas was built in 1910 and dedicated in January 1911.

In 1907 the work was separated from the Northeast German Conference and became related to the already existing Russian work of the Methodist Church, under the direction of Superintendent George A. Simons. Now Methodist evangelization spread to other parts of the Baltic states, but it was no longer under the Germans. Instead it was under the Estonians, Latvians, Lithuanians, and Russians. Hence, in 1909 there was a very effective evangelization on the Island of Ösel by Vassili Täht, who was once a Bible colporteur for the British and Foreign Bible Society, and who had begun to work for the Methodist Church. Congregations were established in the capital of Arensburg and in other places on the island, which Pastor Martin Prikask organized and has served since then. This was the promising beginning of the Methodist work in Estonia.

World War I also affected the Baltic Methodist congregations. It restricted their work but did not destroy it. After the war the congregations provided the foundation for a widespread work of love in the three Baltic states, Estonia, Latvia, and Lithuania, through which many people were aided. Two homes for children are a continuing fruit of this activity. The Latvian Methodist Children's Home in Riga cared for eighteen children, and the Estonian home in Tallinn cared for twenty-two children. The congregations also have increased in number. In 1924 there were fifteen pastors working in Estonia, fifteen in Latvia, and eight in Lithuania, while six were responsible for the work among the Russian-speaking population. In each of the four languages there is a publication, and for the friends of the work in other countries, especially the United States, the superintendent publishes an illustrated newsletter in English two or three times a year.

Until 1924 the Baltic and Russian work had a united church administration. In that year, however, with the approval of the General Conference, it was divided into two Mission Conferences. The Baltic and Slavic Mission Conference held its first meeting in August of 1924 in Arensburg on the Island of Ösel. On this occasion the following was reported: 1,639 church members, 11 church buildings, 15 preaching houses, 3 children's homes and 1 home for refugees, and 50 Sunday schools with 3,272 children and 1,271 youth league participants. At the time of the 1927 annual conference there were fifty districts with 160 preaching stations and 2,122 members. A visit was made to a theological school with a few young men.

Riga is the central headquarters of the Methodist Church in the Baltics. Here and in other places valuable church property has been acquired. Also, a diaconal work has been initiated with a few indigenous young women who have been trained in Hamburg. Although it was initially met with opposition, the work seems to be looked upon favorably today by the governments, other evangelical churches, and among broad circles of the population.

* * * * * * * * *

After the war, the Methodist Episcopal Church, South of the United States began working in Europe. With a view toward the sought-after reunification with the mother church of American Methodism, the church in Europe was in solidarity with the Methodist Episcopal Church, South, which was entrusted with the summons from Belgium, Poland, Czechoslovakia, and Ukraine.[9] During this time of great need, the Methodist Episcopal Church, South performed great works of love wherever the opportunity existed to undertake evangelistic work. Up to now this work has been most successful in Czechoslovakia.

CHAPTER 2

A Methodist Venture in Bolshevik Russia[1]

Donald Carl Malone

On March 17, 1917, a telegram was received in the offices of the Board of Foreign Missions in New York City from George A. Simons in Petrograd. The telegram stated simply, "Church property intact. All well." This communication was the source of much rejoicing, for the primary concern of the Methodist Episcopal Church at the outbreak of the Bolshevik Revolution was the safety of its missionaries in Russia.[2]

George A. Simons and Beginnings

George A. Simons's legacy in the Russian Methodist Mission dated back to 1860 when F. W. Flocken of the Bulgaria mission at Shumla went to minister to the Russians in Tultcha on the Danube, baptizing four Russian children and gaining his first convert, Gabriel Elieff. The first Russian Methodist chapel was built at Tultcha in 1868. Although Flocken found friendly cooperation among the Molokan and Lipovan sects, there was bitter opposition from the rest of the population. The persecution forced Flocken to flee, and the mission was eventually abandoned.[3]

Nevertheless, the Methodist Episcopal Church did not lose interest in having a mission in Russia.[4] The second attempt began in a more natural way—as an extension of the mission work in Scandinavia. In 1887, B. A. Carlson, presiding elder of Finland, received word from Petrograd that a mission could be started there if a preacher were sent. Carlson was not prepared to begin a mission in Russia, so the request was ignored. A year later or more an urgent request was sent, and Carlson went to Saint Petersburg accompanied by Bishop Charles H. Fowler and two assistants.

The work was facilitated by the lifting of restrictions on religious free-dom by the Russian Empire that same year. A preaching hall was rented, and a small society was organized in August of 1888. In 1892 Bishop Isaac W. Joyce separated the Petrograd Mission from the Finnish Mission.[5] However, the response in Russia was not sufficient to maintain a separate mission, and it was soon combined again with the work in Finland.[6]

In 1907 George A. Simons, a popular director of German immigrant work in the New York Harbor Mission, was appointed to superintend the work in Finland and Russia. In 1911, Bishop William Burt reorganized a separate Russian Mission Conference with thirteen preachers, fifteen charges, four buildings, three deaconesses, and five hundred members.[7]

Simons's ministry in Russia was an unqualified success. His followers increased rapidly, and their work extended into social concerns and publishing interests. Methodists in the United States were justly proud of their extension into what was considered the last missionary frontier.[8] Before the Russian Revolution, Simons was awarded the *Russian Red Cross,* was made a *Chevalier of the Order of the White Cross* in Finland, and was made a *Knight of the Order of the Stars* by the Republic of Latvia.[9]

When the Russian Revolution erupted, George Simons saw the difficulty that had to be endured "for the gospel's sake" as an unprecedented opportunity. The Russian people were freed from the dark ages of the Romanov Dynasty, and the free churches were placed on an equal footing with Russian Orthodoxy.[10] If not the enthusiasm, at least the hope of Simons was shared by his church.[11]

The Methodist Episcopal Church Board of Foreign Missions continued to be anxious about Simons, and in spite of a second "All well" telegram, the board recalled Simons and his sister, Ottilie A. Simons, who was working in the Russian Mission with her brother. However, Simons failed to respond to the recall.[12] Simons and his sister did not leave Petrograd until they were ordered to do so by the United States Government in October 1918. Thus the work in Russia was left to Sister Anna Eklund, a Finnish deaconess educated at the Methodist Institute and Hospital at Frankfurt-am-Main in Germany and appointed as head deaconess in Russia in 1908, while Simons remained close by in Finland. The only reports of the Russian work during this period came from two Methodist preachers fleeing to Finland in January and April of 1919. They reported that Anna Eklund and her followers had sold their furniture and were starving, but they were persisting.[13] Sister Eklund was imprisoned for a time, but with the help of Pastor Oskar Poeld, her "young Timothy," the mission did survive.[14] Even in the face of the trial of revolution, Bishop John L. Nuelsen, episcopal leader of the European area, proposed to the 1920 General Conference a strengthening of the Russian Mission because "Russia presents a mission opportunity of unprecedented magnitude and importance."[15]

In 1921 a massive famine struck Russia, and thousands died of starvation. Abandoned and emaciated children wandered the streets of Moscow, and those on the verge of death made their way to the cemetery to be assured of burial in consecrated ground. Dogs and crows tore at the flesh of bodies heaped in pits for mass burial. Hoards of starving people moved across Russia to Moscow where they thought aid was available.[16] Relief from the United States was cautious because of the questionable political motivations of the Bolsheviki, who had seized control of the Russian government, and because it was doubtful Russians had the ability to distribute goods equitably or to distribute goods at all. However, relief came from the American Relief Agency under Herbert Hoover and from many churches and church agencies, including the Federal Council of Churches, the American Friends Service Committee, the Disciples of Christ, the Episcopal Church, and the Methodist Episcopal Church.[17]

The Methodist Mission in Petrograd had been involved in relief work even before the famine. The Methodist foothold therefore proved advantageous when the famine struck. George Simons believed that the best way to counteract Bolshevism was by bettering the living conditions of the Russian people.[18] Simons requested relief funds from American Methodists, and he and Bishop Nuelsen stationed themselves in Finland where they could oversee the work in Petrograd, making frequent trips there.[19] Later the work was transferred from the German Area, under the direction of Bishop Nuelsen, to the Scandinavian Area, under Bishop Bast, because Bast had secured the assistance of the Danish government for the shipment of relief goods through Finland to Sister Eklund and Pastor Poeld in Petrograd. Simons moved his headquarters from Helsinki, Finland, to Riga, Latvia, to be closer to the relief work.[20]

Thus, due to the efforts of George Simons, Ottilie Simons, Sister Eklund, and Pastor Poeld, the mission in Petrograd not only survived the famine but also prospered.[21] Traveling through Russia in the interest of famine relief in October of 1922, Bishop Nuelsen said, "There is a hunger for the bread of life stronger than I have seen anywhere in Europe." He boasted of Methodist progress in Russia and reported that he preached to capacity crowds in Petrograd, ordaining four men there.[22] It was on that trip that Bishop Nuelsen took an interest in a faction of Russian Orthodoxy called the "Living Church."[23]

Russian Orthodoxy, the Provisional Government, and the "Living Church"

The Russian Orthodox Church found itself in a peculiar situation at the time of the revolution. Since the election of the Duma in 1906, the church was in the position of defending autocracy. The abdication of Nicholas II and the establishment of a provisional government placed the church in an uncertain position.[24] The subsequent victory of the Bolsheviki was a disaster for Russian Orthodoxy.

At first the Russian church was hopeful that its position would not be altered under the provisional government. However, even the reaffirming of the Religious Toleration Decree of April 17, 1905, abolishing Orthodoxy's position over Evangelicals, Catholics, Baptists (German Lutherans), sects, and Jews, was not acceptable to the church. The office of Ober-Procurator of the Holy Synod was transferred to the Ministry of Religion and placed in the hands of a liberal, Vladimir Lvov, a member of the old Duma. Lvov promptly removed the old reactionary members of the Holy Synod and replaced them with moderates and liberals.[25] This act was an irritation to the church, but it gave strength to a group of "The Thirty-Two" liberal professors and priests who had been urging for "renovation" of the church since 1905.[26]

This group of "Thirty-two" organized the All-Russian Union of Democratic Orthodox Clergy and Laity in Petrograd under the chairship of the Rev. D. Popov, with Dean Alexis Vvedensky as secretary. However, the power was still in the hands of the conservative Black or monastic clergy, who took immediate measures to protest their position by claiming government recognition and support for the church and church educational functions. The provisional government, however, did not consent to this claim. To protect further the conservative position, an All-Russian Church Conference or *Sobor* was called on August 15, 1917.[27] There were 265 representatives at the sobor, including 91 priests, 11 military representatives, 9 counts and princes, 8 capitalists, 43 peasants, and 6 workers.[28] A number of foreign representatives were also present, including John R. Mott, general secretary of the Young Men's Christian Association and a Methodist, who spoke to the sobor.[29]

To give stability to the Russian church, which had been thrown into a turmoil by the revolution, it seemed necessary to the conservatives, who composed the majority of the sobor, to reinstate the patriarchate.[30] Although the Renovators stalled on this decision, the issue was pressed by the violent upheaval of October 25, 1917, and by fear of a Bolshevik takeover. On October 30, while shots were fired in the streets outside, the decision was made in spite of an incomplete quorum. Metropolitan

Anthony Khrapovitsky, Archbishop Arsenius, and Metropolitan Basil Ivonovich Belevin, former professor of Pskov and Metropolitan of North America and the Aleutian Islands, were nominated. According to the decree of 1634, lots were cast at the Cathedral of Christ the Savior in Moscow, and Nonagenarian Anchorite Alexis drew Belevin's name. Belevin was enthroned under the name "Tikhon" at the Cathedral of the Assumption on November 21.[31]

Patriarch Tikhon proved to be a vigorous opponent of the Bolsheviki. Nevertheless, the position of the Russian Orthodox Church continued to lose ground. Church administration was limited, and the functions of education and birth and marriage registration were taken from the church.[32] The Renovators, on the other hand, who liked Tikhon no better than they liked his office, enjoyed a favored position with both the provisional government and the Bolsheviki. The Renovators had a misguided hope that the change in government would pave the way for a progressive movement in the church.[33]

So the religious situation in Russia became a triangular struggle. The government, soon firmly under Bolshevik control, saw religion as a remnant of the old tsarist regime eventually to be eliminated. The Renovators were seeking an opportunity for their own changes in the shifts of the revolution. The Renovators and the Bolshevik government were aligned in a cooperation of opposites to persecute the Patriarchal Church.[34]

In spite of Patriarch Tikhon's pronouncements against the Bolshevik government, and in spite of popular protests in support of the church, persecutions against the church increased in severity and soon became a national policy. The state, in addition to withdrawing financial support, ordered marriages to be performed by the state, nationalized all church property, and abolished the central administration of the church, forcing local control. To the decree of January 23, 1918, ordering "the separation of the church from the state and of schools from the church," was added on July 6, 1918, "and freedom of religious or antireligious propaganda is recognized for all citizens." Thus, the church was severely restricted. But the state was not restricted in antireligious activity. Churches were closed and priests who resisted were assassinated.[35]

The Famine of 1921 brought even more persecutions. The state took the opportunity to confiscate church property to be sold to feed the hungry poor. The church was willing to give up unconsecrated objects (consecrated objects often had little market value anyway) and to raise funds through its constituency, but the state wanted all. The resistance of Patriarch Tikhon and his priests provided the state an excuse for violence against the church.[36] The Renovators supported the government seizures in pious expressions of the church's obligation to the poor, thus proving their willingness to support the Bolshevik government.[37]

On May 12, 1922, Tikhon was arrested by the authorities for his resistance to and criticisms of the Bolshevik efforts, and also on charges that he had sent consecrated bread to the tsar when he was imprisoned at Ekaterinburg, and that he had supported outside resistance. Tikhon was held at the Don Monastery unable to administer the church affairs. Having foreseen this possibility, Tikhon appointed Metropolitan Benjamin to become *Locom Tenens* should anything happen to him. However, Benjamin had already been arrested and was subsequently executed on July 6, 1922. Therefore, Metropolitan Agathaniel was appointed to sit in the patriarchal chair, with Bishop Innocent to replace Agathaniel. Agathaniel was also arrested, and Innocent was prohibited to travel to Moscow. Thus the way was open for a takeover by the Renovators.[38]

Before Tikhon learned of the impossibility of his successors taking office, he granted the Renovators, who now called themselves the "Living Church," permission to occupy the chancery. With that occupation also went assumed authority. On May 20, 1922, the Living Church formed the Provisional Ecclesiastical Administration, led by Bishop Antonin.[39]

The first action of the new administration was to call a second All Russian Sobor to be convened on August 9, 1922, for the organization of a new church. The Renovators were far from united, however, and in the midst of strife the sobor was postponed until February 2, 1923, and again until April 29, 1923.[40] In the meantime, a power struggle was occurring between three factions: the Living Church, which was the leading body, led by Krasnitsky; the Regeneration of the church headed by Antonius; and the Ancient Apostolic Church under Alexander Vvedensky. Instead of a sobor, secret meetings were held in attempts to work out minor differences, which were primarily concerned with the status of monasticism and married clergy and with the personalities of the leaders. In addition to conflict within the Renovators, there was conflict without, for the Patriarchal Party was still very much alive. To assure a majority of votes at the sobor, the Living Church engaged in an action of purging priests in the Patriarchal Party by reorganization of parishes, imprisonment, and banishment. Many others shunned the sobor because they considered it noncanonical, so when the sobor finally met only a handful of the Patriarchal Party members was present.[41]

The Second All Russian Sobor of 1923 convened on April 29, at the Cathedral of Christ the Savior in Moscow, under the questionable and probably forged endorsement of Patriarch Tikhon.[42] Early on the agenda was the in absentia trial of Patriarch Tikhon, who was found guilty of producing church discord and was defrocked.[43] The sobor also gave support to the Bolshevik government, lifted celibate restrictions on the episco-pacy, formed a decree against superstitious veneration of relics, and adopted the Gregorian calendar.[44]

However, the sobor failed to unite the Russian church and failed to establish the Living Church as the predominant religious body in Russia. The Renovators remained schismatic and were not popular among the laity. This failure was unsettling to the Bolsheviki. The government, unable to shatter the Patriarchal Party and realizing the futility of making a martyr of Tikhon, now sought reconciliation with the expatriarch. The authorities gave Tikhon to understand that if he agreed to make a statement of confession, he would be released from prison. On the eve of his trial, June 15, 1925, Tikhon recanted and agreed not to oppose the Soviet govern-ment.[45] Although there were rumors that the confession was forged, that Tikhon was ill and not responsible for his statements, or that he was forced to sign a statement, apparently Tikhon had only come to realize that his situation demanded a more conciliatory stance.[46]

A reversal in the church then ensued. The Living Church found itself embarrassed by its seizure of power, as the released Tikhon emerged as the natural and still popular leader of the church.[47] With the masses rallying behind him, Tikhon began to form a new church that was synodical and conciliatory. With the help of the new leader of the Renovators, Metropoli-tan Eudokim of Odessa, a union was formed between the Patriarchal Party and the Living Church, retaining elements of both the old and the new. Only a remnant of the Living Church did not join in the union. Both the Apostolic Church and the Union of Church Regeneration refused to unite, but most of the members of both groups went over to the new church.[48]

Although the division in the church continued, the schismatic groups either came into union with the new Russian Orthodox Church or faded into obscurity. Thus the church in Russia was no longer the Living Church but the Holy Synod of the Russian Orthodox Church.[49]

Patriarch Tikhon died on April 7, 1925.[50] On that same day Metropolitan Peter Krutitsky, who had been with the patriarch just before his death, emerged with a questionable testament allegedly signed earlier by Tikhon. The testament named Metropolitans Cyril or Agathaniel as Tikhon's suc-cessor and should both be unable to succeed him, Metropolitan Peter would be the successor. Both Cyril and Agathaniel were restricted from Moscow, so Peter became *Locum Tenens*. A sobor, which Peter refused to attend, was held on October 1, 1925, and Archbishop Sergei of Novgorod was elected patriarch.[51]

Tikhon was patriarch from 1917 to 1925, Sergei from 1926 to 1936, and Alexei from 1944 to 1945. With each came a necessary growing relationship to the Soviet Government—conciliation with Tikhon, recognition with Sergei, and cooperation with Alexei.[52]

Help from North America and Europe

As the breakdown in the Russian Orthodox Church progressed, other religious bodies increased their interest in Russia.

Dr. William Feltner of the Moody Institute in Chicago began training Russian students for future work in Russia at the Russian Bible and Educational Institute in Philadelphia. In August of 1918 he formed the Russian Missionary and Education Society to send two thousand evangelists to Russia and to build a tabernacle, orphanage, and educational and vocational school in Moscow.[53] The ambitious goal was never realized.

Another group taking advantage of the breakdown in the Russian church and of the relaxing of religious persecution after 1918 was the Roman Catholic Church. Although strong in Poland, Roman Catholicism had remained a minor force in Russia because of the strength of Russian Orthodoxy. When the Soviet Government showed open disfavor for the Russian Orthodox Church, the Roman Catholic Church entertained hopes of replacing Orthodoxy by finding favor with the Soviets, and the Soviet Government gave them reason to hope. But their hopes were dashed when the Soviet Government turned against the Catholics, as it had once turned against Orthodoxy, this time in favor of the new form of Orthodoxy, the Living Church.[54]

The Episcopal Protestant Church and the Russian Orthodox Church in North America have been on friendly terms for many years, exchanging pulpits nationwide and exploring possibilities for church union. Therefore, Episcopalians viewed developments of Orthodoxy in Russia with intense interest.[55] The Episcopal Church was among the first to send relief to Russia during the famine, choosing to work through the Orthodox Church instead of independently.[56]

It was Episcopalian Bishop William T. Manning of New York who came to the aid of Eulogius Platon, Russian Orthodox archbishop of the Diocese of North America, when John S. Kedrovsky, archbishop of Kherson and Odessa in Russia and an American citizen, was assigned by the Sobor of 1923 to the Diocese of North America and presented himself on Platon's doorstep with an unsigned document from Tikhon. Because Platon did not recognize the Living Church, he refused to yield his office, and Bishop Manning supported him in the ensuing litigation. The New York Supreme Court at first ruled in Platon's favor, but relying heavily upon the testimony of Louis O. Hartman, editor of the Methodist publication, *Zion's Herald*, later reversed its decision. Again Bishop Manning came to Platon's aid providing the use of St. Augustine's Chapel at Trinity Church in New York for the remnant of Platon's followers.[57]

No denomination, however, became more entangled in Russian religious affairs than the Methodist Episcopal Church. There was no need for Methodists to move into Russia for they were already there before the revolution, and although the Methodist mission was not large, it was strong enough to endure the revolution and the famine.

While on a visitation to the Methodist Mission in Russia, Bishop John L. Nuelsen, one of the three Methodist episcopal leaders of Europe, became intrigued with the Living Church movement, and the Living Church in turn became intrigued with Methodism. Bishop Nuelsen and Archbishop Antonin of Moscow met together in 1922 and concluded that the objectives of their two churches were very similar. Bishop Nuelsen was interested in establishing a church in Russia built upon a social democratic basis, and Archbishop Antonin believed that the experience of Methodists in establishing a free church in America would be valuable to the Living Church. Already a translation of the American Social Creed of the Church (which had its origins in Methodism) was being circulated among the churches in Russia. Dr. Julius Hecker, a Russian-born Methodist scholar, had given Archbishop Antonin a copy of the *Discipline of the Methodist Episcopal Church*, and part of that book was being reprinted for circulation in Russia.[58]

For Nuelsen, the time of his meeting with Antonin was the right time for a revival of religion in Russia. Religious persecutions of the past were subsiding, and a new interest in religion was growing. Nuelsen stood ready to assist in the rebuilding of a new church free of the anarchy and rigidness of the past.[59]

During the meeting, Antonin invited Nuelsen and other representatives of the Methodist Episcopal Church and the Federal Council of Churches to attend the sobor to be held on December 10, 1923.[60] The formal invitation from Vladimir Krasnitsky, president of the Living Church, came to Nuelsen in December 1922, along with a note of gratitude for famine relief.[61] Nuelsen was elated:

> This means that the most rigid and dogmatic church on the globe is relenting and opening the gates to the audience of the Gospel and that now in the critical hour when they are forming their constitution, they do not look to the church that has commanded during the centuries the Seven Hills of Rome; they are looking to the church that has occupied the Eighth Hill of Rome.[62]

The Board of Bishops shared Nuelsen's enthusiasm and issued this statement:

45

The importance and delicacy of the situation thus created can scarcely be over-estimated. It is highly flattering to Methodist pride to be singled out as an expert on organization by the high administrative body of one of the oldest and most numerous churches in the world.[63]

However, the enthusiasm was not unanimous. Bishop Richard J. Cooke, who had followed Bolshevik advances with considerable concern for many years, was not warm to the invitation. Although agreeing that a new church was needed in Russia, and agreeing that the Soviet Government had become more lenient toward religion, he believed that the Living Church was too schismatic to succeed and too much aligned with Marxism to be cooperative with Methodism.[64] Nor did Bishop Nuelsen receive a favorable response when he presented his report to the Board of Foreign Missions in November 1922.[65]

The Board of Bishops requested that the three European bishops of the Methodist Episcopal Church—Bishop Anton Bast of the Copenhagen Area, Bishop Edgar Blake of the Paris Area, and Bishop John L. Nuelsen of the Zurich Area—attend the sobor in February.[66] Also President L. H. Murlin, of Boston University, who had visited George Simons in 1917 and returned to the United States to raise funds to purchase Simons an automobile, and Louis O. Hartman (later Bishop Hartman), editor of *Zion's Herald* and supporter of Nuelsen's relief work in Germany after the Great War, planned to attend.[67] Bishop W. B. Beauchamp and the Rev. John Vancura were appointed to represent the Methodist Episcopal Church, South.[68] In February 1922, Nuelsen, Blake, and Bast met in Berlin to depart together for the sobor in Moscow. However, word was received that the sobor had been postponed until April 15, 1923.[69] At the time the postponement seemed to be only a minor irritation, but the events that were soon to ensue transformed Methodist pride into Methodist embarrassment.

Bolshevik Pressures and Help for the Russian Church

In March 1923, several Roman Catholic priests were arrested for refusing to yield church property for the relief of famine victims, which was regarded as counter-revolutionary action, and were tried in a Soviet court with M. Krylenko as prosecutor. Prominent among the priests were Archbishop Zepliak, head of the Roman Catholic Church in Russia, and a Polish priest, Vicar General Constantine Butchkavitsch, who was also charged with treason as a Polish spy. Krylenko demanded the death penalty for the two priests and for Vicar General Kocheyvo, who had insulted the court by stating that he appealed to a "higher tribunal than yours."[70] Archbishop Zepliak and Vicar General Butchkavitsch were sentenced to death, five priests were given ten-year sentences, eight priests were given three-year sentences, and a choir boy was acquitted.[71]

Early in the morning on March 31, 1923, Butchkavitsch was taken to the cellar of the Cheka (Secret Police) Building and shot in the back of the head. His body was disposed of without Christian burial, and the event was not announced until four days later.[72] Zepliak was sent to prison to serve a ten-year sentence, which he was not expected to live out, and indeed his health began to fail in prison. Three years later Zepliak was released, but he died of pneumonia before he could sail for Rome.[73]

Although the persecution of religious leaders in Russia was nothing new,[74] a wave of protest against the trial of the Catholic priests came from the Pope in Rome, the House of Commons in England, T. P. O'Connor representing Ireland, Premier Sikorski of Warsaw, the Catholic Welfare Council, United States Secretary of State Charles Hughes at the request of U.S. Catholics, the Reformed Rabbis of the United States, and many other religious bodies and national governments.[75]

Although the protests may have given the Soviets reason to ponder, they quickly decided that they should not let capitalists define Bolshevik policy and carried out the execution, followed by an announcement that Partriarch Tikhon would be tried on April 10.[76]

Protests magnified after the execution of Butchkavitsch.[77] The Soviets countered with threats against the Pope, by tightening censorship of news relating to the incident, and by refusing to renew the six-month visa of American reporter Francis McCullagh of the *New York Herald*.[78]

McCullagh was himself a point of controversy. Being the only American present at the trial, he was the sole source of all news that reached the United States. The accuracy of McCullagh's characterization of the trial as a mockery of justice came into question because he was a Catholic. Speaking about Krylenko, McCullagh said, "Of all the blood thirsty, wild beasts I have ever set eyes on, Krylenko is the worst."[79]

So vehement was the reaction of the American people to the story of the Butchkavitsch execution that reached them, that Secretary of State Charles Hughes was forced to cancel the much anticipated visit of Madam Kalinin, the wife of one of the signers of the execution order, to the United States. At the invitation of the American Red Cross, Madam Kalinin was to make the trip as a representative of the Russian Red Cross on behalf of Russia's poor and Russia's children.[80]

Overlooking McCullagh's Catholic sentiments, most Methodists accepted the accuracy of his reports and were appalled by the events.[81] For Frank Mason North, chairman of the Board of Foreign Missions, the reports confirmed suspicions of the insidiousness of the Soviet Government.[82] John R. Mott, general secretary of the Y.M.C.A., and Harold Williams, director of foreign news for the (British) *Methodist Times,* also sided with McCullagh.[83] However, Bishop Edgar Blake and Dr. Louis Hartman believed that McCullagh's Catholic bias had colored the story[84] and agreed with Senator William E. Borah, a proponent for recognition of the Soviet Government, that Butchkavitsch was in fact guilty and that the evidence in the trial gave proof of that guilt.[85]

Hope was expressed by U.S. religious leaders that when the three Methodist bishops went to Russia they would carry a strong reprimand to the Soviet authorities.[86] This hope was based on the mistaken notion that the Methodist bishops shared the sentiments of most religious leaders and that they would have contact with Soviet authorities. It was also spoken without the knowledge that there was now serious question whether or not the visit would be made.

The Butchkavitsch execution embarrassed both the Roman Catholic Church, which had dreams of replacing the defunct Russian Orthodox Church in Russia, and the American Methodists, who sought to evangelize Russia through the organization of a new church to replace Russian Orthodoxy.[87]

Bishop Blake would not be deterred from his original plans, however, even in the face of threats upon Patriarch Tikhon's life, suspicions of involvement with the Soviet Government, and rumors that the project had been abandoned. To him the opportunity was too great to be easily abandoned, and he was determined to go to Russia.[88] When the sobor was called for April 29, 1923, Bishop Nuelsen was unable to attend because of an episcopal appointment, and Bishop Bast was ill. Therefore, Bishop Nuelsen requested Bishop Blake and Dr. Hartman to represent the Methodist Episcopal Church at the sobor.[89]

In the meantime, a secret session of the Board of Bishops, meeting in Wichita, Kansas, denounced Bishop Nuelsen's proposal to assist the Living Church and recalled Bishop Blake. Although Bishop Blake was already on his way to Russia and could not have received the recall, and although each bishop was responsible to the General Conference and not to the Board of Bishops, to the general public Blake's arrival in Moscow seemed to constitute disobedience.[90]

Bishop Blake and Dr. Hartman were sympathetic with most of the decisions of the sobor—approving total separation of church and state, lifting celibate restrictions of the episcopacy, forming a decree against the superstitious veneration of relics, and adopting the Gregorian calendar—but considered the defrocking of Patriarch Tikhon in absentia to be a mistake.[91]

One of the outstanding features of the sobor was the address of Bishop Blake, which he delivered on May 2, and because of which he was made an honorary member of the sobor.[92] In his speech, Blake emphasized the unity of the church, and in that spirit pledged his assistance to the church in Russia in its time of trial. At least by implication, he also pledged the aid of the Methodist Episcopal Church.[93]

> When your call came across the seas we answered with but one desire, and that is to aid the Russian Church and the Russian people. If in anything we can serve you, you have only to ask. Tell us what you want and, so far as our resources will permit, it shall be done.[94]

The Russians did not hesitate to ask. Since the revolution, all of the theological academies operated by the Russian Orthodox Church had been closed, leaving theological education one of the critical problems of the church. Soon after Blake's address, Bishop Antonin, Metropolitan Peter, and Archbishop Vvedensky requested the advice of the Methodists on training for priests. Blake readily promised to raise $50,000 in the United States between January 1, 1924, and January 1, 1927, upon Bishop Nuelsen's approval, to be used for the opening of a theological academy. Until the school could be opened, and for those who could not attend a school, Blake set up a plan for training ministers by correspondence courses, using professors of old theological academies who were now scattered throughout the country. This system was patterned after the Methodist course of study in use in the United States. Blake and the members of the sobor also formed a Board of Education for the Russian church with Bishop Nuelsen as a member.[95]

However, the Board of Foreign Missions at its annual meeting on November 19, 1923, refused to endorse the pledge. An attorney, William H. VanBenschaften, who served on the board as chairman of the Finance Committee, made a resolution that was adopted by the board:

> It is resolved that it shall be the policy of the Board of Foreign Missions of the Methodist Episcopal Church to carry on its work in Russia, in general, through the direct channels of the board of our church, and that every provision possible as to both workers and finances be made for such work. And it is further resolved that the board shall not conduct any of its work in Russia through the new Russian Orthodox Church nor have any working connection or relation with, nor financially assist that church.[96]

However, Hartman proudly announced that funds were already being raised anyway, and that the assistance of the Board of Foreign Missions was not needed. Appeals were being made through articles and advertisements in church periodicals to establish the *Zion's Herald* Russian Fund for the project. Nine of these were Methodist publications and eight were publications of other denominations. Two Methodist periodicals refused to cooperate on grounds that aid to the new church was aid to the communist government.[97]

When the first payment was due at the beginning of the year, $3,000 was sent to Russia for the opening of the theological school in Moscow, and another $33,000 in pledges had been obtained.[98]

The Moscow Theological Academy was reopened on Sunday, November 25, 1923. The school, which was founded in 1913, had been closed by the Bolsheviki. Metropolitan Eudokim was to be the head of the seminary, and the staff consisted of six theological professors, one Greek teacher, one modern language teacher, one secretary, and a librarian. The professors were Bishop George Dobronrovov, Professor Popoff, Alexander Vvedensky, Dr. Julius F. Hecker (a Methodist minister), Metropolitan Eudokim, and Bishop Krassatin. Fifty students had enrolled the first year, and it was expected that the enrollment would soon reach one hundred. The reopened school gained enough acceptance by the Russian government that its three-year curriculum was printed in *Izvestiya*.[99]

On March 16, 1924, Metropolitan Ryazan opened a second seminary at Leningrad (Petrograd) on the *Zion's Herald* Russian Fund. This was the second step in the plan to found seminaries across the country in Hamel, Odessa, Kharkov, Ekaterinodar, Saratov, Zlatoust, Tomsk, and Irkutsk.[100] The fund also enabled the publication of a monthly paper, *The Christian*, by the Moscow Theological Academy.[101]

On a visit to the two schools in 1925, Bishop Nuelsen wrote to Hartman that both were progressing well. Later, in 1926, Nuelsen, while visiting the Moscow Theological Academy, reported that theological education in Russia was very limited and was still in need of support from American Protestants, without whom there would be no theological education. Nuelsen felt that the school lacked evangelical fervor, which made Protestant support all the more critical.[102]

The gratitude of the Russian church for Methodist support was genuine. An unexpected cablegram was received on May 10 at the 1924 General Conference. It was signed by Metropolitan Eudokim, and read:

> The Holy Synod sends fraternal greetings to your great Conference, trusting that the Holy Spirit will guide you wisely at this time of unprecedented need for world peace. Our church will never forget the Samaritan service which Bishops Blake, Nuelsen, Doctors Hartman, Hecker, and your whole church [have] unselfishly rendered us. May this be the beginning of closer friendship for our churches and nations.[103]

At the death of Patriarch Tikhon in 1925, the new chairman of the Holy Synod of the Russian Orthodox Church, Metropolitan Seraphim of Moscow, wrote to Bishop Nuelsen:

> The services rendered by Bishops Blake and Nuelsen and by Drs. Hartman and Hecker and by the American Methodists and other Christian friends will go down in the history of the Orthodox Church as one of its brightest pages in that dark and trying time of the church.[104]

However, in the United States there was serious reservation about the project. In the first place it seemed that the Board of Bishops' recall of Bishop Blake constituted a rebuke to those who framed the proposal. Bishop Blake claimed that the recall was not as important an issue as the public made it to be. The Board of Bishops claimed that the visit to the sobor was not as important as the public made it to be, characterizing it in a public statement as "only a friendly visit."[105] Still, the controversy raged. Some admired Blake, Nuelsen, Hartman, and Hecker for their courage and foresight, and others believed that they failed to understand the ruthlessness of the Soviets and had been taken in. Rumors were spread that Bishop Blake had been pickpocketed in Moscow, and that he had made pro-Soviet statements.[106]

So heated was the controversy among Methodist bishops that a closed door meeting of the Board of Bishops was called in December of 1923 at Simpson Methodist Church in Brooklyn to settle the matter. The bishops emerged smiling, having reached a compromise resolution containing neither a reprimand nor an apology, but simply thanking Bishops Blake and Nuelsen for their work in Russia.[107]

Bishop Nuelsen suggested a major shift in Russian work at the General Conference of 1924. Although the Russian Mission had grown in membership from 825 to 3,212 in the past four years, it seemed that the $6,000 per year spent for the Russian Mission could be more effectively used in assistance to the Russian church. George Simons was operating effectively with headquarters in Riga and was permitted to travel in Russia. Sister Anna Eklund continued her work in Leningrad. Publications were being printed in Latvia, Estonia, and Lithuania. However, the mission, although remarkably strong in the Baltic, had retreated primarily to that area.[108]

Therefore, Nuelsen proposed that evangelical leaders be sent to Russia to assist the Russian church, that a leading Methodist professor and a leading Methodist pastor be sent each year to teach in a Russian theological academy, and that six to ten Russian theological students be brought to study in American schools each year.[109]

The Fate of the Russian Work

Nuelsen's proposals were never to be realized, for the $6,000 per year allotment was already rapidly dwindling. In 1926 Bishop Nuelsen reported that, in spite of the reduction in funds, Anna Eklund and Oscar Poeld were still working in Leningrad, and that the Talonpoika brothers had begun work in Ingermanland. Because of the opportunity in Russia, other denominations were beginning to do the work that Methodists were unable to fund. Although Nuelsen did not regret that others were doing the work, he still believed that "Russia needs Methodism."[110]

The yearly conference in Riga in 1927 marked the twentieth anniversary of the Russian work. Simons was honored for his service and looked back upon the history of the mission with pride. However, the future looked bleak. Apportionments to the mission had been cut by 50 percent, and membership had dropped to 2,122. Still Bishop Blake, who spoke at the conference, was hopeful. He spoke of the strategical importance of the mission and announced his intentions to attempt to raise a jubilee fund for the mission in the United States.[111] By the end of that year the Methodist mission was in full support of the Soviet Government.[112]

Bishop Nuelsen and Bishop Blake complained bitterly about the cut in mission funds at the 1928 General Conference.[113] Nuelsen said:

> We are doing the best that is possible under the circumstances, but I am bound to state that it is very little—not creditable to the great Methodist Church.

He went on to say that "Methodism is marking time in Russia."[114]

The Russian Mission continued to decline and eventually retreated to Estonia. At the outbreak of World War II, the mission was cut off from its mother church and became independent. Although the church was very small and was under Soviet persecution, it remained faithful and was respected by other religious groups.[115]

In 1963 Bishop Odd Hagen of Stockholm was permitted to visit the virtually forgotten Estonian church for the first time since the war and to hold its first annual conference in twenty years. From his visit came the remarkable report that Methodism in Estonia not only survived the hardships of the war and the Stalin era, but also had been legalized by the Russian government (April 1961), was one thousand members strong, and was growing.[116]

It is difficult, if not impossible, to trace the effect of Methodist influence upon Russian Orthodoxy. However, Metropolitan Nikodim of Leningrad and Novgorod, who was instrumental in the Russian Orthodox Church's decision to enter the World Council of Churches, was educated in the late

1940s through a correspondence course arranged by the Leningrad Theological Academy.[117]

Conclusion

The courageous behavior of those who sought a new form of mission to Russia is not unusual in Methodist history, nor is the controversy surrounding that activity. The episode typifies American Methodism: Cautious and traditional yet bold and innovative, highly structured yet individualistic, proud and self-preserving yet ecumenical and cooperative. Those same characteristics are evident in Methodism even today.

Two approaches can be seen in the Russian Mission: On the one hand there was the traditional evangelistic outreach, and on the other there was an attempt to assist indigenous Christians to develop their own ministry. Both approaches had their value, but now the results of both approaches seem almost negligible. Nevertheless, one can safely say that Methodism left its mark on Russian soil.

CHAPTER 3

George A. Simons and the Khristianski Pobornik
A Neglected Source on Methodism in Saint Petersburg[1]

John Dunstan

Vasilevski Ostrov

On May 16, 1703, on one of the tiniest of the swampy, wooded islands of the Neva delta in northwestern Russia, Peter the Great laid the foundation stone of a fort and ordered the building of a city. How Russia thus cut through its window into Europe, at the enforced cost of thousands of lives through flood, fire, and pestilence, is a familiar epic whose harrowing aspects time does little to alleviate. But Saint Petersburg rose: first directly to the north of the fort on the island now known as *Petrogradskaya Storona* (Petrograd Side); almost simultaneously to the south, across the River Neva, which we think of as the mainland and the heart of modern Leningrad; and later to the southwest on another island over the Malaya Neva.

Two and a half centuries before, a merchant named Vasili Selezen had owned lands on this island, and it was probably from him that *Vasilevski Ostrov* (Basil's Island) derived its name; it is first so called in a document from the year 1500.[2] Peter fortified the island's eastern tip in 1703, and in 1709 he presented it to Prince Menshikov, governor general of the new city. Near the fortifications Menshikov promptly erected a wooden palace, which was replaced over the years 1710-14 by a lavish stone palace. Menshikov turned part of the forest into gardens and orchards and cut through a vista to the western extremity of the island, where the Neva river pilots had their huts. This later became known as the *Bolshoi Prospekt* (Great Avenue);[3] and it was here, two hundred years later, just as the Great War was breaking out, that the Methodist Episcopal Church finally secured a property of its own, at no. 58.

54

In the meantime Vasilevski Ostrov had changed its face. In 1715 Peter decided to turn the island into a new Amsterdam, with rectangular blocks intersected by tree-lined canals.[4] Within ten years a quarter of the territory had been covered with houses, mostly wooden ones laid out in so-called "lines," and because Peter regarded it as the future municipal center, foreigners had been ordered to move there from other areas of the city. Although the few canals that existed proved insalubrious and in 1766, were filled in, and the island was too inconveniently placed ever really to take off as the city center, it acquired considerable commercial importance.[5] The foreigners remained, a fact of great significance for our incipient theme. A French Roman Catholic chapel was established (with a somewhat wayward priest)[6] and likewise a Lutheran church for the German population, and it still standing at the corner of Bolshoi Prospekt and First Line.[7]

We linger briefly on the "lines," because they will recur in our story. By the 1760s they were crossed, to the north, by two other avenues—the *Sredni* (Middle or Central) and *Maly* (Little)—and extended to the Sixteenth Line, nearly halfway across the island. The grid pattern and the use of numbers rather than names seems more American than European, but there are differences: the "lines" refer specifically to the houses along the streets, so that the Eighth Line, for example, faces the Ninth Line across the same street. Originally they were to have been two streets separated by a canal.

For the next hundred years residential development remained very slow, but the emancipation of the serfs in 1861 brought in its train enormous industrial growth, which apart from brief periods of stagnation in the early 1880s and around 1900, continued to the end of the imperial era. The island was still one of the two most popular areas for foreign residents, and the part of it initially settled (between Sredni Prospekt and the Neva to the south) although its social composition was very mixed indeed, commanded the highest rents in the city outside the center.[8] Around the turn of the century growth was more marked in the predominantly working-class district to the north, but overall, the population density was rising because of the replacement of small wooden houses with large tenement blocks of up to seven storys with courtyards and wells.[9] The actual number of foreigners had changed little, and adjacent areas of the city were similarly populated; but Vasilevski Ostrov remained the focus of business and cultural life.[10] Both the stock exchange and the university were there. So were factories, whose workers lived in dark doss-houses and dank basements. Many of them were former peasants from the Finnish-speaking villages outside the city. The considerable social diversity of the island's population was to be another factor in the later history of Methodism in the Russian capital.

The Beginnings of Methodism in Saint Petersburg

The history of Methodism in Saint Petersburg is bound up with that in the Nordic countries, all of which received it as a result of work among Scandinavians, frequently sailors, in New York. This is how Methodism first reached Finland in 1859. Systematic missionary work in Finland, however, did not begin until the 1880s, with a third phase of outreach associated initially with a Swedish local preacher named Karl Lindborg. In 1881 he became leader of a Methodist society in Nikolaistad,[11] where the first Finnish church was opened the following year. About the same time he was invited to preach in Saint Petersburg, apparently among the large Swedish community there; and thus 1881 and 1882 mark the Methodist Episcopal Church's earliest witness in Russia.[12]

The first ordained Methodist missionary to work in Saint Petersburg was Bengt August Carlson (1833–1920), an American of Swedish birth. In 1869 he had been one of the two men sent to open up Methodist activity in Sweden. In 1884 he was transferred to similar duties in Helsingfors (Helsinki).[13] The sources are contradictory as to whether Carlson originally visited the Russian capital in May 1889 or a year earlier,[14] but that need not detain us now. The first reference is a contemporary one of 1888: "Rev. B. A. Carlson writes from Helsingfors, Finland, April 7th, that he has just received a call from St. Petersburg, Russia to go there and preach the gospel. We may yet hear of a redeemed Russia."[15] Bishop Mallalieu made a preliminary visit to Saint Petersburg in the same year, and later expressed his hopes of seeing a Methodist missionary established there to serve in a few months the Swedish population;[16] and after the Swedish Annual Conference of 1889 Carlson arrived with Bishop Fowler. On August 9 they rented a convenient preaching room in the Vasilevski Ostrov district (we do not know the precise site) for thirty rubles a month, Carlson paying the first quarter from his own pocket. On the morning of September 17 the work began; Carlson preached on Luke 10:28 to a crowded room. The need and the opportunity were manifest.[17]

But to make a permanent appointment to Saint Petersburg was easier contemplated than done. According to Carlson, the men available regarded the prospect with as much enthusiasm as a posting to Siberia. As presiding elder of the Finland District, Carlson had responsibility for the work and had to content himself with monthly visits. On November 10 the sacrament of the Lord's Supper was celebrated for the first time in a Methodist service in Saint Petersburg by a society of seven probationary members who would soon be joined by four more.[18] One of them became a local preacher and acting pastor of the society.[19]

In 1890, at the request of Bishop Fowler, the Board of Missions granted $250 for Saint Petersburg, and in 1892 the General Conference resolved that "the Swedish Annual Conference may set apart the work in the Russian Empire, and organize the same into the Finland and St. Petersburg Mission."[20] But as far as the Russian capital was concerned, this did little to help. Already the Methodists had lost their hall through a shortage of funds;[21] there were language problems, for the work was among Finns and Swedes who tended not to understand one another; and the Methodists were not allowed to advertise their services and could spread word of them only by very discreet visits to people's homes. Carlson, in his memoirs, hints at a lack of corporate self-confidence.[22] Difficulties are certainly suggested by the membership figures. Late in 1890 there were twenty members (eleven full members, nine probationers);[23] in 1897, twenty-seven (eight and nineteen, respectively);[24] in 1898, seventeen (thirteen and four);[25] and twenty in 1904.[26] By 1894 the Finnish work was taking a prominent place, and there were several conversions. But the fourteen new members received that year clearly did not last long. Although August Ek doubled as preacher at Saint Petersburg and Viborg in 1895 and 1896, for the next two years the former was listed as "to be supplied."[27]

When Carlson, who for his children's sake had returned to his native Sweden in 1891 following his wife's death, came back to Saint Petersburg in 1902 as district superintendent, he was evidently dismayed by what he found. The tiny group was reduced to meeting in a room where lay-preacher Strandroos lived. Carlson was invited to preach for the Methodists in the English Congregational Church[28] (presumably what was conventionally known as the British-American Chapel). Carlson felt that the Methodists should have such a base for themselves and that the present funds, though scanty were being wasted. A similar plea was put to the General Missionary Committee by Carlson's successor, J. William Häggman, in 1905.[29] But in fact there had been serious legal constraints on evangelical action.

Saint Petersburg Methodism: A New Era

At last, in 1906, the situation in Russia began to improve. This followed the Edict of Toleration of April 1905, which gave religious minorities the right to exist, though not to seduce the Orthodox faithful. Secret missionary activity by the North German Conference in Russian Lithuania could now come into the open, and soon work began also in Estonia and Latvia, though their history cannot be considered here. (Estonian Methodism continues to this very day.) Thanks to the energy of the bishop in charge of

Europe, William Burt, the General Missionary Committee allocated an extra $1,000 for the work in Russia, and a Finnish- and Russian-speaking pastor, Hjalmar F. Salmi, born in Saint Petersburg, educated at a Methodist school in Finland, and with practical experience of ministry among Finnish Americans, was appointed to the city. In March 1907 he obtained permission to hold public meetings in the Saint Petersburg province on the condition that he avoid political issues and he extended his preaching to some Finnish-Russian villages, where a revival began.[30]

In October Salmi was joined by George Albert Simons.[31] The new superintendent of the Finland and Saint Petersburg Mission was born in La Porte, Indiana, in 1874. He was the son of a Methodist pastor who as a former sailor had been converted by reading a tract on the Bible handed to him in a Glasgow street. After working as a bank clerk and helping his father in his spare time, Simons decided to follow in his father's footsteps and successively trained at Baldwin-Wallace College, Berea, Ohio; New York University; and Drew Theological Seminary. He became a minister in 1899 and served various charges in the New York area. Bishop Burt broached the idea of working in Russia to Simons soon after the Edict of Toleration was issued, but Simons at first resisted, and more than two years passed before the call came clearly early one morning: "I can do all things through Christ which strengtheneth me."[32] Russia was in a notoriously unsettled state, but Simons's slowness of response betokens common sense rather than cowardice; events showed him to be a man of courage, resilience, and enthusiasm. When he arrived in Saint Petersburg, he discovered that the legacy of the 1890s consisted of a Swedish meeting of "ten aged women and a feeble man, not one of whom belong to our church."[33] Although these soon allowed themselves to be blown away by the winds of change, all sorts of new work began.

In 1908, within a few weeks of his arrival, Simons began to publish a quarterly missionary magazine in English entitled, *Methodism in Russia*, printed in Rome and distributed from the Methodist Press there. The first issue, dated January-March 1908, mentions preaching in Finnish, Swedish, and Russian at Saint Petersburg, and in Finnish at the Khandrovo Circuit of six places, where Salmi' s evangelistic campaign had resulted in over 150 conversions.[34] Salmi, fluent in all three languages, was listed as the pastor, living at 33 Bolshoi Prospekt and assisted by local preacher Strandroos, while the "First Methodist Episcopal Society" met at 15 Tenth Line. This was the first of three temporary meeting places before the society could acquire its own building; it had opened for services on November 3, 1907. Simons himself was living in the city center at 24 ulitsa Gogolya (Gogol St.), where one J. Grothe had a bookstore, which as an agency for Protestant publications served as the depository of Methodist literature, selling Bibles, books, and tracts in English, Finnish, German, Russian, and Swedish. During his first four months, Simons had attended the annual conference of the New Molokans, an offshoot of a sect originating in 1760 and similar to the Dukhobors; visited Methodist congregations in Finland and in Lithuania; and revisited Western Europe to promote interest in the work.[35] *Methodism in Russia* was, of course, explicitly designed for the same purpose.

But what of the need for light and learning of the Russians themselves? The Finnish- and Swedish-speaking members and inquirers had access to Methodist journals printed primarily for use in those countries. We have noted that special funds had been authorized for the work in Russia, and Hjalmar Salmi's command of Russian symbolizes a new departure. The next step was to publish an evangelical magazine in the Russian language. It was soon to be taken.

The *Khristianski Pobornik* as a Christian Magazine

Methodism in Russia had presumably been printed and distributed in Rome partly because of existing facilities there and partly because the evangelization of the Orthodox in Russia remained legally forbidden. Although preventive censorship had been formally abolished and new journals could be published without permission, it was not difficult to fall foul of the law. But as 1909 approached, the church was about to acquire legal status,[36] and thus Simons must have felt sufficiently confident to bring out his second new magazine. The first monthly issue of the *Khristianski Pobornik (Christian Advocate),* consisting of eight pages, appeared in January 1909. It was edited by Salmi and published from apartment 12 at 18 Ninth Line, to which Simons had recently moved.

In 1910 Simons reported that the *Pobornik* was published in an edition of 1,000 copies, with a further thousand to be published at Christmas, Easter, and conference time. Its subscribers included the Orthodox Synod, the Orthodox Seminary, the Department for Foreign Relations, and leaders of various churches. He also told a story about it:

> One of our converts in St. Petersburg, having charge of a vodka dispensary, whose contract with the government would not be up for about a year, hence could not become a member of our church; [but he] has made a practice of giving [away] a copy of *Khristianski Pobornik* with every bottle of vodka, thus counteracting the evil effects of the spirits with a spiritual antidote![37]

For a content analysis the author had access to an almost unbroken set of *Khristianski Pobornik* recently discovered at the Leningrad Public Library and spanning the years 1909-1917. Whether it continued after 1917 is not known.[38] There are twelve issues for each of the years 1909 and 1912 to 1916; 1910 and 1911 have eleven issues each, including a double issue; and for 1917 there are four single and two double issues but those from July to October are missing. The average number of pages per month, including eight months in 1917, was 10.3. During the nine years there are five successive editors, and from February 1915 until June 1917 there is a special English-language section probably edited by Simons himself averaging slightly over half the length of the Russian part. A classification scheme previously devised by church magazines has been adapted for this purpose; occasionally the content of a piece overlaps and is then notionally divided between categories.

The *Khristianski Pobornik* as a Russian-language journal was always predominantly instructional in its functions. In October 1910, with growing political reaction, new regulations were introduced curbing Protestant outreach, and this seems to have increased the safer devotional and theological content, while keeping input of a missionary or a pastoral nature to a fairly modest level. Successive editors maintained a low profile. Nobody would suspect from reading these pages that the number of strikes in Russia rose from 222 in 1910 to 4,098 in the first seven months of 1914! What we have classified as home and local items are generally reports of meetings in the Russian or Finnish societies or the conference: they do not reveal plans to campaign for the conversion of the Orthodox. The very few references to fund-raising are strictly for charitable purposes or concern for China, where Orthodoxy scarcely had much at stake. In 1911, articles appeared praising the tsar's grandfather, Alexander II, who was assassinated thirty years earlier just after he signed a decree that would have set up a representative assembly.[39] Assuming Simons had a hand in editorial policy, it must have been considerably easier for him to praise the "Tsar-Liberator" than the emperor's reactionary successors.

With the coming of the Great War, the picture changes somewhat. Censorship, or at least self-censorship, must have been at work in 1914; although war broke out in August, there is no mention of it until December, though the new name of Petrograd (less German-sounding than Sankt-Petersburg) is first used in the September issue. In December there is a photograph of Ensign Adalbert Lukas, one of the ordained men serving what we must now call the Petrograd society, and a picture of Christ comforting a wounded soldier on the battlefield.[40] The two items were more closely linked than might have been realized, for Lukas had already fallen, though nobody heard about it until March.

After 1914, however, more and more was reported about the war, and the topical articles and miscellaneous news items together increased from an all-time low of 2.8 percent in 1914 to 10.9 percent in 1915 and over 26 percent in 1916–17, although the 1917 issues examined cover only two-thirds of the year. The English section during its brief existence had primary functions that were basically different from the Russian: to encourage American-Russian solidarity—although that was an increasingly evident subsidiary function of the Russian section—and to provide a local news service for the American community in Petrograd.[41] Its attention to Christian teaching was not insignificant, but it was minor, dropping to 15.4 percent in 1916. Topical features and miscellaneous short news items, combined with biographical articles that were usually about locally prominent Americans such as Ambassador George T. Marye[42] or Henry Dunster Baker, the commercial attaché,[43] comprised 52.3 percent of the content in 1915 and increased to 71.5 percent in 1916. Some pages were devoted to service and pastoral work, such as medical war relief and temperance, social care increasingly the last-mentioned following the 1914 decree on prohibition, and this was true of both sections. But the English one fell on early casualty to the unheavals of 1917.

Apart from changes in content likely to have resulted from exogenous influences, those apparently attributable to a change of editor are minor and probably indicate personal tastes. When Hjalmar Salmi relinquished the editorial chair to Vladimir Datt in August 1910, sermons ceased abruptly and articles became more numerous and shorter. In November 1911 Datt was replaced by N. P. Oksochski, evidently an individual of serious demeanor; the fiction introduced by Salmi in January 1910 and intermittently sustained by Datt was cut out as soon as it could be, back came the sermons in abundance for the next two years, and study materials in the form of Sunday school lessons were lengthened so much that they sometimes occupied nearly half of the issue. The brief incumbency of A. A. Lukas[44] saw the inception of a series of sermons by Simons, and that of I. A. Tatarinovich, beginning in June 1915, is marked by a penchant for verse, ranging from the religious poetry of the Grand Duke Konstantin Konstantinovich Romanov to translations of the "International Sunshine Song" and "When Johnny Comes Marching Home."[45]

The *Khristianski Pobornik* as a Source of Saint Petersburg Methodism

We move now to a consideration of the *Khristianski Pobornik* as a source on the life and outlook of Saint Petersburg/Petrograd Methodism, drawing on additional sources as appropriate. We shall first survey the day-to-day activities of the Methodist Episcopal Church there and the development of the work up to the beginning of the Soviet era, and then turn our attention successively to its doctrinal emphases and the formation of a Methodist consciousness, and to missionary strategy and relations with the secular authorities.

A. Daily Life

During 1908 the First Methodist Episcopal Society moved from 15 to 37 Tenth Line, an apparently detached two-storied wood and brick building with attics, its side of seven bays facing the street; the front of five bays was approached through a walled courtyard.[46] It was owned by the Jewish Orphans Home.[47] In 1909 Simons moved to a nearby address (apartment 12, at 18 Ninth Line) to supervise the work more closely. The Methodists had Sunday services in six languages (German at 10:00 A.M., English at 11:30 A.M., Russian at 3:45 P.M., Swedish at 5:00 P.M., and Finnish and Estonian at 6:00 P.M.); a morning Sunday school held in several languages; and weeknight meetings in Finnish (Monday at 7:30 P.M.), Estonian (Tuesday and Friday at 8 P.M.), English and Russian (Wednesday at 7:30 P.M.), and German (Thursday at 7:30 P.M.).[48]

When Simons delivered his report to the 1910 Conference of the Finland and Saint Petersburg Mission, he was able to claim a total congregation of 500, of nine different nationalities, including eighty full members and fifty-two adult probationers, most of whom had been meeting in class once a week for instruction by him. Testimonies could be heard in five languages. In addition, the superintendent was averaging four sermons each Sunday, holding a Bible class for Russians on Wednesdays, speaking to a German group on Fridays, and giving a three-hour catechism class on Saturday afternoons for five boys and four girls who had voluntarily appeared for it. Their three-year course comprised biblical and church history and the history, catechism, doctrines, and discipline of the Methodist Episcopal Church; some of them might join the ministry. The Sunday school, with 175 scholars and teachers, was run by Vladimir Datt, with a board of eight men and seven women teachers to help him. It included Bible classes for various nationalities. Simons led a class for some fifty Germans aged from fourteen to fifty. In the previous year, the Sunday school had raised 175 rubles, of which nearly half had gone to China to support the new Saint Petersburg Day School for boys there. The society as a whole had raised over 3,200 rubles for self-support, benevolent and missionary purposes.[49]

The home missions and Christian service activities of the Saint Petersburg society merit fuller attention. As well as the parts of the empire already mentioned, there had been outreach in Karelia, terminated by the authorities, and west of Mariinsk on the Trans-Siberian Railway.[50] In 1910 the latter work had just started through the initiative of August Karlson, a British and Foreign Bible Society colporteur who had made contact with the Methodists when visiting the capital and studied their faith and practice.[51] By 1914 he was preaching in seven widely dispersed villages, and in one of them, Vambolsk, a prayer house was being built. Martin Prikask, another of Simons's preachers, made the nine-day journey there to open it in December. He helped to finish the prayer house in temperatures of 40-47 degrees centigrade, but it was ready for Christmas Day. He recorded that the local people were in a very sorry situation. The place had been settled for seven years; some had built little houses, but others were still living in caves; there were no schools for their children, and during the long winter they all lived together with their animals. The spiritual life there was at the same low level. Karlson's son Paul formed a choir, and the Petrograd friends sent them an American organ.[52]

Back in the capital, as we saw in the introduction, there was also poverty and squalor. To the relief of this, Methodism made a contribution, which earned wide respect. Sister Anna Eklund, a deaconess of Finnish birth who had trained in Germany, joined Simons soon after his arrival. Within months she had gathered four other sisters about her, and they had a cholera epidemic on their hands. This meant that they had already begun to be known by November 1908 when the *Vifaniya* (Bethany) Deaconess Home was opened in a five-room apartment, no. 10, at 44 Third Line.[53] Morale was high; the only difficulty was a shortage of funds for the work and for the two-year training of the younger sisters.[54]

The range and extent of Bethany's activities can perhaps be best summarized from a statistical report filed by Sister Anna in the summer of 1911. Over the previous year they had accumulated 256 days and nights of nursing in private houses and thirty-six night duties, treated 148 paying and non-paying massage patients, undertaken 345 visits to homes and hospitals, made gifts to 305 people at Christmas and Easter, and given clothing and bread to 400-500 people a week during the summer.[55] A few weeks later she was appealing for bread, clothes, firewood, and medicines for them.[56] In 1913 a children's home named after Ottilie, Simons's mother, who had recently died in Saint Petersburg, was opened at Khandrovo;[57] one of the deaconesses was in charge of this and also a small day school.[58] When the war came, Simons issued appeals for shoes and clothing for Methodist relief work among refugees and destitute families.[59]

In 1909 Sister Anna also assumed responsibilities for the sale of Methodist literature. The following summer Simons reported on his first ten months of book publishing. The *Standard Catechism* (called in Russian *Sushchnost veroucheniya*, i.e., *The Essentials of Doctrine*) had been translated and published in an edition of 5,000 copies; the translation of the 1908 edition of the *Doctrines and Discipline of the Methodist Episcopal Church* was nearing completion, and the first part had been printed. A pamphlet entitled *The Methodists: Who They Are and What They Want* had appeared in a Russian edition of five thousand copies and an Estonian edition of three thousand. Some of Wesley's sermons had also been translated into Russian; and Estonian and German hymnbooks had been published too.[60]

Very few data have come down to us on how and to what extent the Saint Petersburg Methodists managed their society's affairs. Obviously, in a missionary situation that had suddenly begun to evince such vigorous renewal that sixteen years later the renaissance was authoritatively taken for the start,[61] it was to be expected that the missionary leadership should assume the dominant role. By March 1909, however, there had been sufficient progress to organize an official board (*tserkovny sovet*, literally church council) consisting of eight men and Sister Anna.[62] Its chairman was Robert Albertovich Mertins, a bank clerk and native of East Prussia who had come to Saint Petersburg at the age of ten. But after one year as chairman, Mertins died of consumption at age forty-nine. One of the speakers at his funeral referred to his harsh background and great goodness.[63] We do not know how significant a proportion of the membership the lower middle class comprised, but the hardness of Mertins's life must have been fairly typical of the members. The Finns, in particular, were an impoverished group.[64]

Thus we have a picture of vibrant activity, with recurrent glimpses of its poverty-stricken setting. By 1911 the development of the work justified the formation of the Russian Mission, separate from the new Finland Conference, and earned a grant of $1,500 towards a printing press, but in general, Simons's regular pleas to the Board of Foreign Missions went unheeded, and the appropriation for Russia was the smallest of all.[65] Truly it was amazing what faith could do when funds were wanting.

An exceptional windfall, however, came on the eve of the war. Prior to that, after a four-year sojourn at 37 Tenth Line, the Methodist meeting place had been moved late in 1912, following government interference, to 3 Malaya Grebetskaya ulitsa, on Petrogradskaya Storona, the island to the northeast of Vasilevski Ostrov.[66] The new location, fairly close to the bridge linking the two districts, was known as Fyodorova's Hall, after its owner. Simons then received a gift from an American benefactress, Fanny Nast Gamble, which enabled him in 1914 to realize the long-cherished dream of buying a property. This property was 58 Bolshoi Prospekt, on the southeast corner of its junction with Twentieth Line. Simons, who had been living at the latest address of Bethany (34 Ninth Line) for a season, soon moved in and set up his headquarters. After months of waiting, permission finally came on December 20, 1914, to open the "prayer house." Six days later, 125 people came to the first meeting and an invitation to "English-speaking friends and strangers without a church home" promptly appeared in the *Pobornik*; open house would be kept for them on Thursday afternoons.[67]

After the dedication services on March 1, 1915, a note in the English section of the magazine described the church as modest but homelike and large enough for 200 persons: "it is hoped that a large Central Building with a commodious auditorium will be erected in the not too distant future."[68] A more unrealistic scenario can scarcely be imagined; a less unrealistic one could hardly be expected.

It would be tedious to enumerate the minutiae of changes in the church's life between 1909–11 and 1917. We will restrict ourselves to trends in the primary form of corporate activity, the Sunday services and weeknight meetings.[69] The earlier pattern of worship in six languages does not seem to have been maintained from 1912: Swedish and Finnish disappeared from the list then and Estonian a year later. Against this, there was growth in the German work (two Sunday services and two meetings on other evenings in 1912)[70] and in the Russian work (increasing to four or five weekly meetings in 1914).[71] In 1923 it was reported that Russians of German origin, mainly professional people, and Russian artisans formed two separate groups of members, between whom there was very little contact.[72] This may well have been true of the pre-1917 situation. The outbreak of war put a discreet stop to activities in German. Since Protestantism was identified with Germany, Simons publicized and developed the American connexion. Work in English took on new life with a Sunday evening service and the unusual evangelical device of English language classes, including hymn singing and Bible reading on Monday evenings, with Simons teaching the University Class and his sister, another Ottilie, teaching the beginners. A hint that these attracted a somewhat better-placed audience occurs in the record of the presents given to the teachers, ranging from "a rare set of Turgenev's works" to a Thanksgiving turkey.[73]

B. Emphases in Worship and Doctrine

Although no detailed accounts of the form and content of the Saint Petersburg society's worship appear to have survived, it can be deduced from the *Khristianski Pobornik* that it was in the mainstream Methodist tradition, with much attention to the sermon and to congregational singing, and the same is undoubtedly true of the doctrine. The need for gospel preaching was the keynote of Simon's first report;[74] there are occasional references to hymns in the meetings;[75] the Estonian and German hymnbooks have been mentioned. From time to time the *Pobornik* printed Russian translations of well-known hymns, such as *Jesus, Lover of My Soul* and *Low in the Grave He Lay*, and a Russian book of about one hundred translated favorites appeared in 1913.[76]

The journal lost no time in acquainting its readers with Methodism's doctrinal emphases. It began with four celebrated sermons by John Wesley: Salvation by Faith, The Almost Christian, Scriptural Christianity, and Justification by Faith.[77] Simons contributed a lengthy three-part article on conversion[78] and followed it up with Wesley on the New Birth.[79] We have already perceived the distinctively Methodist character of the book publishing program. Other efforts to develop a Methodist consciousness ranged widely. There was a significant amount of historical material, with related biographical articles on luminaries such as George Whitefield and the Countess of Huntingdon,[80] and Francis Asbury on the centenary of his death;[81] Methodist news, with much conference reporting, items such as the opening of the Central Hall, Westminster,[82] and letters on American Methodism from that later controversial figure Julius Hecker;[83] the emphasis on temperance noted earlier; and the choice of none other than Mark Guy Pearse as the first storyteller. One wonders what those Russian peasants or ex-peasants made of the English village Wesleyans who were "Mister Horn and his friends."[84]

C. Strategy and Relations with the Authorities

As we have seen, Russian Methodism began on Vasilevski Ostrov. The choice of this location, the abode of foreigners, epitomizes the initial approach. Russia was missioned through the non-Russian-speaking population and from the countries where their forebears had originated; Finns and Swedes were both shepherds and flock. Russia was regarded as a vast field of opportunity, but in a vague manner, and in the late nineteenth century the specifics of advance there appear to have been little discussed. True, the Board of Missions was short of funds at the time, but there were other constraints that did much to determine both the foothold approach and the powerlessness to stride forward. Work among ethnic Swedes and Finns was tolerated, but mission to the Russians was forbidden by harsh legislation.[85] A law of 1894 betokened a worsening climate: the *Stundists* (originally meaning Baptist; this term came to be applied to all Protestants) were deprived of the right of assembly[86] and were persecuted. But the small scale of the Methodist activity, so much criticized by later missionaries, was in effect its salvation from the attentions of officialdom.

The situation had changed by 1907, when Nicholas II's Easter Decree of 1905 was, temporarily at least, making things easier for Protestant denominations. Simons clearly saw Methodism as providing a great light for a nation walking in darkness.[87] Under the 1905 legislation, the Orthodox were for the first time permitted to transfer to another denomination, and Orthodoxy was for Simons a write-off.[88] So he regarded it as essential to develop Russian-speaking work, not only in Saint Petersburg, but also in the emergent Methodist activity elsewhere. His command of German meant that another important non-native group could now be catered to, until the political situation prevented it. Preaching was backed up by extensive publication. Simons drew on the services of experienced colporteurs and made it a priority to train indigenous Russian-speaking pastors and lay preachers. Except for primary education, the Orthodox Church had traditionally been little concerned with social matters before 1905; here, too, there was a backlog of need to supply. Methodism's social involvement included the deaconess work at Saint Petersburg—nursing, visiting the sick, helping the poor—and this took on additional significance during and after the Great War.

How successful was this strategy? Certainly the relaxation of the law gave the Methodists their chance, and socio-economic circumstances provided much scope for action. On the other hand, the Edict of Toleration was increasingly disregarded in practice and considerably vitiated by the regulations of October 4, 1910. Thus, we must not exaggerate what Simons was able to achieve in the face of despotism: although, almost on the eve of the war, new work was begun around Yamburg (Kingisepp) and Volosovo to the west of the capital, membership in Petrograd, with fewer than two hundred full and probationary members, and elsewhere remained small.

The Methodist response to these later constraints was, in effect, to keep in favor with the authorities where possible, and to proceed discreetly where not. Under the 1910 regulations, permission had to be obtained for all church meetings except services, all meetings had to have a policeman present, and children's services and catechistic instruction were banned.[89] The last-mentioned was initially disregarded, and later circumvented, for the *Pobornik* was still advertising its Sunday school classes in Russian, among other languages, in January 1911.[90] Two years later, apparently after a period of enforced suspension, this was slightly disguised as "Bible Hour for Adults and Youth,"[91] and from January 1916 more so as "International Bible Lesson."[92] But from a casual reference in an account of the Christmas celebrations of 1916, we know that there was a large Sunday school in Petrograd and others round about: the Petrograd society had raised the money to provide 300 parcels for 115 children in the Sunday school there and 185 in the village Sunday schools.[93]

It is very interesting to watch the *Pobornik*'s changing attitude to events during 1917. The occasional contributions from 1911 honoring the Romanov Dynasty and presenting the verse of Grand Duke Konstantin have been noted; this is prudential deference to the imperial family. But after the

February Revolution and the abdication of Nicholas II, the journal immediately adopted a totally different tone, which faithfully reproduced the typical American reaction to the turn of events. It is seen as what Kennan terms "a political upheaval in the old American spirit: republican, liberal, antimonarchial."[94] Thus the April-May issue included the Russian and English text of a proposed new national anthem;[95] an account of a mass meeting in the Duma (State Council) on the occasion of the United States' entry into the war, at which Simons spoke; a report of the first of a series of open-air meetings in the church garden; a poem by Aksakov entitled "Free Speech," which had been banned for seventy years;[96] and in the English section, an article by Simons on "Russia's Resurrection"—"from the gloomy tomb of despotic tyranny and medieval terrorism into the joyous light and life of freedom and democracy."[97] The next issue had a Russian translation of Ebenezer Elliott's "God Save the People."[98]

These were Simons's main concerns, but there is a subsidiary motive that reflects America's, and indeed her allies', attitude to Russia's continued role in the war. In his speech at the mass meeting in the Duma, Simons's theme was America's strong moral consciousness, which she now offers to her allies.[99] The United States government expected not only that Russia would become a stable democracy, but also that she would play a reinvigorated part in the common cause against Germany. In point of fact, while the provisional government had the administrative experience, the Soviets held the real power, and many socialists saw the war as irrelevant. The country was politically riven. Yet in his article Simons goes on to say: "It was the wonderful unity of purpose, strength of will and quick action of the men and women of various classes who saved the day in Russia." But those were the heady days of March. Such sentiments are no longer detected in the November-December issue.

Epilogue

And there, at the end of 1917, the *Khristianski Pobornik* apparently ceases. The United States' new-found popularity (if we can believe the April-May issue) is even shorter-lived. In August 1918 the United States is reluctantly involved in the allied intervention at Archangel, and in October George A. Simons is recalled by order of the United States government. Yet the Board of Missions envisions a future for Russian Methodism: it sees it in terms of opposition to Bolshevist influences, but apart from education and medical work the perception of the way ahead is vague.[100] And Methodism does have a future in the USSR, with nearly 2,300 members and probationers by 1928.[101] But this must be its apogee. It is the start of the First Five-Year Plan and the concomitant atheistic onslaught. The church building vanishes with the reconstruction of Bolshoi Prospekt. By 1931, even the doughty Sister Anna has fled; and the work based in Leningrad appears to cease altogether in 1939.[102] Its history during the 1930s is utterly obscure; that of the 1920s is patchy, colorful, and largely untold. But at no other time is it as well documented as in the nine years of the *Khristianski Pobornik.*

CHAPTER 4

The Methodist Episcopal Church, South, in Siberia/Manchuria 1920–1927[1]

Dana L. Robert

In May of 1920, the Board of Missions of the Methodist Episcopal Church, South, authorized the opening of a new mission in Siberia and Manchuria. The elderly missionary bishop, Walter Russell Lambuth, pioneer of Methodist work in China and Japan, called the entry into Siberia "the greatest missionary opportunity of this generation."[2] Lambuth's words proved to be prophetic. Within a few years, the mission boasted thousands of members among the Chinese, Korean, Japanese, and Russian people. By 1925, the Korean section of the mission had 3,600 adherents gathered into twenty-six churches, thirty-five Sunday schools, two youth leagues, and twelve Women's Missionary Societies.[3] Near Harbin, Manchuria, Methodists had founded six Russian churches by 1927. The Russian Methodists in Harbin ran a high school, a business institute, an elementary school, a medical clinic, a women's social center, a child protection league, and a theological seminary that trained men and women for ministry.[4] Methodist work in Siberia and Manchuria seemed to deserve the confidence placed in it by Bishop Lambuth.

Yet at their May, 1927 meeting, the Methodist Board of Missions, under Bishop Ainsworth, voted to close the Russian work in Siberia and Manchuria. Before the summer was over, the missionaries had sold the property, transferred the money, and shipped lock, stock, and barrel out of Harbin. The most vivid memory of missionary George Erwin was that of pulling from the station on the Chinese Eastern Railway as dozens of Russians stood sad and bitter on the platform until his train was out of sight.[5] A Russian preacher pleaded for many, when in the Board of Missions journal he begged that the mission be reopened:

Suddenly and unexpectedly our wings were cut, our hearts wounded by the telegram from Bishop Ainsworth. Close the mission! Why? How? We do not know. What could we do, what could we say? We wept and prayed. We hoped it was not so. Our hope was in vain. Schools disposed of children, children were cut off from cheap and religious education. Clinic lost for the Methodists, part of the churches closed, and missionaries were withdrawn. Our spiritual leaders are withdrawn. We are left alone. We are like children without parents.[6]

Today, the Siberia-Manchuria Mission rates no more than a line in histories of Methodism. Yet, historically, the mission is important for the portrait it paints of a little-studied refugee community—that of exiled Russians who fled the Bolshevik Revolution. The story of the mission shows how Russian refugees used the church to help them cope with hopelessness, starvation, persecution, and massive unemployment. The personal and printed documents from the mission, most of which are in Russian, represent a hitherto unexplored source of information, not only for the refugee history, but also for the history of Protestantism among Slavic peoples in Asia.[7] Sadly, the closing of the Siberia-Manchuria Mission also illustrates how the southern Methodist bishops of the early twentieth century exercised arbitrary power over Methodists in other parts of the world.

The Beginning

The Siberia-Manchuria Mission began as an effort to reach an estimated 1,400,000 Koreans who had migrated to Siberia for economic and political reasons. During the famine of 1870, Koreans began slipping over the border to find new farmland. Initially, those who were caught by the Korean government were beheaded, but whole villages of farmers continued to defy the law in the effort to secure the rich and unpopulated fields and forests of Siberia. After the Japanese occupation of Korea in 1910, more farmers fled the country. Enterprising Koreans transformed swampy areas of Siberia and Manchuria into rice fields.

An estimated five thousand of the migrating Koreans were Methodists, and their brothers and sisters back in Korea were eager to send them missionaries to help them establish their own churches and to educate their children.[8] In November of 1920 Bishop Lambuth and the Korean Annual Conference sent several missionaries, both Koreans and Americans, to explore the possibilities of Methodist work among the unchurched Koreans of Siberia and Manchuria. Methodist work spread rapidly among the emigrants: within nine months, there were 1,291 Korean members gathered into thirty churches with thirty-one Koreans licensed to preach.[9]

In addition to Korean work, Bishop Lambuth had long desired to reach Russians. Following World War I, the Methodist Episcopal Church, South, had undertaken relief work among European refugees in Belgium, Czechoslovakia, and Poland. The Woman's Missionary Society established soup kitchens in Warsaw and sent millions of dollars worth of soap, shoes, and clothing to refugees. Many of the needy in northern Poland and Czechoslovakia were ethnic Byelorussians (White Russians), one of Poland's largest minorities.[10] Although the Methodist Episcopal Church, South, had originally entered Poland to do only relief work, the positive response to Methodist assistance among some Byelorussians led Bishop Lambuth and others to hope that the church could enter Russia proper for evangelistic work.[11]

During the Russian Revolution and civil war that began in 1917, the Bolsheviks soon gained control over western Russia, but it took them a few years to extend their grip over Siberia and the eastern provinces. From the beginning, as avowed atheists, the Bolsheviks persecuted the Orthodox Church and accused it of being a pawn of the tsars. Even though in the early years they were more tolerant of Protestantism than of Russian Orthodoxy, Lenin and the Bolsheviks did not let the Methodist Episcopal Church, South, begin evangelistic work in Russia. The Methodists had to remain content with relief work on Russia's western border and with hopes that a few converted refugees might be able to sneak back into the Soviet Union where they could evangelize secretly.

Siberia, however, was not yet under communist control. Bishop Lambuth believed that in the aftermath of the Revolution, Russia hung like a ripe plum waiting to be plucked by the Methodists. He believed that the Orthodox Church had been discredited by its association with the tsars, by its seemingly unintelligible liturgy, and by its "superstitious" customs. Lambuth felt that the disillusioned Orthodox Russians, suffering under the Bolshevik yoke, were ready for the Protestant gospel. Perhaps by entering Siberia, Methodist missionaries could gain access to Russia. In describing Lambuth's dream of Russian penetration, his biographer wrote:

> The political and social conditions made mission work impossible in Russia proper; but Siberia was then withstanding the spread of Bolshevism, and it was possible to reach Russians from that quarter. It was a strategic move on his part to drive a wedge from the east at the same time we were approaching Russia from Poland on the west as far as conditions would permit.[12]

Lambuth's scheme in 1921, then, was a grand Methodist pincer movement to drive Protestantism into Russia from both sides. His underlying assumption was that Orthodoxy was a dying religion and that Russians, now freed from its grasp by the Revolution, would eagerly embrace Methodism as a replacement.

The needs of Korean and Russian refugees would have been inadequate to draw the Methodist Episcopal Church, South, into Siberia had it not been for the Centenary, a fund-raising drive that increased the budget of Foreign Missions by four million dollars from 1918 to 1921.[13] 1918 was the centennial year of Methodist missions, and the General Conference of that year voted that $35 million be raised for missions over the next five years. Southern Methodists were in an optimistic and aggressive mood after the successful fund drives of World War I, and the Centenary fund was oversubscribed. By 1924, 281 new missionaries had been sent overseas, nearly doubling the mission force.[14] As part of the Centenary, the Methodist Episcopal Church, South, set a goal of one million converts and one hundred thousand family altars. The slogan of the Centenary summed up its appeal: "When two million Methodists go from their knees to any task, it shall be done."[15]

The result of the Centenary was significant overseas growth. The first new mission to be opened under Centenary pledges included the aforementioned work in Poland. The second centennial thrust was the Siberia-Manchuria Mission. Even the international branches of southern Methodism caught the centennial spirit. Every Korean Annual Conference had a Centenary chairman who collected funds and backed mission work to the Koreans of Siberia-Manchuria. In 1924, the China Conference opened a mission to the Chinese in Manchuria.[16] Although it initially was a part of the Siberian-Manchuria Mission, the Chinese mission soon became completely supported by the China Annual Conference. In all, the Centenary years represented a major outpouring by American, Korean, and Chinese Methodists into the new Siberia-Manchuria Mission.

The Russian Work

The Russian section of the Siberia-Manchuria Mission opened its doors in Harbin, Manchuria, the provincial capital of the northernmost province of China. In 1921, Harbin was the center of one of the largest European populations in Asia. At least one hundred thousand Russians and Poles shared the city with Chinese, Korean, and Japanese immigrants. Manchuria itself was caught in a Japanese-Chinese-Russian struggle for sovereignty. At stake was the Chinese Eastern Railway, the vital link in the Trans-Siberian Railway between Vladivostok, Russia's major Pacific port, and western Russia. Also at stake were the rich farmlands in central Asia. Although the Chinese Eastern Railway cut across Manchuria, which was nominally controlled by China, practical control of the railway lay in Russian hands until 1905 when Japan won the Russo-Japanese War. Many Russians had migrated to Manchuria to work on the railroad and on the new industrial concerns that sprang up along its path. The number of Russians had swelled after the Revolution of 1917 when refugees from Bolshevism crowded into Harbin, the largest city along the railway. In the city of Harbin Red and White factions were constantly struggling against each other. Simultaneously, the Japanese began to militarize the railway zone in their preparation for war against China.[17] Into this situation arrived the H. W. Jenkins, a Methodist Episcopal Church, South, family from the South Georgia Conference.

The second center for Russian Methodist work was an equally dangerous location. During World War I, when access to Russia had been cut off by the German front to the west, Vladivostok became a strategic center for shipment of war materials to Russia. The Bolsheviks first gained control of Vladivostok in March of 1918. But by June, an uprising of Czech soldiers with Allied backing managed to retake the city from the Soviets. Japanese, British, and American troops landed to aid the Czechs, ostensibly to protect their interests against German prisoners of war, whom the Allies feared would try to seize Siberia. President Wilson aided the citizens of Vladivostok through the Y.M.C.A., the Red Cross, and with agricultural and labor advisers. An American warship lay anchored in the Vladivostok harbor much of the time in case the American consul needed to make a quick getaway.

The missionary J. O. J. Taylor arrived in Vladivostok to minister to Koreans.[18] Soon he had recruited a fellow Georgian from his home circuit. The Rev. George Erwin was one of the last missionaries appointed by Bishop Lambuth before he died in 1921. The Erwin family arrived in Vladivostok on May 15, 1922.[19] All the original American missionaries assigned to the Siberian-Manchuria Mission—Taylor, Jenkins, Erwin, and their families—were supported by the Centenary funds of the South Georgia Conference. George Erwin traveled north of Vladivostok to supervise the Korean work of Nikolsk, but he soon became interested in the plight of the Russian refugees and began to minister to them also.

The situation of the Russian refugees tore the hearts of the missionaries. Beggars filled the streets of Vladivostok, and thousands huddled in refugee camps fed by the American Red Cross. Homeless Russians lived in railroad boxcars along sidetracks. Tuberculosis, malnutrition, and curvature of the spine affected the children. Many of the refugees were Russians from prosperous homes who had fled east to escape the Bolshevik terrors.[20] Although the Methodists had arrived to bring spiritual food to the Russians, they soon realized that the great physical needs of the people had to be met as well.

Late in 1922, Vladivostok fell to the Bolsheviks. Americans, Russians, and Japanese crowded into the harbor ships and left the city to the Reds. George Erwin recalled being the only American he knew on the streets of Vladivostok when the Bolsheviks marched in. First came the cavalry on horses that were skin and bones. Then shuffled in the barefoot soldiers, most in rags. Within three days, Erwin recalled, the Bolsheviks were well-dressed with shiny new boots plundered from the city.[21] Although the Bolsheviks confiscated the Methodist property in Vladivostok, they permitted worshipers to hold church services. Sunday school and other meetings had to be held in private homes. Of the three young Russians who had volunteered to become Methodist ministers, the Bolsheviks imprisoned one.[22]

Within a few months of the Bolshevik conquest, it became obvious that the position of the American missionaries was untenable. The Erwin family left for Harbin in February of 1923, and the Taylors were forced to depart soon afterward. With them went some of the Russian Methodists. The Methodists that remained in Vladivostok, mostly Koreans with a few Russians, experienced persecution over the next few years, including the imprisonment of pastors and leading Christians, the closing of churches, and the forcible organizing of young children into atheistic clubs.[23]

By the spring of 1923, all Russian Methodist work had been concentrated in Harbin, at least temporarily safe across the Chinese border from Bolshevik control. The first Methodist missionary in Harbin, H. W. Jenkins, was able to engage the Russians quickly by meeting needs for education and employment. Many of the Russian refugees in Harbin were people desperate for practical training that would help them find jobs. The economy of Harbin was severely strained by overcrowding and a concomitant lack of employment possibilities, and many educated Russians were eager for teaching or tutoring jobs, even at low salaries. Refugees also needed language instruction to qualify them for admission to the United States or to other countries. They did not know when the civil war might spill over into Manchuria and force them to emigrate to some other part of the world. They were people on the move who desired nothing more than a safe home and a secure job, both of which were scarce in Harbin in the 1920s.

By the time the Erwin family arrived from Vladivostok in early 1923, Jenkins had built a missionary compound on Tilenskaya Street, which contained missionary apartments, classroom space, and educational equipment. Soon the Methodist Institute opened in the compound with seventy pupils.[24] Most of the adults who attended the night school studied English. In its business department, the Institute offered bookkeeping, English typing, and Russian typing. By 1925, the annual enrollment in the Methodist Institute was 744.[25] Graduates of the vocational school quickly found jobs that enabled them to migrate to such places as Australia, Canada, or the United States. In the Methodist Institute, the mission was filling perhaps the greatest need of those it had come to serve—that of helping them to gain the skills to be able to leave war torn Asia as quickly as possible. Through the Institute, the Methodist Episcopal Church, South, became a conduit for Russian emigration all over the world. One convert of the mission, Gregory Yasinitsky, called it a " 'channel of hope' for the Russian people."[26]

Other educational enterprises included a high school of ten grades and an elementary school. The American consul considered the Methodist high school to be one of the finest in the city.[27] The Methodist schools were popular among Russian parents, but their children had to endure dingy storefront rooms and the scant Methodist supplies in order to gain a Christian education. Letters home from the missionaries stressed the substandard nature of the educational facilities and the need for more money to improve light and ventilation in the classrooms. The schools were nevertheless free for the needy and thus helped to educate children who otherwise would have received no education.

One of the most appreciated Methodist works for children was the Child Protection League, founded by Russian Methodists to rescue the estimated eight thousand Russian children in Harbin. Many children of Harbin were homeless war orphans, or even if they had families, were subsisting on water and black bread. Members of the Child Protection League donated a fixed sum of money per month to help house, feed, and educate orphans. By 1925, 110 Russians had joined the Child Protection League and gave monthly out of their poverty to help those less fortunate, both Chinese and Russian children, in Harbin.[28] The mission ran soup lines for the poor and also fed children in the winter.[29] A medical clinic with four doctors, four dentists, and three pharmacists was treating seven thousand patients a year by 1926.[30]

By 1927, the evangelistic wing of the mission had opened six churches in Harbin and along the railway. The evangelistic goal of the mission was to found churches as close as possible to the Soviet border so that Russian Methodists, some of whom were Soviet citizens working on the railway, could make forays into Soviet territory. The Methodists wanted to be in a good position to evangelize the Soviet Union if the political situation permitted.

The success of each church depended on the pastor, who had to rent a building before he could organize a congregation. Often the establishment of a Sunday school was the first step toward gathering a congregation.[31]

Since the Russian Orthodox Church had no activities for children, the Methodist evangelists could reach nominal orthodox parents through children's work. The odds against collecting a successful congregation were high in the face of the frontier drunkenness and immorality, the hostility of pro-Bolshevik Soviets, and the disdain poured on the Methodists by Orthodox Christians who considered them to be sectarians. Only great sacrifice by the Russian Methodist preachers made the churches possible. Although they received only a fraction of the salary paid to the missionaries, the Russian preachers gave their energy, their health, and in one case their lives for the goal of evangelizing Russia.[32]

The young Russian preachers, supervised by the missionary George Erwin, received their theological education at the Bible Institute run by the missionaries and by visiting professors from Methodist schools in Korea and China. In the 1925 school year, the Bible Institute enrolled fourteen persons—nine men and five women. The Institute offered courses in church history, English, systematic theology, Old Testament, New Testament, homiletics, Methodist polity and history, and the study of Russian literature. Those who attended the Institute did so on top of carrying a full pastoral load of teaching Bible classes, running Sunday schools and choirs, and preaching sermons.[33] The women who attended the Bible Institute did youth and women's work.

The first Bible Institute graduate ordained by the mission was Gregory Yasinitsky, who had fought for Russia during World War I and then was imprisoned by the Bolsheviks for refusing to join them. Though sentenced to death, Yasinitsky was freed by Czech forces who revolted in Siberia. Yasinitsky joined the White Army under Admiral Kolchak. After being deceived by the Bolsheviks into a fake truce, 126 officers of Yasinitsky's regiment were bayoneted and thrown into the Hoy River. One of the few survivors of the massacre, Yasinitsky fled to Harbin and became an early convert of the mission. Raised in Ukraine as a *stunde*, or Moravian, Yasinitsky was already a Protestant and so was put in charge of teaching the Bible in the Methodist schools.[34] Yasinitsky's refugee background was typical for the twelve men who eventually became Methodist preachers.

The vast majority of the converts came to the church from a Russian Orthodox background, but a few were already Protestants. Person-to-person evangelism and Bible teaching brought most members in by profession of faith. Frequent revivals by missionary evangelists kept the fires of conversion stoked hot.

In the context of Harbin in the 1920s, many curious young Russians visited Methodist services out of boredom.[35] Some of them stayed to join one of the Epworth leagues sponsored by the various Methodist churches. The Epworth leagues were the forerunner of the Methodist Youth Fellowship, and in them teenagers found social identity and a sense of Christian purpose for their lives. On February 14, 1926, there occurred probably the most interesting Epworth League meeting in Methodist history. The five Epworth leagues of Harbin—one Chinese, one Japanese, one Korean, and two Russian—held a union service at the Central Methodist Church of Harbin. Each Epworth League president gave a speech in his own tongue, which was then translated into English and from English into the three other languages. The missionary George Erwin summed up the significance of the intercultural gathering when he reported in *The Missionary Voice*: "The program impressed me with the universality of the religion of Christ more forcibly than I have seen ever it demonstrated before."[36]

Women's work in the churches was supervised by two missionaries from the Woman's Department of the Board of Missions of the Methodist Episcopal Church, South, Sallie Browne and Constance Rumbough.[37] They organized missionary societies, Bible classes, Sunday schools, Girl Scout units, and other work for women and girls. Through the missionary societies, Russian women helped the poor of Harbin and helped to evangelize their neighbors. They paid half the salary of a Chinese Bible woman for the Chinese Methodists in Harbin. Several of their number decided to train for formal mission service. In the summers, the women held month-long church camps so that children of Harbin could get fresh air, exercise, and intensive gospel training.[38] In 1927, a laywoman from Virginia endowed the Jane Brown Evangelistic Center. This gave young women a safe place to live and to go for music lessons and other wholesome entertainment.

News of the world mission activities spread by word of mouth and through the sale of the mission paper. From 1923 to 1925, the mission published a Russian version of the Nashville-based *Methodist Christian Advocate*. The paper had a local section that reported on the progress of the mission, but it was largely a translation of articles from English. The popularity of the *Advocate* encouraged the mission to publish its own paper. In August of 1925, it began the *Methodist, the Bulletin of the Siberia-Manchuria Mission of the Methodist Episcopal Church, South*, as a replacement for the Russian *Advocate*. The *Methodist* contained photographs and news of Russian Methodists and missionaries. Church, educational, and charitable activities were reported in its pages. Bible studies, sermons, and testimonies by mission members made the bulletin a significant evangelistic organ throughout Manchuria and Siberia.

The End

By 1927, the Russian branch of the Siberia-Manchuria Mission seemed well established. Members and adherents numbered in the hundreds.

Twelve Russian pastors administered the religious work, and the mission employed numerous Russians as doctors, nurses, and teachers. The mission was like a home to many of the displaced emigrants. The Rev. George Erwin supervised the evangelistic work, and his wife Vada kept the books for the mission and taught school. The Rev. H. C. Ritter, former professor of Nanking Theological Seminary, had replaced H. W. Jenkins as coordinator of the educational enterprises.

In 1927, the mission seemed on the edge of a breakthrough: the first convert had volunteered to evangelize inside the Soviet Union. Bishop Lambuth's dream continued to inspire missionaries and converts, both of whom wanted, for different reasons perhaps, to enter the Soviet Union to evangelize Russians. The dream of converting the Russian people to Christ, and perhaps in the process undercutting Bolshevik atheism, animated the pages of the mission *Methodist*. Copies of the *Methodist* mysteriously crossed the Soviet borders. Manchurian Methodists hopefully read reports of Methodism in Moscow and Leningrad and of other Protestant groups in Siberia. And now in 1927 a Bolshevik soldier was ready to defy the authorities and preach the word in the Soviet Union. Mr. Zaharedsky had been a nominal Roman Catholic who had fought with "the Red Army from Petrograd to Vladivostok and was wounded ten times."[39] He settled in a small railroad town where he became a barber and the president of the local Bolshevik Union. Meeting the Methodist group in Tsitsikar, Mr. and Mrs. Zaharedsky were converted and decided, despite persecution by local Bolsheviks, to enter Russia. Zaharedsky represented the first Soviet citizen able and willing to cross the borders to attempt to capture the Soviet people for Methodism. All that was needed was to raise money for his support. The ideological *raison d'être* of the mission seemed on the verge of fulfillment.

Then in May of 1927, Bishop Ainsworth, newly in charge of the Siberia-Manchuria Mission, recommended that it be liquidated.[40] The Board of Missions voted for closure at the annual meeting and telegrammed the missionaries, instructing them to sell the mission compound and to return to the United States. The Woman's Board transferred Rumbough and Browne to Poland. It was left to George and Vada Erwin to shut down the work. After turning over some of the Methodist work to other charitable organizations, George Erwin left for a tour of Methodist missions en route to Georgia. Mrs. Erwin spent three more weeks closing the mission. She put the mission money and papers into a money belt and wore them out of the country. Mrs. Erwin led an entourage of her three children and about a dozen Russians across Manchuria to Korea, across the Pacific, and to the United States. She traveled by rail from British Columbia to Minnesota and on to Georgia, dropping off emigrants as she went. Because of the anti-

Russian bias of United States immigration officers, most of whom were former military men, Mrs. Erwin had an extremely difficult time getting the Russians into the country.[41]

The Russian Methodists petitioned to continue the mission, but to no avail. They stood by helpless and angry at all their sacrifices for the work, as the missionaries pulled up stakes and left Manchuria, never to return. Those who could take advantage of the missionaries' departure used them as a one-way ticket out of Harbin. But most of the converts had to remain to face an uncertain future without Methodist support.

The reason given the Russian Methodists for the close of their mission was lack of funds. Several missionaries accepted this explanation at face value.[42] It was true that the Board had not received all the Centenary funds that had been pledged and had suffered a 40 percent budget cut from 1924 to 1926. But decisions about where to cut the budget were made according to other financial criteria. As the newest mission field of the Methodist Episcopal Church, South, the Siberia-Manchuria Mission was vulnerable. Newness, however, still does not explain why the entire operation was shut down instead of budget cuts being felt more evenly across the board.

Elmer T. Clark, in his 1929 mission history of the Methodist Episcopal Church, South, argued that Bolshevik persecution had necessitated the closing of the mission. Although the Bolsheviks harassed mission converts, they did not control Harbin in 1927, and Clark's reasoning seems faulty.[43]

Another possible reason for the closing stems from the fact that the mission accounts were transferred to work among ethnic Belorussians in Wilno, Poland, and by 1927 it seemed that Belorussians living near Wilno might respond to the Methodist gospel. Esther Case, administrative secretary for Foreign Fields, argued in the November 1928 issue of *The Missionary Voice* that funds were transferred from Harbin to Wilno under the mistaken impression that the Belorussians of Poland were the same group as the "white" Russians of Manchuria. Methodists in the United States believed they were merely consolidating two missions for the same people into one. In fact, however, the mission board eliminated work among political "White Russians" in Manchuria, and then transferred the resources to ethnic Belorussians (also known as "White Russians") who lived in Poland. When Browne and Rumbough of the Woman's Board arrived from Harbin, they were forced to learn an entirely new language and culture because the Belorussians were ethnically different from the Manchurian refugees.[44]

The mistake was perhaps costly in terms of Methodist expansion. The Board terminated a successful mission to work among Belorussians who were so attached to the Orthodox Church that they uniformly opposed the Methodists. By 1933, the Woman's Board of Missions had to transfer its Belorussian work to Poles. In the words of historian Noreen Tatum, "When

Methodist work was changed over to the Polish group, it was due to a lack of response of the White Russians and a growing response of the Poles."[45]

In the 81st Annual Report of the Board of Missions, May 1927, the refugee status of the Manchurian Russians was suggested as a reason to terminate the mission and to transfer its resources to Little White Russia in Poland. It was reported that,

> When the Russian Mission was opened, our object was to make a gateway into Siberia. There are now legal difficulties in the way of doing this. The fact that the large Russian population here is migratory raises the question as to whether we should continue our work there or direct our money and interest to Little White Russia as a more favorable approach to the Russian people.[46]

The Board argued, then, that permanent Methodist church-planting was impossible among people whose major goal was to leave Harbin as soon as possible. The Board's decision to shut down the mission was made in the interest of the Methodist Episcopal Church, South, as an institution rather than in the interests of the Russian refugees for whom the Siberia-Manchuria Mission had become a community and a source of hope. The decision to liquidate the mission was a top-down decision made without consulting either the group of missionaries or the Russian Methodists.

The primary mover behind the decision to terminate was Bishop William N. Ainsworth, who succeeded Bishop Boaz as missionary bishop over the Far East. Both converts and missionaries recalled that in contrast to Bishops Lambuth and Boaz, Bishop Ainsworth was hostile to the mission from the beginning. Gregory Yasinitsky believed that Bishop Ainsworth was not a mission-minded man and that he failed to realize that Methodist converts witnessed for Christ and organized believers wherever they migrated. Yasinitsky believed that Ainsworth favored the Orthodox Church and felt Methodist work to be unnecessary.[47] Missionary Vada Erwin also had negative memories of Bishop Ainsworth—that he refused to visit Harbin because of his fear of cholera and that he was responsible for funds being diverted away from Harbin.[48] Regardless of whether these negative impressions of Bishop Ainsworth were accurate, it is a fact that he proposed before the Board that the mission be terminated. Considering the monopoly of power held by Methodist bishops, it is unlikely that anyone on the Board of Missions would have opposed him. A strange twist of the situation was that as a member of the South Georgia Conference, Bishop Ainsworth eliminated the mission of his own parishioners and friends.[49]

In retrospect, the decisions to close the Siberia-Manchuria Mission and transfer its funds to Little White Russia were tragic. First of all, the bureaucratic manner in which the decision to terminate was made is a typical example of American chauvinism. The original missionaries to Manchuria were meeting the needs of Russian refugees by assisting them to construct schools, social centers, charitable facilities and to plant churches. Then out of bureaucratic concern for institutional longevity rather than human need, the Bishop back home closed the mission without even consulting the Russian Methodists under its care. The failure to take into consideration the opinions of indigenous Christians was all too frequently a common attitude among American church personnel in the late nineteenth and early twentieth centuries. An irony of the situation was that the transfer of funds to Little White Russia was made in belief that Methodist work in Poland would be more permanent than among Manchuria refugees. Yet not only did the Belorussians of Poland reject Methodism, but World War II destroyed mission work in Poland as well. Among Hitler, Stalin, and Polish Catholic resurgence, American Methodism in Poland had a difficult future.

The major reason that the Siberia-Manchuria Mission should not have been closed was the tenacity with which converts clung to the Methodist Church after the missionaries withdrew in 1927. In March of 1928, the Woman's Missionary Council received a letter from four members of the Ladies' Missionary Societies in Harbin. In the letter, the women told of how there were four ladies' missionary societies with one hundred members who had raised $2,500 over five years to help needy children. Three Russian women had trained for full-time Christian work at the now defunct Bible Institute. The letter closed with the words, "Will you accept us among your midst, our dear Sisters, will you teach us what we do not know yet, will you take interest in the worn out soul of a Russian woman, in her sufferings in the recent past and in her joys in the present new life?"[50]

Despite the withdrawal of American support, the Russian preachers continued their evangelistic work—even after the Japanese invasion of Manchuria of 1931.[51] Several converts left all they had and crossed the border into the Soviet Union to preach the gospel and to plant evangelical churches. One can only surmise that the brave evangelists eventually lost their lives in one of Stalin's prisons. Fellow Russian Methodists continued to beg for support of Bishop Lambuth's dream, but to no avail.

A few missionaries managed to keep contact with Methodists in Harbin until Soviet communists invaded Manchuria in 1945. The women missionaries who had been transferred to Poland sent packages to children in Harbin. Although the Methodist Church did not substantially assist its struggling Russian members, on occasion individual missionaries helped various Russians to escape from Manchuria. As late as 1957, the Rev. and Mrs. George Erwin assisted a destitute couple in their eighties to leave Harbin for a room in a World Refugee Home in Ireland.[52]

Today there are an estimated thirty-seven Russians left in Harbin, down from a population of 100,000. Under the Japanese occupation, many Russians used Japanese passports to flee Manchuria. After Soviet troops marched in, half of the Russian population was forcibly deported to remote Central Asia. During the Cultural Revolution in China, the few Russians that remained were persecuted by the Chinese. The Chinese destroyed the Russian burial ground, Nikolayevsky Cathedral, and Russian homes. There are few signs left of what once was the largest European community in Asia.[53]

Perhaps the Mission Board was technically correct when in 1927 it closed down the Methodist mission to Manchuria; it is true that no Russian Methodist churches remain there today. There are, nevertheless, an unknown number of Protestants in the Soviet Union, some of whom are the fruit of Methodist evangelists who crossed the borders in the face of death. The undaunted spirit of Russian Methodism also continues to live in emigrant communities in the United States, Canada, Australia, continental Europe, and Latin America.

CHAPTER 5

The Evangelical Church in Latvia
S T Kimbrough, Jr.

The history of the Evangelical Church (*Evangelische Gemein-schaft*) is important to the whole of United Methodism's story in Russia, since this church merged with the Church of the Brethren to form the Evangelical United Brethren Church, which subsequently united with The Methodist Church in 1968, the result being The United Methodist Church.

The move of the Evangelical Church into the Baltic region was primarily through the impetus of its North Germany Conference. Even though German-Russian members of the church in Dakota had written of the desperate need for a Christian mission to Russia, the American church gave no immediate response. Already in 1899 Bishop Breyfogel, in a speech to the General Conference declared, "The *Evangelische Gemeinschaft* stands on the Russian border and looks eastward."[1] These words expressed the hope of responding to a "Macedonian call" to Russia.

In 1908, the Rev. G. Baehren of the North Germany Conference was invited to Riga, Latvia by a Russian of high standing.[2] After the Board of Missions had approved acceptance of the invitation, Baehren made the journey. Upon his arrival, much to his surprise, he met a family who had attended an Evangelical church in Berlin. As there was a sizable German-speaking population in Riga, it was natural for the Evangelical Church to envision a role there.

In 1909, a request from Riga for a missionary was received by the North Germany Conference. Two years would pass, however, before it could fulfill it. Nevertheless, in October of 1909, the Rev. R. Kücklich, a presiding elder, made an initial visit on behalf of the conference.

During the following year another visit to Riga was made by Bishop Breyfogel and the Rev. Max Richter of the North Germany Conference.

Together they traveled to a number of Russian cities, including Saint Petersburg and Kiev. Like the Rev. Baehren, they too encountered Germans: Brother and Mrs. Linz[3] and Brother Werner, who had been associated with the Evangelical Church in Germany, were now living in Riga for business reasons and very much desired a pastor. In 1910 they planned a week of evangelization and invited the Rev. Max Richter to Riga to preach. Richter provided a vivid account of his stay there in an unpublished letter (February 11, 1910) to his wife.[4] The services in various surroundings were held in German, Latvian, and Russian. Of particular interest are the services in Russian, as most accounts of the Evangelical Church work in Latvia mention only work in German and Latvian. However, Baron von Stackelberg, who directed mission work among the Russian population, invited the Rev. Richter to preach to a large group of Russians, and the Baron translated for him.

At the annual meeting of the Board of Missions in the United States in October of 1910, the decision was made to begin officially the mission work in Latvia, and the Woman's Missionary Society agreed to pay the salary of a missionary.[5]

Riga was a strategic business center of the Baltic. It covered an area of about 65 square kilometers, and before World War I had a population of over four hundred thousand. It is situated on the Daugava River just seven miles from its mouth and some 560 kilometers from Saint Petersburg. At the time the Latvian work of the Evangelical Church was established, Riga boasted approximately four hundred factories and some ninety thousand workers. The city's commercial importance was a key factor in attracting German business personnel.

The North Germany Conference saw the potential for its outreach in the city and appointed the Rev. Reinhold Barchet, who at the time was assigned to an Evangelical church in Wanne, to be a full-time missionary in Riga. With his arrival in Riga on May 11, 1911, the work of the Evangelical Church in Latvia began.

The Rev. G. E. Epp provides the following description of the origin of the Evangelical Church mission in Riga.

> After due consideration the Board of Missions resolved that our Church enter Russia as a mission field, and that the city of Riga (now in Latvia) constitute her first field in that country.
>
> The North Germany Conference declared its willingness to supply the missionary for this important new enterprise, and the Woman's Missionary Society generously offered to furnish the means of support. Rev. Reinhold Barchet was the missionary appointed to undertake the important task of locating and organizing the new work. He and his wife arrived in Riga on May 11, 1911. New and unusual problems confronted the missionary. While

private devotional meetings were allowed, only twenty-five persons were permitted to attend. After repeated efforts both in Riga and Petrograd, the new missionary finally succeeded in securing permission to organize a society with a legally prepared constitution, said society having the name Evangelical Association-White Cross. In the first paragraph of the constitution the purpose of the society was stated as being to contribute toward the moral uplift of the people in accordance with the principles of the Word of God. In order to fulfill this purpose permission was given to organize auxiliary societies, to erect benevolent institutions, and to publish literature in all parts of the Russian empire. The society elected Brother Barchet president and he was privileged to deliver addresses in all halls rented by the same.[6]

The work of The Evangelical Church in Latvia must be viewed in two stages: (1) before World War I (1911–1914), and (2) after the war (1918 onward).

Before the War

On September 12, 1912, the "Evangelical Association-White Cross" was officially recognized and registered by the government. The first task was to procure locations for meeting. Ten days later, on September 22, only about one and one half years after Barchet's arrival, the Evangelical Church in Riga celebrated its first communion service in a newly rented hall. The same afternoon and evening it opened its first Sunday school and held a service of dedication.

It was not long before civil authorities began to send a representative to the meetings to hear the Rev. Barchet's sermons. Nevertheless, they did not interfere with his work so that, at least among the German-speaking population, the work grew, enabling the official organization of a congregation before the end of 1912. By 1913, adult, youth, and children's work had begun, including a Sunday school.

In 1913 Barchet also began mission work on the other side of the Daugava River at Agenskalns. On Dec. 14, 1914, the second Evangelical Church meeting hall was dedicated in Riga. While the membership of Riga and Agenskalns was reported as seventy-five in 1914 and the future looked bright indeed, World War I began, Barchet was conscripted for military service by his homeland, Riga was drastically affected by the tragedies of war, and the work was discontinued. The hope Barchet expressed in his report on the work in Riga to the North Germany Conference of the Evangelical Church at its meeting in 1914 was, at least for the moment, not to be realized: "Our goal: mission among the Russians of Russia! May God soon open the doors for us!"[7]

After the War

War ravaged Latvia and, although it declared its independence from Russia on November 18, 1918, it was extremely vulnerable. Eller reports: "Of the million refugees, hardly 300,000 returned—the rest perished.[8] Ten thousand farms were destroyed; industrial machinery was removed into Russia. The population exodus is portrayed thus: in 1910 there were 2,552,000; in 1914 there were 1,930,000; and in 1936 there were 1,800,000."[9]

During the terrible war years what had become of the mission work begun by the Evangelical Church in Riga? "A few sisters, under great hunger, and self-denial, succeeded in saving some of the furniture of the chapel and parsonage from the ravages of the Russians and later of the Bolsheviks."[10] During Barchet's absence there were primarily two groups of sisters—German (Agenskalns) and Latvian (Slokas iela [iela = street], Riga)—that took over the work.[11] During the war any ongoing work was due also in part to the efforts of Brothers Linz[12] and Werner, as well as Baron von Stackelberg.

When the war was over and independence had been declared, suffering was by no means at an end in Latvia. With the economy in shambles and a poverty-stricken population, high taxes and few exports (some birchwood and agricultural products), Latvia was in extreme need and vulnerable on almost all fronts. Christianity had survived in this context, but its followers' sufferings were not passed. Otto Michaelis provides a gripping account of the desperate situation in Riga.

> The collapse of 1918 resulted in the withdrawal of German troops from the Baltic nations. Now Bolshevism could raise its head without resistance. Unhindered the red flood waltzed over the land. Armed resistance was no longer possible. What would happen now?
> At dawn on January 3, 1919 there was a meeting of the Riga pastors. Provost Eckhardt, who a few weeks later would pay for his faith with a martyr's death, spoke. Three days before in his sermon on New Years Eve he had told his congregation that the only thing which could help them in this time of need is the willingness to be a martyr for their faith. As long as Christians give in to every movement which recklessly pursues its goals, things could never be better. Christians must show their opponents that they too have goals to pursue. In this same spirit he now spoke from the heart to his fellow pastors: What will become of the members of our congregations, who cannot flee, if their leaders abandon them? That afternoon the first Bolshevik mob led a parade with the red flag through the streets of Riga and from that point on there was a reign of blood and fear. It began with the prohibition of religious teaching and prayer in the schools, and with the desecration of the churches from whose pulpits the Communist leaders gave blasphemous speeches. Finally it resulted in a terrible bloodbath. Within a period of four and one half months in the city of Riga the number of

executions rose to 2,654! This is the number of deaths in a single city! Bolshevism saw in the Lutheran pastors its most dangerous enemies. Thirty-two pastors went to their deaths for the gospel and because they were Germans. They did not doubt the words one of them preached to his congregation shortly before his death: "The Lord needs the death of his own time and again as the most precious seed of his kingdom."

As word of these events reached Germany, it struck a people who were inwardly crushed, like someone who is ill, suffering and tortured by pain and no longer can muster the energy to empathize with the suffering of others. However, this news was so horrendous that even those who had become numb and indifferent were moved. The effect was doubled. For once the eyes of the German Christians were opened. They received a terrible report of the satanical passion with which Bolshevism sought to obliterate all Christian life. Even so the Baltic martyrs had shown that there is another who is stronger than death, of whom Luther in rejoicing over the progress of the gospel in the Baltic nations once had written: "Christ is wonderful."[13]

Already in his district report to the North Germany Annual Conference dated May 2, 1918, however, G. Baehren expressed the hope that the work of the Evangelical Church might begin once again in Riga.[14]

On November 18, 1918, independence was declared and the nation of Latvia was born. At this time no foreigners could obtain residence permits, hence Reinhold Barchet, who though wounded in the war had survived and wanted to return to Riga to reopen the work of the mission, could not return. However, in 1919 he did make two exploratory visits to Riga, found the remnants of the work meeting in private homes and regularly in Agenskalns,[15] and was greatly heartened by same. Nevertheless, he realized that the time was not yet right to begin again.

In the fall of 1920, the Board of Missions asked Bishop Heinmiller and B. R. Wiener, its field secretary, to examine the work of the church in Europe.[16] Wiener and Barchet then traveled to Riga, as reported by the former.

We arranged for a visit to Riga immediately upon conclusion of the session of the North Germany Conference. Permission was granted, and after two nights and one day of travel from Berlin, Brother R. Barchet and I [B. R. Wiener] arrived safely on Wednesday morning. Brother Bahn, a young brother who had been looking after our interests there recently, and who had been advised of our coming, met us at the station and informed us that there had been three services announced for us that day, a union service for the next day, and again three for Friday, the last day of our stay.

Our services without exception were well attended. The audiences were composed of Christians from the inner circle of believers of various names. However, among these there were quite a number who hold to the Evangelical Association. It may interest you to hear that our name, *Evangelische Gemeinschaft*, is so popular in Riga that various other fellowships of believers have adopted it as their own. We have no objection providing they will bring no dishonor upon it and will later unite with us in church fellowship.

We left Riga not only with the firm conviction that the responsibility for the Christianization of this splendid old city and a very large part of old Russia, now in part divided up into various smaller countries, rests in a measure upon the shoulders of the Evangelical Association, but also, with the belief that this part of the world will be a very fruitful field for the missionary programs of the church.[17]

Wiener's subsequent report recommended: (1) continuance of the mission, (2) appointment of a missionary, (3) purchase of property, (4) bilingual work (German and Latvian), and (5) possible appointment of an American superintendent. All of these were eventually fulfilled with the exception of the fifth recommendation. Barchet recommended that Waldemar Steinert be assigned as a missionary to Riga. Wiener proposed Steinert to the Board of Missions, which approved him. He took up his post in June 1921 and was ordained deacon at the North Germany Conference of 1923.

The minutes of the Mission Society of the 1921 North Germany Annual Conference reported the lack of meeting places and workers, high rental prices, and the spiritual and physical hunger in Latvia. R. Barchet described his trip to Riga from March to April and how he preached almost every day, and on the last Sunday more than four hundred people attended. The minutes state that, as of 1921, the Evangelical Church had two meeting halls in Riga, where the work was conducted in the German, Latvian, and Estonian languages. It was also reported that the current political situation prohibited the appointment of preachers of German citizenship/origin to work in Latvia, hence, the hope was expressed that a qualified person might be sent from the church in America.[18]

On May 17, 1922, the Latvian government recognized the Evangelical Church as a church, and on January 11, 1923, it officially recognized the Evangelical Church as a free church, which meant that it could conduct its work unencumbered in the future. The church was duly incorporated as an ecclesiastical body with all juridical rights and privileges provided by Latvian law.

Riga

In Riga, the Rev. Steinert was assisted in children's and youth work by Mrs. Hannah Heinrichsen. On April 1, 1922, the Evangelical Church opened its first kindergarten. Even so, "during the winter many children [were] unable to come for want of clothing and shoes."[19] At first, the Rev. Steinert restored the German-speaking work and was assisted in the Latvian language mission by a Brother Fischer. Mrs. Steinert held Bible classes also in Latvian. In the city of Riga proper, the Evangelical Church rented two meeting halls where preaching services were held regularly. The worship services and classes of instruction were well attended. The rental costs were extremely high, for the government placed no restrictions on the hall rentals, although it did on other properties. This was a heavy burden for the mission. On Pentecost Day 1922, a new meeting hall with a seating capacity of 125 was dedicated in Agenskalns across the river from Riga, where work was begun before the war and miraculously continued during it.[20]

The reports that came from the Latvian work in central Europe and the United States were filled with hope and anticipation. The future seemed bright. In a report of his recent trip to Riga dated March 9, 1922, Reinhold Barchet wrote:

> Since I have been here I have been conducting evangelistic services every day; many hundreds of people have visited the meetings. If I gave heed to all the petitions and invitations which I have received, I could spend another six months in the work right here. Rev. and Mrs. Steinert, who are laboring under the signal blessing of God, are confidently looking forward to the time when an American missionary may be sent here to help build the kingdom. Soon the doors of Russia will be opened again for missionary work and our church ought to be ready to enter them when that time comes.[21]

Before the end of 1923, two new Latvian-speaking congregations were established. In the fall one was begun with nine charter members at Sloka, about two hours away from Riga. "The meetings are well attended, on an average from twenty-five to thirty persons, however, they are all very poor people, many of them are fishermen."[22] A second Latvian-speaking congregation began at Sarkan-Daugava, with seven charter members and two services on Sunday (11:00 A.M. and 3:00 P.M.), a Bible study on Wednesday evening, and vesper services on Saturday. The minutes of the Mission Society of the 1925 North Germany Annual Conference reported the establishment of these two new mission stations.[23]

After the church was approved as an official ecclesiastical body, and with appropriation of some foreign funds, church leaders began the search for church property in Latvia. Property was purchased in Riga on Brivibas iela, and the new meeting hall and building were dedicated there on September 23, 1928.

Kuldiga

Work was expanded also to Kuldiga, a small city of some eight thousand people, of which some two thousand were Jews, fifteen hundred were Germans, and the rest were Latvians. The Rev. Eugene Schwenk was licensed to preach at the 1923 North Germany Conference session and was assigned to Kuldiga.[24] At the same conference it was reported that a mission worker and his small congregation in Kuldiga had decided to join the Evangelical Church.[25] At this time, the Latvian work was placed under the supervision of the Berlin District of the North Germany Conference. During the year 1923 seventeen new members were added to the church.[26] Agenskalns reported twenty-nine active members and fifty-one associate members. Sunday school attendance totaled two thousand, the Junior E. L. C. E. one thousand, and the girls organization four hundred.[27] Steinert reported ten active members at the Slokas iela preaching station (seating capacity of 150, with services in German) and nine associate members, and a total annual attendance of 461. It was with a particular source of joy that he reported: "Two young women have gone to prepare themselves at our Berlin institution for Deaconess work."[28] Furthermore, "three young men from Kuldiga attended the session of the North Germany Conference in 1924 and requested admission to the Theological Seminary at Reutlingen, Germany."[29]

Sister Berta Engels began an independent Latvian Evangelical congregation in Kuldiga, which eventually merged with the congregation of the Evangelical Church in that city. When the Rev. Schwenk was assigned to Liepaja, Sister Engels remained in charge of the work in Kuldiga. She was a particularly gifted woman who held the work in Kuldiga together, especially when difficulties seemed insurmountable. The spirit of the work in Kuldiga is captured aptly by Bishop S. J. Umbreit, who described a trip he had made there:

> Here we were greeted warmly by Brother Arnack and family, sister Berta Engels and sister Lindwart. . . . Our hall is well located and spacious, although the entrance could be better. . . . By Wednesday evening the first worship service in this district was held in German. The hall was filled with a sizeable congregation. Poems, songs, and a gift of flowers preceded the sermon. The people here take very seriously the Great Commission of the Master.[30]

Superintendent Wilhelm Mohr reported of Kuldiga: "Those who attend the worship services are primarily from the city. Considerably more than 100 fill the lovely hall. A large number of young people, who also organized a Latvian choir, are an indication of the hope which this work portends."[31]

Not everything moved smoothly in Kuldiga, however. The minutes of the Mission Society of the 1925 North Germany Annual Conference indicate that there had been some difficulties in the Kuldiga work. The majority of the members in a small independent congregation there, which was registered under the name of *Blau-Kreuz* (Blue Cross), desired to become members of the Evangelical Church. Their leader, Preacher Rabe, however, had resisted such action and had refused to withdraw in favor of the merger.[32]

It is important to note that two significant Latvian Evangelical Church workers came from the Kuldiga congregation: the brothers Hans and Rudolph Kalnmalis.

Liepaja

The third primary station of work, in addition to Riga and Kuldiga, was established in Liepaja, also a port on the Baltic Sea. This once extremely busy city had a population at the time of about fifty-eight thousand, of whom some five thousand were Germans. Many Jews also lived in Liepaja. Numerous languages were spoken in the churches of the city. The Rev. Schwenk was appointed to Liepaja in 1923 and soon opened two preaching places. He registered the following report in the *Evangelischer Botschafter*.

Of course, we are not the first ones in Liepaja. Other congregations have been organized along side the large Lutheran and Reformed Churches and, therefore, much fruit has already been stored in heaven through these efforts. Nevertheless, we believe that we also have a contribution to make in the building of God's kingdom. In addition to the five fairly large Baptist congregations there are also Methodists, as well as three Moravian congregations which are active. The German language is represented by a Lutheran Church and a German Baptist congregation. There are also Old Apostolic and Adventist congregations, the Salvation Army and small beginnings in other directions. In our newly begun work, conducted at the outset in German, we have much to rejoice about in spite of many difficulties. In our very pleasant meeting hall, which has been made inviting and furnished well to our needs by sisters, brothers, and friends, we have experienced many blessed hours. Even though some seed has fallen by the way, some has fallen on good soil.

Through the fine leadership of our small Martha organization (raffles, handwork) we have come into the possession of a beautiful organ-harmonium, for which we had longed for quite some time. Its lovely sound now fills every heart with joy. These places of which we report are not famous and they will not one day play a great role in history, nevertheless we hope with the souls here gathered to lay the foundation for prosperous and fruitful work for the Master. Our small choir does its best to enhance the beauty of our worship services.

Eben-ezer! [meaning in Hebrew "stone of victory"] With great joy we were able to inscribe this beautiful word on our cornerstone in this lovely Baltic Sea country. That will be the name of our parish hall. With the joyful hope that our God will continue to help us, we are now in the midst of building. It is a beautiful piece of earth, which God has given us. We hope to be able to hold the dedication at the beginning of October and then a full report will follow. For faith intercessions we are very grateful. [33]

By 1928 the property at Juliannas iela 54 in Liepaja had been purchased. It was a sizable lot with two buildings or houses on it. One was built along the side of the lot and one at the back. The latter one was converted into a chapel that could seat about four hundred people.

There was a decided effort to reach the Latvian-speaking population, as Wilhelm Mohr reported in the *Evangelischer Botschafter:* "Sister Berta has worked very diligently and translated large portions of the cathechism into Latvian. We need more workers for Latvia, a Latvian cathechism, a Latvian church polity, and a Latvian *Botschafter.*" [34]

Hope Against Hope

After a tour of the Evangelical Church work in Latvia, Bishop S. J. Umbreit concluded his 1927 report with these words of hope:

> Our work in Latvia has great possibilities of expansion. In the area of Liepaja there are many Germans, and, if one considers the Latvian population, one must say that the harvest is great. May God be gracious to our fellow workers and brothers and sisters in Latvia and give them victory in all things.[35]

The Latvian work of the Evangelical Church was by no means destined for victory in all things. At first it seemed that all would indeed run relatively smoothly. When the government began to be progressively suspicious of foreign organizations, however, it was clear that the rising spirit of nationalism necessitated making the work as indigenous as possible. Hence, it was recommended that the workers all be Latvian, with the exception of the superintendent.[36] The Latvian mission was also given its own identity separate from the European work, although the European bishop retained episcopal responsibility for it. All of these actions were approved by the Board of Missions.

Property was also bought for the building of a church in Liepaja, but the situation there was complicated by the fact that government officials prohibited the Rev. Schwenk's further residence because he was not a Latvian citizen.

The minutes of the Mission Society of the 1929 North Germany Annual Conference included the following membership report for the Evangelical Church in Latvia:[37]

Riga	68
Liepaja	70
Kuldiga	58
Total	196

The 1931 minutes reflect a slight variation of these figures:[38]

Riga	60
Liepaja	76
Kuldiga	63
Total	199

Just as it seemed the work would suffer greatly because of the government restrictions, the Rev. Rudolph Kalnmalis, a Latvian, was assigned in 1930 to the work in Liepaja. He was the first indigenous pastor. However, already during this same year in the city of Riga, the Bolsheviks began their ravage of Latvia.

A careful record of the work in Latvia is more difficult to reconstruct during the years 1930 to 1940. Still, the report of Superintendent Wilhelm Mohr in 1931 is an excellent description of the forces that were making the work of the mission difficult, the status of the work itself, and the signs of hope.

> The results and consequences of war and revolution, the rapid spread of anti-Christian culture from the West, especially the influence of Bolshevism, not to speak of a growing nationalism, a stagnant Christianity, a general spiritual dearth, and the love of sinful living, are all strong hindrances to a church with a real spiritual message. However, our calling to Latvia is in full force, and the promises of God will yet be fulfilled. Jesus, the strong hero of Golgotha, owns his word and will stand by his work, if we prove obedient and faithful. There are signs of progress, not phenomenal to be sure, for each bit of progress must be made by strong wrestling with the enemy of our souls,—every sinner must be snatched from his terrible claws. The land surely needs the gospel, and the Lord will certainly revive his work during these years.
>
> At present there are two men and four women in our Latvian Mission. For some years we have tried to secure a German and locate him in Latvia. Unfortunately the laws of Latvia have thwarted every such attempt. However, we did not desist from our endeavor, and now have good prospects of success. We work three mission stations, and own two rather desirable pieces of ground of some dimensions. In Riga there is a fine mission building, including a preaching hall and parsonage. It was dedicated September 23, 1928. There is still a debt of $1,000 on this property. Ebenezer Chapel and a parsonage are located in Liepaja.
>
> The chapel was dedicated on September 30, 1928. Worship services are held regularly in both the German and Latvian languages. This property is encumbered with a debt of $6,900. In Kuldiga,[39] which includes several appointments, both languages are also used. At present this charge is served by a woman missionary.

Our membership currently is 196. There are in addition 275 friends of the work. In all about 700 persons are under our influence. There are Sunday Schools, young people's organizations and a number of women's missionary societies connected with our church organizations. This is our work at present, and hopefully we are sowing seed for harvests in the future. Our hope is in God, who will prosper the work of our hands![40]

The American publication of the Evangelical Church, *Evangelical Missionary World*, listed the work in Latvia and its workers under missionary appointments through the May issue of 1935, but then Latvia is no longer listed and without explanation.

In the late 1930s the work of the Evangelical Church in Latvia came under growing pressure from a rising nationalism, the threat of Bolshevism on one hand and Nazism on the other. With Hitler's rise to power came the summons to Germans living abroad to return to their homeland, which drained the German population from Latvia, especially those who were a part of the Evangelical Church.

Still, in 1934 the Rev. Steinert spoke of their hope amid the suffering: "Perhaps you think we have turned to stone, since you have not heard from us for so long, but blood is still flowing through our veins in spite of the many crises and emergency rules."[41] In the same article in the *Evangelischer Botschafter*, Steinert described some evangelization weeks they continued to hold.

The attempt of the Board of Missions in 1938 to give the Latvian work its own identity as a separate work and the 1939 contribution from the Evangelical Church in America of $2,250[42] were not enough to save it. When the Soviets took over, nationalized the church properties, and severed contacts with the outside world, members of the church in central Europe and North America were left to wonder about the fate of the faithful few who remained, those who could not or did not flee.

Nevertheless, the reports in the *Evangelischer Botschafter* during the 1930s indicate that, until the end of the decade, the work was proceeding with hope and determination. In 1932 the Seventh Faith Conference was held in Liepaja, with Bishop S. J. Umbreit and Superintendent Mohr in attendance. From time to time evangelization weeks were held with guest preachers from Germany, such as the Rev. Drews, District Superintendent Goebel, the Rev. Brachmann, etc. A 1938 issue of the *Evangelischer Botschafter* also carried a long report by Wilhelm Steinert regarding the visit of Bishop John S. Stamm to the various locations of the Latvian work of the Evangelical Church. During a worship service in Agenskalns Bishop Stamm appointed a young Latvian preacher, Bernhard Schkobe,[43] to the Latvian congregation in Riga. At this time, the Rev.

Steinert was seventy-six years of age and still fully engaged in the Latvian work.

In 1938 the Latvian mission came under the jurisdiction of the American bishops. The repatriation of Baltic Germans by Hitler reduced the membership of the Evangelical Church in Latvia by more than 50 percent. R. Kalnmalis, who became superintendent of the Latvian work from 1938 to 1940, continued the work until the circumstances of war made it prohibitive. Then he and Pastor Schkobe fled to Germany with some of the church members, while Sister Berta Engels and other members were sent to the interior of Russia.[44]

The following are the 1939 statistics for the Latvian work:

3 pastors: R. Steinert, Hans and Rudolph Kalnmalis
223 members
5 preaching stations: Riga, Kuldiga, Liepaja, two additional
570 worshipers (including friends)
4 Sunday schools with 210 children
2 deaconesses
2 buildings for worship: Riga, Liepaja

Who knows the full story of suffering that followed? Only those who endured it. But here is the testimony of Olga Erfurt, which is no doubt that of many whose lives were changed and enriched by the Evangelical Church, which had the vision of witness, evangelism, and service to human need in Latvia from 1911 to 1940.

I am delighted to share some thoughts with you about congregational life in Riga, the capital city of Latvia. In Russia, where we lived immediately prior to coming to Riga, my parents regularly attended the worship and other events of the Moravians. Now we were looking for a congregation here, which was similar to that church both in its biblical understanding and congregational life. This we found in the Evangelical Church.

We children attended the Sunday School and the children's organization. All of the children in our family were dedicated in the Evangelical Church, which had very good relations with the Blue Cross and the Methodist Church. The youth and congregational meetings with the congregations from other Latvian cities were always special events for us. We were especially happy, when a preacher from Germany would come for a week of evangelization or for some other occasion. This was always a special opportunity for the chorus and the guitar ensemble.

As I look back today, I am thankful for the lovely time in our church and community in Riga.[45]

Appointments in Latvia 1911–1940

There follows a listing of the appointments of the Evangelical Church in Latvia from 1911 to 1940.

	Riga	Liepaja	Kuldiga
1911	R. Barchet		
1912	R. Barchet		
1913	R. Barchet		
1914	R. Barchet		
1915			
1916			
1917			
1918			
1919			
1920			
1921	W. Steinert		
1922	W. Steinert		
1923	W. Steinert		
1925	W. Steinert		
1926	W. Steinert	E. Schwenk	Arnack
1927	W. Steinert	E. Schwenk	Arnack
1928	W. Steinert/Neubauer	E. Schwenk	Arnack
1929	W. Steinert/Neubauer	E. Schwenk	Neubauer
1930	W. Steinert/Schwenk	R. Kalnmalis	Berta Engels
1931	W. Steinert/Schwenk	R. Kalnmalis	Berta Engels
1932	W. Steinert/ Schwenk	R. Kalnmalis	Berta Engels
1933	W. Steinert/ Schwenk	R. Kalnmalis	Berta Engels
1934	W. Steinert/H. Kalnmalis	R. Kalnmalis	Berta Engels
1935	W. Steinert/H. Kalnmalis	R. Kalnmalis	Berta Engels
1936	W. Steinert/H. Kalnmalis	R. Kalnmalis	Berta Engels
1937	W. Steinert/Schkobe	R. Kalnmalis	Berta Engels
1938	W. Steinert/Schkobe	R. Kalnmalis	Berta Engels
1939	W. Steinert/Schkobe	R. Kalnmalis	Berta Engels
1940	W. Steinert/Schkobe	R. Kalnmalis	Berta Engels

It is also important to note the service of deaconesses in Latvia. Sister Berta Engels served in Kuldiga from 1925 to 1940 with educational, pastoral, and preaching responsibilities. Sister Lindwart was also assigned for a number of years to the work in Kuldiga. Sister Marta Beier served in Riga from 1926 to 1939 in charge of youth work and social services.

CHAPTER 6

The Rise and Fall of Methodism in Lithuania and Latvia

S T Kimbrough, Jr.

Methodism moved across the Baltic region from Germany to Finland and on to Russia during the last years of the nineteenth century. Barclay and Copplestone cover the broad strokes and many details of this movement.[1] Certainly the Methodist work in Finland, the Baltic states, and Russia is intimately related through Methodism's connection and the way it related to the connection. There are, of course, many political factors that unite this history, particularly those relating to the old Russian Empire, World War I and German occupation, the Bolshevik Revolution, and the establishment of the Soviet Union. While the Baltic region's history is interrelated by such political factors, especially those pertaining to domination by other peoples, the political turmoil of the Baltic states during much of the twentieth century has made the telling of the story of Methodism there difficult. In the previous chapter, the work of the Evangelical Church in Riga, Liepaja, and Kuldiga, Latvia, has been described.

The story of Methodism in Estonia is now being told by such authors as Heigo Ritsbek[2] and Mark Elliott.[3] Estonia is, of course, the one country of the former Soviet Union where Methodism survived Communism as an organized church. But what do we know of Methodism in Lithuania and Latvia? Ritsbek says:

> When Estonia, Latvia and Lithuania were incorporated into the Soviet Union in August, 1940,[4] the Soviet authorities had formulated plans concerning the religious organizations. They accepted the existence of the Russian Orthodox Church, the Baptist Church and in the Baltic settings the Lutheran and Roman Catholic Churches. The Seventh-Day Adventists, quite unlike mainline Protestantism, were somehow tolerated. No other denominations were to be

allowed to exist. The Salvation Army, the Moravians and some other religious organizations were closed. The Methodist churches in Latvia and Lithuania were liquidated.[5]

What do we know, however, about Methodism in Latvia and Lithuania during the years between 1927 and 1940[6] (i.e., from the time the work of the Methodist Episcopal Church in Saint Petersburg and the Methodist Episcopal Church, South, in Manchuria/Siberia came to an end)? It is well known that the Methodist Episcopal Church superintendent, Dr. George A. Simons, was forced to retreat to the Baltic states and that Methodism survived to the present in Estonia. There is, however, much yet to be discovered and told of the Methodist story in Lithuania and Latvia. As has already been stated by this author, in the reports of the Evangelical Church's *Evangelischer Botschafter*, there is evidence of a Methodist presence in Riga, Kuldiga, and Liepaja, Latvia, in the early 1930s.

There follows a brief review of some of the known facts about the Methodist Church and its work in these two countries.

Beginnings of Methodism in Lithuania and Latvia

When the Baltic states were liberated from the old Russian Empire due to World War I and the Bolshevik Revolution, an extremely difficult period followed. Even though the first free elections in Latvia were held in April of 1920, the country and its neighboring states were not destined for free self-rule.

The past had been one of foreign domination. For example, the people of Latvia had been made serfs by the Teutonic knights and the Poles had taken over in 1561. Then came the Swedes in 1621 and the Russians in 1710. The landed aristocracy of the German Baltic barons dominated Latvia and surrounding regions during the old Russian Empire, but in the wake of World War I and the Bolshevik Revolution they were run out of the country.

Lithuania

At the turn of the century there was a religious awakening in and around Kaunas, Lithuania, which eventually led to the formation of a Methodist congregation there. Most attempts to trace the birth of Methodism in the Baltic states, including Copplestone's research, infer that the Lithuanian beginnings were the direct result of German Methodist missionary efforts, particularly by the Northeast German Conference. However, that is not accurate.

As just indicated, at the turn of the century there was an evangelical movement in the area of Kaunas, Lithuania, among the German-speaking population, which eventually led to a merger with German Methodism. However, it is clear from conference records and other documents that the first Methodist congregation in Lithuania (Kaunas) arose from an independent evangelical movement within the country, which began without any direct influence from Methodism, although German evangelization in the late nineteenth century played a part. When German Methodist Pastor Heinrich Ramke visited Kaunas in 1900, it was because a group of independent German-speaking Christians there invited him.

There are two documents which assist greatly in telling the story of Methodism's beginnings in Lithuania: 1) The *Programm zur 25 jährigen Jubiläumsfeier de Bischöflichen Methodistengemeinde zu Schanze-Kowno. Litauen. Vom 1. bis zum 3. November 1925.*[7] *(Program for the Twenty-fifth Anniversary Celebration of the Methodist Congregation in Kaunas-Sanciai,[8] Lithuania, from November 1 to 3, 1925)* and 2) an illuminating description of the origin of the first Methodist congregation in Kaunas, Lithuania by Emma Robbert, whose parents were two of its founders. She relates how the congregation began, thrived, survived, suffered, and was discontinued.

The *Program for the Twenty-fifth Anniversary Celebration of the Methodist Congregation in Kaunas* provides this account of the beginning.

> In 1893 God inaugurated a marvelous awakening in the area of Kaunas. Many souls found peace with God. Those seeking salvation gathered regularly to study the Word of God, although they had no permit to do so. In a packet of publications from the Methodist Publishing House in Bremen [Germany], Brother Jant found a copy of the articles of faith of the German Methodist Church. What a discovery and what a surprise to everyone! These articles of faith were read at a time of testimony and someone commented, "Yes, that is who we are."
>
> In 1900 they contacted the Methodist Publishing House in Bremen with the request to meet and hear a Methodist preacher. This led Brother Heinrich Ramke of Königsberg [Germany], who is now the director of Bethany Diaconal work, to them in Kaunas. He was given the task of visiting Lithuania to learn who these people were.
>
> The Rev. Ramke came and was warmly received by the small Kaunas congregation. At the first gathering there were exchanges of ideas, and questions were raised about the confession of faith, Christian experience, etc. At the conclusion, the Rev. Ramke commented, "You are already Methodists without knowing it."[9]

A copy of Emma Robbert's account written in German is to be found in the archives of the Evangelisch-methodistische Kirche of Germany in Reutlingen. It is published here in English for the first time.

The Methodist Church in Kaunas,[10] Lithuania, founded 1900, discontinued 1941[11] due to the repatriation of the Germans in Lithuania

I, Emma Robbert, born Durchholz, grew up in the Methodist Church in Kaunas, Lithuania, so to speak, and I was very happy there. Because it lies close to my heart that the church was closed due to the repatriation of the German Lithuanians, I have decided to record my memories of the beginnings of the Methodist Church in Kaunas. It could be that one day, someone from a younger generation will be interested in our church in Kaunas. Hence, I provide the following report:

The Non-Methodist Beginning[12]

My memories of the beginnings of the Methodist Church in Kaunas, Lithuania go back to the year 1899, or more properly said, when I was three years old. My mother told me what happened before then. She knew everything exactly and told me what I have recorded in the following account.

As a young girl my mother, Magdalena Durchholz, born Brenneiser, was already interested in religion, and in the house of her parents devotions and church attendance were regularly practiced. Her father was particularly strict in such things, however, she knew nothing of conversion at the time. They were devoted *Lutherans*.

When my mother, the youngest of the children, was sixteen years old, her father, Johann Brenneiser, sold his farm in Kybartai to a Mr. Tietz. He was forced to do so, because none of his children wanted to take it over. My grandparents received lifetime residential rights from Mr. Tietz and my mother, as the youngest, remained with them until she married.

At the time there was a very active religious movement, particularly among the farmers in the country. The new neighbor of my grandparents, Mr. Tietz, belonged to this group. He was almost always travelling with the farmers and hence did not take care of his farm. For that reason he was ridiculed by everyone and laughed at and, as was the custom of the time, perceived as crazy and mocked as a hypocrite [or religious fanatic].

My grandparents were, as I have already said, devoted Lutherans and wanted also to die as a part of that faith, but my mother had thought much about that. There must be some truth to it [the religious movement among the farmers]. The people cling to the Bible, preach repentance and conversion, and pray so freely from the heart, not according to the prayer book, as my mother was accustomed to do. Mother wanted to explore further.

It was not long before my mother married and moved to Kaunas. In Kaunas at the time there was a group, which gathered in houses and went out with its speakers or preachers (what they called themselves at the time I do not know) into the countryside over the weekend to hold mission meetings. Sometimes they would stay gone for an entire week. Because my mother was interested in the group, she was invited to the gatherings. Once she went with a friend over a weekend to a farm to one such meeting to observe everything.

101

However, she only went once and never again. She did not like it. The people were too self-righteous for her, too pious. Everyone who did not belong to their group they considered to be a sinner. They sat with drooped heads, criticized and damned everyone who did not do the same. My mother found no peace in these circles and searched further.

The majority of the proclaimers of the Word [which we shall designate here as *Bible Christians*] came from Memelland/Prussian Lithuania. My mother knew the names; I have forgotten them all unfortunately. There is only one name which I recall: *Schimansky*. He was a very simple man, but a faithful and true servant of God. Also he only evangelized in the homes of those who would receive him. God blessed his ministry, for many were converted and remained together, prayed and studied the Bible. Among these were also my parents and Brother Karl Pieper. Brother Pieper was a gifted speaker and the leader of the meetings. God blessed his ministry. The circle became larger and larger and the need of more space grew.

Actually all of them belonged to the Lutheran Church. On Sunday they went into the old city to the church but in addition they gathered regularly in their houses and conducted Bible study. Brother Karl Pieper was in charge of the spiritual leadership and my father, Friedrich Durchholz, was in charge of business matters.

At that time the Lutheran Church was built in Kaunas-Šančiai. All of the Germans, who lived in this outlying community, were supposed to assist with the building. Of course, it was the converted who began it in the hope that they would now have a gathering place. My father was chosen as the house administrator. Everything went well. Soon the building was finished with a worship hall and an apartment for the custodian. Once a month, Propst Dobbert came to Sančiai on a Sunday afternoon and held a worship service and on the other Sundays and weekdays the leadership was shared by the local members. Soon a choir and a Sunday school were begun. Gradually the *Bible Christians* had everything in their own hands in the Sančiai place of worship. It was a very lively work; God blessed it. The Propst was also pleased and happy about the diligent coworkers. He invited them to meet with him and organized a committee which was to provide a monthly evaluation of the work. Everything seemed to be fine, but as sometimes happens, the devil does not sleep in such cases. It did not take long before quite a few people found the *Bible Christians* to be too pious, because they preached repentance and conversion and warned against addiction to alcohol, etc. That was too much. Those who voiced the criticisms were surely good Christians, who went every Sunday to church. What they did otherwise was no one else's business. The result was that they went to the Propst and made accusations against the *Bible Christians*.

The Propst then called together the committee of the Sančiai congregation and asked them about their activities because of the criticisms which had been made. They reported everything to him—how they worked, sought order, and proclaimed only God's Word. The Propst found nothing bad in their work and said they should continue in the same manner. But the complaints of their enemies did not stop and finally they persuaded the Probst, for the sake of peace, to ask them to stop preaching. Thereafter the brothers and sisters withdrew and gathered once again in their houses, but the opposition did not cease. Now the opponents made their accusations to the police. As soon as a meeting began, the police were already present in order to disperse it, because gatherings in their homes were forbidden.

Sometimes the police arrived when the brothers and sisters were kneeling in prayer. Then they stood there quietly until they had finished. They saw indeed that nothing bad was being done and left. Once one of the brothers from the area of Memel, in other words a foreigner, was also present. The police wanted to arrest him and take him to the police station. Then all of the men prepared to go as well. One of them took a Bible and all proceeded to the police station. The police chief questioned them. They told him what they had done and showed him the Bible. The policeman who arrested them confirmed what was said. Then the police chief said: You may pray, that is not forbidden, but you should not meet in your homes, as such gatherings would have to be registered with the police. He let everyone go. My father laid a ruble unobtrusively on the table. The police chief was satisfied. So the work continued under difficulties. If they ministered with the Word elsewhere, then my father would inform the police accordingly.

The number of people attending the meetings became larger and larger, as well as the need for space. There were a number of property owners in the group who made space available. My parents did the same, although our apartment only had one room and a kitchen. Our family consisted of four persons, my parents and two children.

Early on Sunday we children were taken next door to our neighbors and everything was moved out of our apartment. They had to make seating space for the people. My father had made boxes and benches, which would be set up especially for this purpose, and then the meeting room was ready. Nothing was too difficult and everything was done gladly. In the evening the benches were then taken out and the room was once again made into living quarters. That is the way things continued.

Meanwhile the brothers and sisters had asked the proper authorities for a meeting permit and it was granted. That meant they had to become a part of some congregation. As one says, the child must have a name. Brother Pieper contacted a number of different congregations and invited pastors from Germany, who usually held a week of evangelization, generally in one home. They were very trying, because of what I have already said about moving things in and out of our apartment [during an evangelization week that meant every evening] and because of so many people in one room, which was not exactly pleasant.

The services lasted generally more than two hours, since at each one time was devoted to prayer and testimony. Afterwards we children, who had gone to sleep at our neighbor s house, were awakened and often we went home crying.

The meetings were always well attended. The people often stood outside under the windows, because there was no more space inside.

One of the strongest relationships developed with the brothers and sisters of the Chrischona congregation near Memel. The preacher of the congregation was named Kmita. He was often invited and roomed with the Pieper family. He would stay with us during the day and receive those who wanted to speak with him. In the evening there were always evangelization services, which would continue for one a week. (I would like to add that during these years our family increased by one member.)

103

The Methodist Beginning

Then it happened that Brother Pieper became extremely ill. In Kaunas there was no treatment for him and the doctors recommended that he go to Königsberg, which he did. In Königsberg he came into contact with Methodist brothers and sisters through the magazine *Evangelist*. At the time the pastor of the Methodist congregation in Königsberg was Pastor Ramke. Brother Pieper told him about the Kaunas work and that they needed an official relationship to a congregation. Pastor Ramke said happily: After all that you have told me, you are Methodists! Brother Pieper had found the connection they sought. When he returned home and told the brothers and sisters about this, they decided unanimously to join the Methodist Church. Thereafter Pastor Ramke was invited to Kaunas. He came, listened to and saw everything, and promised to communicate the entire matter to Bishop Nuelsen, which he did.[13]

From that time on the Kaunas brothers and sisters maintained a connection with the Methodist Church in Germany. There was great joy as the news arrived from the bishop that he had approved receiving the Kaunas congregation into the German Methodist Church. The first Methodist preachers to travel to Kaunas were Ramke and Bergmann. Thus the Kaunas Methodist Church was born.

To God's honor and out of gratitude for God's blessing and help, the first congregational celebration was held in the year 1900[14] in our meager apartment. At the time I was three and one half years old. I had the great honor and joy of taking part in this celebration, even to read a poem. It was very short, a verse from the page of a calendar and it went well. I can remember that I was put on a stool so that everyone could see me. From that time on I can remember everything.

The work of the congregation progressed. The church discipline was introduced, the first reception of members took place and probationary members were also received.

Now it was time for a larger meeting room. Brother Mossack, who was the wealthiest member of the congregation at the time, bought a house with a number of apartments and made a large room out of two apartments and two smaller adjacent rooms, which could be used when the large room was filled. And so the problem of a meeting place was resolved. God had made it all possible.

Now there was still a need for a pastor. In July 1905 the first pastor from the German Conference [Northeast] was assigned to us. It was Pastor Georg Durdis from Liegnitz, who was unmarried at the time. He began the work with the full engagement of his energies and not only as preacher, but as teacher and reformer of the old Sančiai customs and traditions. He ministered to the old and young, not only in the congregation, but outside it. Soon he was known to all the Germans in Sančiai and also recognized and valued. Particularly the youth gathered around him. He founded the youth fellowship and the choir. A pedal harmonium was purchased and he accompanied the congregational singing on it. Everyone was happy and grateful.

At that time the daughter of Preacher Schaarschmidt in Germany was very active and known as an evangelist. This young lady, Maria Schaarschmidt, was invited by Pastor Durdis to Kaunas. She came and quickly captured the hearts of the young people. There was a great awakening particularly among the young. Many were converted and became a part of the congregation. She was invited often and later married Pastor Durdis and remained in Kaunas. Then both of them continued the work there with joy and blessing.

Under the leadership of Pastor Durdis our lovely church was built (1910–1911) and dedicated.[15] Pastor Durdis had also made the building plans himself and assisted with the work on the interior. The construction cost a lot of money and work. At first a piece of property had to be bought and a construction permit procured. That was not easy. Credit had to be obtained because many of the members of the congregation were workers, who had difficulties earning enough to live, but their love for God and God's work made them ready to sacrifice. All sacrificed what they could. Some laid their watches and jewelry on the table as a sacrifice to build the church. The men worked on the construction after their working hours late into the night.

Unfortunately other difficulties arose: the adjacent property belonged to the government railway system. According to the law a building erected on the congregation's property had to be at least ten meters from the property line. The construction plans for the church called for a wing which extended almost to the property line. The railway system protested against this and the building of the wing was stopped. However, the brothers and sisters did not give up and turned directly to the Tsar himself with the request for the approval of the building plans as foreseen. A miracle happened. The Tsar approved the building of the church to extend almost to the property line of the government property. The document even bore the signature of Tsar Nicholas II. Once again God's presence was revealed.

Pastor Durdis led the congregation for six years and then was assigned elsewhere. In his place came Pastor Heinrich. He was only in Kaunas for a year and then moved to Kybartai. After him Pastor Ludwig was assigned to Kaunas. All three of the pastors mentioned here were killed during the First World War.

Methodism did not remain merely in Kaunas. It spread to Kybartai and from there to Pilviškiai. Meanwhile the Methodist Church in America had begun work in Russia. Dr. Simons from America had been appointed as superintendent with a residence in the city then called Petersburg. Our new bishop was Dr. Burt, who once held a conference in Kaunas. On that occasion I had the opportunity to meet him.

All of this happened before the First World War and we were an active and blooming congregation.

The First World War

On Sunday, August 2, 1914, the government announced that war had broken out between Russia and Germany. We Germans were shocked. Up to that time the Germans were always regarded as friends and valued by the government authorities. Now there was war. What would become of us? That was our concern. As long as the battles were on German soil, things went well. However, as the front came closer and the Russians had to retreat, the atmosphere changed. We were suddenly in danger. Could there be spies among us? At the time we were Russian citizens, but the Russians no longer trusted us.

One day someone told us secretly that those who had a connection with Germany were being sought. My father was on the list. He was considered particularly dangerous, because he had registered all of the visiting pastors' names with the police. My father was to be arrested and sent to Siberia. During that week my father was serving on a defendant committee in a war trial. My brother, who brought the terrible news, set out immediately to tell my father. We realized that we would have to flee and began to pack the most essential things for a quick departure.

Escape from Kaunas

At this point I would like to include something about our escape, and that of other Germans, from Kaunas, because it is through the flight of the Germans that our church work there was discontinued. Both of these things are bound together.

When father came home, he brought a car he had rented, because we were afraid to travel by train. We could be discovered. Unfortunately we could not leave that day and when evening came the driver refused to drive at night. So we had to wait until the next day. At daylight on the morning of September 15, 1914 we fled. We left everything behind, except for the hand luggage we took with us.

Along the way we met a few Baptist families, who, as we learned, were also on the list of the police. All of us had only one wish: to get out of the Kaunas compound as fast as possible. Thank God, we were fortunate to get through the iron gates of the compound. The sentry was distracted because there were so many refugees and they had more than they could do. No one checked us. In the evening we arrived at Jonova and decided to overnight there and on the next day to travel further with the train to Vilnius. When we arrived at the train station the next day, we learned that the railway system was closed to civilians, since it was being used for military troop transport. We were forced to remain in Jonova and were able to find an apartment very quickly.

After a short while, we learned that the Kaunas compound's Commander had declared that all Germans living in Kaunas had to leave. Although Jonova was also a part of the compound's jurisdiction, only the German men sixteen years of age and older had to leave the town. Women and children could remain. My father and two older brothers had to leave. They decided to go to Riga and from there further into Russia. My mother, my two younger brothers, and I remained in Jonova until the orders came in June 1915 that also the German women and children had to leave the area. We decided to travel to Vilnius where we met other members of the Kaunas Methodist Church, and the Nausner family, who also were Methodists. Also our pastor Ludwig and his family were already there. We decided to remain in Vilnius and rented a small apartment. We wanted to stay there until the end of the war.

In August 1915 the German troops captured Kaunas and in September they also occupied Vilnius. On the one hand, we were happy over the fact that

Vilnius was in German hands. We were relieved that the Russians could not persecute us any more. On the other hand, we were separated from our relatives. We received no news from father or our brothers. Over three years passed and we heard nothing. Not until 1918, when the war was over, did they all come home.

Return to Kaunas

The hope of returning to our home was high. We contacted the German command, which authorized our return to Kaunas and placed a military vehicle at our disposal. The soldiers brought us as far as Landvorovo and from there we travelled by train to Kaunas. On September 15, 1915 we arrived in Kaunas. After a year's absence, we were at home again.

Kaunas was not destroyed. Also our house and lovely church escaped damage. But everything which was not absolutely stationary and secured in its place had been stolen. With the help of the police we found the most essential pieces of our furniture with some of the local citizens who had not fled. We were able to furnish our apartment with the essentials.

We were the first of our congregation who returned home. Gradually the flock began to gather; we only lacked the shepherd. Pastor Paul Ludwig had been killed during the war.

Among the German soldiers there were also believers, who had used our empty church. They were not Methodists, but they went from house to house looking for the stray sheep. They were happy when they found German-speaking people. It was not long, however, before we received permission from the German military to use the church again. Soon a small congregation had come together. It consisted not only of Methodists but also of Baptists and Lutherans. The soldiers who were Christians also ministered to the Word. Soon a Double Quartet and a youth group were begun again. Unfortunately the soldiers stationed in Kaunas changed frequently but there were always new ones who joined us.

When the German military left Kaunas in 1918, most of the members of our congregation had already returned home. Hence, our work could begin again.

The first pastor assigned to us was Alfred Hühn. We had experienced God's help and could now sing with joy:

> Die Sach ist Dein, Herr Jesus Christ,
> die Sach an der wir stehen,
> Und weil es Deine Sache ist,
> kann sie nicht untergehn![16]

The work of the Methodist Church in Kaunas continued.

After the war, Lithuania became independent and we had nothing more to do with Russia. Superintendent Simons moved from Petersburg to Riga and as a result Methodism became known in Latvia and Estonia. A theological school was opened in Riga where Baltic pastors could be educated.

After the war evangelical work began among the Lithuanians. Through Pastor Oskar Kaufmann the first Lithuanian congregation was founded in Biržai. Soon thereafter a congregation was begun in Siauliai with services in Lithuanian and German.[17] In 1922–23 a primary German-speaking congregation was established in Tauragė

Soon a Baltic and Slavic Missions Conference was established with the episcopal residence in Stockholm and Dr. Wade as bishop. From that point on we belonged to this conference.

In 1925 under Pastor Rudolf Brenneiser the Kaunas congregation celebrated the twenty-fifth anniversary of the Methodist Church in Kaunas.

The Kaunas congregation had a large Sunday School (ca. 200 children), which was attended not only by children of Methodist members but by children from the Lutheran Church. Also the youth group was very active. The same may be said of the church choir, which was extremely well known and very popular in Kaunas among the Germans. Our singers did their best to the glory of their Savior, as did the brass ensemble. The Lord blessed our ministry—we experienced that often.

The following pastors served the Kaunas church before the First World War: Georg Durdis, Heinrich, Paul Ludwig. After the war there were: Alfred Hühn, Rudolf Brenneiser, Tautorat, Emil Blum, Oskar Kaufmann, Richard Mett, Karl Mett, Richard Lupp, Kostas Burbulys, Plitscheweit and Serge Mosienko.

The Second World War

When the Second World War broke out in 1940, our pastor was Serge Mosienko. In June of that year the Russians occupied Lithuania. That changed things in Kaunas to such an extent that Pastor Mosienko had to leave. He fled to Germany. In 1941 there was the tremendous repatriation of Germans from the Baltic states and other countries. They left everything in order to return to their homeland.[18] Unfortunately from that time onward Methodism in Lithuania was discontinued. Our Kaunas church stands empty and abandoned, and the Communists have removed the cross from the steeple. There are still some congregations in Latvia and Estonia, however, no German-speaking ones.

In the summer of 1941 the war began between Germany and Russia. Kaunas was taken over by the Germans. Because I spoke Lithuanian and Russian, I was sent to Kaunas in 1943 in a service capacity. This gave me the opportunity to observe the circumstances. It was a sad picture! Although Kaunas was not heavily damaged, there was a very tense atmosphere.

Shortly after their takeover of Kaunas the German troops made a storage room out of our church. They put the benches outside in the yard where they had been rained upon and demolished. Brother Müllerschkowsky, who had also returned to Kaunas, wrote to Bishop Dr. Melle in Berlin-Lichterfelde and he received a notarized power of attorney dated August 16, 1943 from the lawyers Dr. Kiesel and Dr. von Krause of the Berlin State Court W 8 designating him as the person authorized to be the administrator of the German Methodist congregation in Kaunas, Lithuania. Brother Müllerschkowsky took it then to the General Commissioner of the occupied East Sector, Dr. von

Rintlein. He authorized that the left wing of the church be cleared out immediately. Then Brother Müllerschkowsky began a renovation of everything: the difficult task of regluing all the pieces of the benches together, etc. We were small in number but our joy was great. Pastor Richard Lupp was assigned to Kaunas at this time, so we had a pastor. He led the worship services and even the choir. Harry and Loni Owald were confirmed by Pastor Lupp. However, it was not long before the war front drew closer and on July 4, 1944 we had to leave everything behind and return to Germany.

I settled with our family near Danzig in a small village. In March 1945 the Russians reached us and, because we were born in Russia, shipped us off to Russia again in November 1945. What a miracle it is that in Kaunas we succeeded in escaping from the train, which was on its way to Siberia. We still had relatives in Kaunas, the Owald family, who took us in, in spite of the prohibition. From Mr. Owald I learned that just after the departure of the German troops the Catholics had cleaned out the church and furnished it as a Roman Catholic Church with the name *Svento Kzimiero Baznyca*. However, that did not last long. The Russians confiscated the church and made a movie theater out of it. When we arrived, it was still being used as a movie theater. I never went inside but my daughter Edith did go there once. It was a very sad experience. Soon the movie theater was closed. Apparently it was not profitable. The church then became living quarters for students and a so-called "community dwelling." The latest change is that the custodian installed four windows in the wall behind the place where the pulpit once stood. I have no idea what it looks like inside today. The outside looks very neglected. Also the dwellings next to the church were about to cave in, when we left Kaunas again in 1959.[19]

Now I have written down everything that I remember. It makes me sad that our blessed work in Lithuania came to such an end. How happily we had sung so often, *Die Sach ist Dein, Herr Jesus Christ*. Will that hymn one day be heard there again? That is the question, but with God all things are possible.

Nürnberg, September 7, 1977
Emma Robbert, born Durchholz

According to Emma Robbert's account Pastor Heinrich Ramke of the Northeast German Conference accepted the invitation of the independent congregation in Kaunas of which Mr. Pieper had told him when he was in Königsberg. In 1900, during the waning years of the Russian Empire, Ramke visited the Lithuanian city to meet the congregation. Bishop Nuelsen, however, has stated that the small independent congregation in Kaunas did have contact with the Methodist publishing house in Bremen before the congregation became Methodist. The records of the Northeast German Conference show that in 1905, Georg R. Durdis was appointed as the pastor in Kaunas. Copplestone reports that a year later, 1906, there were thirty-eight members.[20]

In 1907 Pastor Durdis founded a congregation in Kybartai near the German border, which became an Episcopal appointment not long thereafter. A beautiful brick chapel, that would seat two hundred worshipers, was built by the congregation, particularly through the efforts of three men: Hemke, Unterberger, and Räder.[21] It was dedicated on February 7, 1909 by Bishop William Burt.

This was the first Methodist house of worship to be built in Tsarist Russia. Because the town of Virbalis was to close to Kybartai, Bishop Nuelsen and others often referred to the Methodist chapel as being in Virbalis. The records of the Baltic and Slavic Mission Conference list the appointment, however, as Kybartai. In 1908 Kybartai reported only three to four members.

Pastor Durdis also expanded the Methodist work to Vilnius. *The Annual Report of the Board of Foreign Missions of the Methodist Episcopal Church for the Year 1907* reported:

> Work has also been begun in Wilna [Vilnius] and Landwarowa. Wilna is an important city, three hours' ride from Kowno [Kaunas], having a mixed population of some 200,000 people. A baroness from Saint Petersburg with her two daughters has rented a hall, which we have been using thus far, but we must have a chapel here before long. The services are held in Russian and German. People from all classes and conditions attend these meetings, including army officers, engineers, railroad officials, soldiers, physicians, students, and peasants. The churches represented are Greek Catholic, Roman Catholic, Lutheran, Baptist, and Methodist. We need a regular preacher here. Thus far Pastor Durdis and his wife, who is an evangelist, have tried to keep up this work in addition to their services in Kowno, Wirballen [Virbalis], and Landwarowa.[22]

While some outside assistance from America and Germany was received for church construction, as in Kaunas, the Lithuanians sacrificed everything materially possible to build Methodist houses of worship.[23] The work in Kybartai/Virbalis was primarily German-speaking and it progressed well.

As indicated Pastor Durdis also began work in Vilnius, but in 1918 a section of Lithuania which included that city was annexed by Poland. Methodist work did develop in Vilnius but after the annexation, due to the Comity agreement of the Methodist Episcopal Church and the Methodist Episcopal Church, South, it was administered by the latter through its work in Poland.[24]

With the outbreak of World War I in 1914 the work of the Methodist congregations in Lithuania came to a standstill. German Lithuanians were in grave danger and under suspicion of the Russians as spies of the German government. Numerous Methodists in Kybartai and Kaunas were of German descent and their names invoked the wrath of the Russian authorities. Many were arrested, put in jail or exiled. Others were forced into the interior of Russia for hard labor or military service. Those who could, fled to Vilnius or elsewhere. On the outskirts of Vilnius a small Methodist refugee congregation was begun.

The German army began to threaten the Russian Baltic front and by midsummer 1915 it overran the military installations and city of Kaunas. Kybartai and Virbalis were devastated by retreating Cossacks who had quartered there. They ravaged the German settlement, raised most of the buildings, and even destroyed much of the Russian settlement. They plundered the remaining houses but surprisingly the Methodist chapel survived. Yet, when Bishop Nuelsen visited the sacked area, he found only one Methodist family and a widow. For the sake of protecting the property Nuelsen then placed Kybartai/Virbalis under the superintendency of the Berlin District.

Under the German occupation the Methodist work began to revive. This was due in part to the efforts of some German soldiers, who were Christians. They were not Methodists but they took an interest in helping rebuild the work. In Kybartai, for example, Sergeant Chaplain Kormannshaus began to preach and a private named Ley organized a large choir. Others helped with the Sunday School and youth group.

In spite of this renewal it was a difficult period for Methodism, for there was a lack of resources for the churches and communities. At this time the mother Methodist Church in America sent food and other supplies, although much was confiscated or stolen before arriving in Lithuania.

In 1918 Lithuania became independent and the German troops withdrew. Finally the German Lithuanians could revive Methodist work on their own initiative. A primary concern, however, was whether the new government of a country with a population that was over 80 percent Roman Catholic, would limit the work of a free church. Miraculously the Methodist work expanded and new congregations were established in Pilviškiai,[25] Tauragė, Biržai, and Šiauliai.

The Methodist Episcopal Church in Pilviškiai was founded on July 29, 1921. The congregation built a wooden frame building on Dariaus-Gireno Street (number 40) with an apartment and a sanctuary. Dr. George A. Simons, superintendent, dedicated the building on February 21, 1926.

In 1922 Pastor Alfred Hühn came to Tauragė, rented a movie theater, and conducted evangelistic meetings.[26] A number of the converts belonged to the local Lutheran Church. Not long after these meetings the Methodist congregation in Tauragė was founded on Nov. 1, 1923 through the efforts of the families Lupp, Meier, Mirau, and others. Money to build a beautiful little church[27] was donated by an American Methodist woman by the name of Mrs. Young. The church, with a seating capacity of three hundred, was dedicated on December 20, 1925 by Dr. George A. Simons, superintendent. A parsonage was also built by the congregation.

111

The membership of the Tauragė Methodist Episcopal Church grew to seventy-one members until 1941, when the congregation was essentially liquidated through German repatriation. From this small faithful church during the two decades of its existence came two Methodist pastors, Richard Lupp[28] and Arthur Leifert, and six deaconesses, Nina Barkowksy, Emma Beutner, Martha Haak, Sina Kaufmann (daughter of Pastor Oskar Kaufmann), Nina Ratinski, and Anna Schneiderat.

In 1923 the first Lithuanian-speaking Methodist congregation was established in Biržai[29] by Pastor Oskar Kaufmann. A meeting place, with some eighty seats, was rented at number 3 Kestučio Street. The second indigenous Lithuanian congregation was begun in 1929 in Šiauliai. At the outset there was no place for the Methodists to meet in Šiauliai and a well known Jewish citizen named Frenkel, who owned a leather factory, provided the congregation a lovely room at no cost or obligation in his factory for its meetings.[30] For a time space was rented at number 17 Lydos Street, with room for about seventy worshipers. After Kostas Burbulys, who was also trained in upholstery, became pastor, he purchased a house[31] in which the Methodist Episcopal congregation had its own meeting room. In addition to his pastoral duties Burbulys also taught at a local trade school of upholstery and interior design to supplement his pastor's salary of $10 per month.

A small fraternal group of Christians, that was founded in 1920 in the village of Butingė, officially became asasociated with the Methodist congregation in Šiauliai in 1939. It owned its own meeting house and consisted of twenty members, all of whom were indigenous Lithuanians.

In 1937 Methodist work was also begun in Marijampolė by Pastor Oskar Kaufmann. The small group of ten members met in his home, which was about four kilometers from Marijampolė. The work was affiliated with the Methodist Episcopal Church in Kaunas.

According to the records of Superintendent Serge Mosienko, dated January 13, 1940 and located in the Lithuanian State Archives in Vilnius, the Methodist congregation in Vilnius, which was begun by Georg Durdis while serving as the pastor in Kaunas, worshiped in rented space at number 4 Ofiarno Street. After 1939, when Vilnius once again was a part of Lithuania, Mosienko reported that there were fifty members in the congregation, 90 percent Polish and 10 percent White Russians and others. All were Polish citizens. The pastor was the Rev. Jan Petrovsky.

The period from 1918 to 1941 was indeed the blossoming period of Lithuanian Methodism. In 1922 the first brass choir was founded in the church of Kybartai. The purchase of sixteen instruments was made possible by contributions from America, Germany, and the superintendent's office in Riga.[32] In 1925 and 1928 brass choirs were established also in Pilviškiai and Kaunas respectively. All of the Lithuanian brass groups became members of the German organization "Bund christlicher Posaunenchöre Deutschlands" and some of the choirs joined the corresponding German choral organization "Christlicher Sängerbund Deutschlands." In 1923 two pastors, Tautorat and Mett, published a song book, *Giesmiu Knyga*, of which there are at least two surviving copies.[33] Other publications of the Methodist Episcopal Church in the Lithuanian language of which there are still extant copies include: *Methodistai kas jie yra ir ko jie nori*,[34] *Episkopales Metodistiu bažnyčiu pagrindinis Katekizmas*,[35] *Krikščionystes Sargas*.[36] A Lithuanian translation of the *Discipline of the Methodist Episcopal Church* was also completed.

Latvia

In 1910 Riga, Latvia, was listed as a Methodist appointment. It is not surprising that Methodist leaders were drawn to this beautiful, bustling city, called the Pearl of the Baltic. It was strategically located on the Daugava River, with a population of some five hundred thousand and only about 560 kilometers from Petrograd, in a country about one and one half times the size of Switzerland. The city had been founded by Albert, Bishop of Livonia, in 1201. Before World War I it was filled with factories and thousands of workers. Six daily newspapers were published in five languages: Russian, German, Polish, Yiddish, and Latvian (Lettish). By 1925, however, the population had diminished by 150,000.

In 1911 Georg R. Durdis was transferred from Kaunas to Riga, where he rented a hall and began work. In another Latvian city, Liepaja, Durdis met a Moravian pastor by the name of Alfred Freiberg, who through correspondence with George A. Simons became absorbed in Wesleyan and Methodist literature. As a result, his independent society sent three young men to be trained by Simons for Methodist evangelistic work in Latvia.

During this period "the congregations in the Russian territories of Finland, Estonia, Latvia and Lithuania and in Russia proper suffered economic deprivations. . . . but those that suffered perhaps most bitterly from being close to military operations were those in Kaunas and Kybartai, in Lithuania."[37]

In 1921 the Rev. Alfred Freiberg, the Moravian minister mentioned earlier, and his congregation of 125 united with the Methodist Church in Liepaja, Latvia. This was the beginning of Latvian-speaking Methodism. Like the congregation in Kaunas, Lithuania, the main body of the Liepaja Methodist Church had its origin outside Methodism and through contact with Methodists and the Wesleyan tradition discovered its authentic identity. Dr. George A. Simons has provided an interesting account of the move toward and acceptance of Methodism by Pastor Freiberg and his congregation.[38]

Some ten years ago the pastor of an independent society of Lettish believers in Liepaja began familiarizing himself with the history and literature of Methodism. Liepaja was formerly the chief western part of the old Russian Empire, but now belongs to the Republic of Latvia. Through the Russia-America Line, whose steamers plied regularly all year round between Liepaja and New York, Liepaja was actually Russia's most immediate point of contact with the new world across the seas. Rev. Alfred Freiberg was the name of the young, enthusiastic and energetic pastor. He and his people were all native Letts and were known as a detached Moravian Society or *Brüdergemeinde.* Pastor Freiberg learned that the Methodist Episcopal Church had already established Headquarters in the Russian capital in 1907, and soon he was corresponding with the superintendent of the Russian Mission at Saint Petersberg. He began reading the *Khristianski Pobornik* (Russian Christian Advocate), the *Discipline,* Wesley's sermons, and other Methodist literature. He also ordered our church periodicals from America, Switzerland and Germany. Then he became acquainted with our preacher in Riga, now the capital of Latvia. It was not long before Pastor Freiberg discovered that he and his flock of Moravian believers were really Methodists! Although not affiliated with our church, he sent us three young candidates to be trained for the Methodist work among the Letts. They were but a brief time at the seminary when the war frustrated that plan. Then followed a sad series of kaleidoscopic events in Russia and the Baltic Provinces. The Methodist work that had been inaugurated in Riga was unfortunately suspended in 1914, and thus the Liepaja friends were for a long time cut off from all Methodist affiliations. In the meantime, however, the undaunted resourceful Lett of Liepaja was laying foundations for Lettish Methodism, fully persuaded that the Methodist Episcopal Church was the one providentially called to satisfy the spiritual needs of thousands of Lettish believers who had already abandoned the petrified State Church.

"Of course, strictly speaking, I was as yet no Methodist preacher," Brother Freiberg recently confided to the writer, "but inasmuch as the war had interfered with certain cherished plans of mine, I set out to work for the church of my heart's desire, and simply considered Doctor Nuelsen my Bishop and Doctor Simons my superintendent!" Here was truly a case of genuine soul affinity.

Soon after the armistice Brother Freiberg was again able to communicate with the Bishop and the writer. The Moravian Methodist courtship was not to go on indefinitely! Plans have been made to have the Bishop and myself perform the wedding ceremony, but as the *episcopos* could not come the joyous duty devolved upon the writer.

The crowning climax of this consummation devoutly to be wished was announced for Sunday, April 17, 1921. It was a dreary, rainy day. The chapel, a hall that had been made by pulling down a dozen partitions and putting in it some strong pillars, was crowded with more than three hundred devout listeners. It was just the kind of building one might expect early Methodists to meet in. In this quaint old building tucked away behind large warehouses facing the water-front, one finds a veritable labyrinth of rooms, indeed a building that would have appealed to a Dickens or Hawthorne for descriptive purposes, yea, even an ideal place for frolicsome children to play hide-and-go-seek! And here it was where the Moravians of Latvia and the Methodists of America found each other!

At the opening service on this historic Sunday, Pastor Freiberg reminded his people that April 17th was a most noteworthy day for them in three respects, (1) being the four-hundredth anniversary of Luther's visit to Worms, (2) the sixteenth anniversary of the Tsar's Ukase granting religious liberty, and (3) the organizing of the first Lettish Methodist Church in Latvia! Compliant with the Pastor's request, the writer preached from the text "For whatsoever is born of God overcometh the world! and this is the victory that overcometh the world, even our faith." (1 John 5:4) This is the motto of the Lettish Methodists in Liepaja.

Then followed the session of the Sunday School, where 150 bright-eyed Lettish boys and girls promptly answered all questions propounded by the writer. One girl stepped forward and graciously thanked the Methodist Church of America for sending clothing, shoes and milk to the needy children of Latvia.

At the afternoon meeting the subject was "Methodism a true child of the Reformation." Thereupon followed a special service exclusively for members of the Society, on which occasion the writer related the romantic story of Wesley's association with Moravian believers on his ocean voyage, in America, and his conversion in the Moravian meeting place in Aldersgate, London.

It was truly a brilliant scene when, in the name of Bishop John Louis Nuelsen of Zürich, the writer received one hundred twenty-five Lettish believers into the membership of the Methodist Episcopal Church, adapting the Ritual for this unique occasion. There should have been one hundred fifty persons in all, but some twenty-five members living outside of Liepaja were unable to come on account of the inclement weather. These absentees have since been received into the Methodist Church by the pastor. The ages of these Lettish Methodists range from twenty to fifty-five, fully half of them being men.

In administering the Sacrament of the Holy Communion, the writer was assisted by the Pastor and his colleague, Carl Beike, and Brother H. Soete, our first three Lettish preachers. It was verily a pentecostal hour, never to be forgotten. After the service of this blessed day, scores of Lettish Methodists grasped my hands and with tears in their eyes thanked the Methodist Church of America for heeding the Macedonian call for spiritual and material help. These Letts are good linguists, most of them understand both Russian and German.

During the same year (1921) that Pastor Freiberg's congregation in Liepaja officially became Methodist, the property in Riga on the street named Akas iela (13) was obtained, and in 1922 the spacious Central Hall at Elizabetes iela was procured.[39] The Central Hall functioned as a Youth Headquarters, educational institution (theological seminary), and general headquarters for the Methodist Church in the Baltic region.[40]

115

The organizing session of the Russian Mission Conference, under the leadership of Bishop John Nuelsen, was held at Khapsalu in 1921 and the conference sessions of 1922 and 1923 in Riga and Kaunas, respectively. The following excerpt from Dr. Simons's report at the annual session of the Russian Mission Conference held in Riga, July 26-31, 1922, provides an excellent overview of the beginnings of Methodist work in the Baltic region and Russia. It was published in *Methodism in Russia,* a quarterly bulletin published at Riga under the title "What God Hath Wrought."[41]

In the summer of 1907 Dr. George A. Simons was appointed Superintendent of the Methodist Episcopal work in Finland and Russia, then known as the Finland and St. Petersberg Mission Conference. He had his headquarters at Petrograd. In 1911 the Russia Mission was organized and the Finland Conference launched, Dr. Simons and his Russian co-workers retaining their membership in the latter. In 1921 the Russian Mission Conference was organized and Dr. Simons appointed Superintendent of the same. It all seems like a dream, these first years of our Methodist pioneer work in Russia, Siberia[42] and the Baltic States. We began with three preachers, Hjalmar Salmi, a Finn, born and educated in St. Petersberg, Georg R. Durdis, a German, and myself as the first and only American clergyman sent to Russia for administrative work, having no property, no literature, no work except a small group of German-speaking Methodists in Kaunas (now the capital of Lithuania). During the nerve-racking years and revolutions in Russia three preachers sacrificed their lives in the Allied cause. With an appropriation of one thousand dollars and having to cope with all kinds of embarrassments and obstacles, my motto has been the faith-inspiring word of Saint Paul, "I can do all things through Christ which strengtheneth me" (Phil. 4:13).

At the annual meeting of the Russian Missionary Conference and Baltic Mission in Kaunas, Lithuania, August 1-5, 1923, its last meeting before division into separate conferences, the following statistics were reported:

> 37 preachers and workers in attendance
> 44 preachers total in the conference
> 66 appointments and 103 preaching places
> 59 Sunday schools with 162 officers and teachers
> 4,327 attendants
> 17 church buildings and 11 parsonages; value = $400,000 and debt free
> 11 candidates preparing for ministry; 17 waiting to be enrolled
> 9 deaconess candidates with 8 young women on waiting list

In 1924, with Bishop Bast as the episcopal leader, the Baltic and Russian work was divided into two conferences: the Baltic and Slavic Mission Conference (BSMC) and the Russian Mission Conference.

The Baltic and Slavic Mission Conference (BSMC)

Rarely in the history of Methodism has there been a conference that exemplified the inclusive nature of the church as the BSMC did. In the fifteen years of its existence, 1924–1939, within a delimited geographic area, (Lithuania, Latvia, and Estonia) it brought together people of diverse ethnic and cultural backgrounds, operated with five official conference languages (Lithuanian, Latvian, Estonian, German,and English [Bishop Wade spoke only English]; of course, many also spoke in Russian). The Rev. Richard Lupp has described the annual sessions of the BSMC as linguistically fascinating, with the five official languages. "When the bishop spoke," Lupp said, "translation was made into German, since almost everyone spoke German. Often when the bishop or the person presiding said, 'Let us pray,' you heard all mother tongues simultaneously. Therefore, everyone knew the first line of the Lord's Prayer in all the languages."[43]

The districts of the BSMC conducted intensive programs of evangelization, social outreach (meals for the poor, orphanages), and education (schools for poor children and advanced education for adults—laity and clergy).[44] The Lettish Methodist Children's Home was established in Riga and the Estonian Methodist Children's Home in Tallinn. The interest in children's work was so strong that the Russian Mission Conference, which preceded the BSMC, established the position of manager of child welfare, to which Mr. John Witt was appointed.

The BSMC also founded the Methodist Training Institute, a theological school to train clergy, in Riga, Latvia, which opened in the fall of 1923. Almost all the clergy spoke at least one or two languages besides their native tongue. Literature was published in Russian, Lithuanian, Latvian, and Estonian, including four editions of the *Christian Advocate* in those languages, plus a quarterly bulletin in English for a time.

Interestingly, the BSMC had visions of the unification of the Methodist Episcopal Church and the Methodist Episcopal Church, South, in the United States. Such visions were often articulated in its publications and in the exchange of guests and evangelists between the BSMC region and the mission work of the Methodist Episcopal Church, South, in Vladivostok (Siberia) and Harbin (Manchuria). For example, a guest preacher for the 1924 BSMC was the Rev. Nicolai Pöysti, who trained under Simons in Petrograd, but was then working for the Methodist Episcopal Church, South, among Russians in Harbin, Manchuria. In Harbin Pöysti was also editing a Russian periodical, *The Methodist Christian Advocate*. The last line of the caption next to his picture in *Methodism in Russia*, the quarterly bulletin, April-May-June (1924) reads: "God hasten the day of the Methodist unification which will bring this talented and beloved brother back to us!"[45] In the same issue at the top of page eight are pictures of Bishops William Burt, John L. Nuelsen, and W. B. Beauchamp. The following text appears beneath the pictures:

> It was under Bishop Burt's far-seeing and inspiring leadership that the Methodist work in Russia was officially inaugurated. He despised not the day of small beginnings. In 1912 he was succeeded by Bishop Nuelsen who has had the joy of seeing this Mission develop in spite of the many harassing kaleidoscopic vicissitudes of the Great War and Revolutions. Note this re-markable result: Our Russian work is now in six countries—Russia, Estonia, Latvia, Lithuania, Poland and Ukraine! It is in the latter two countries that the greathearted, statesmanlike Bishop W. B. Beauchamp of the Methodist Episcopal Church, South has been laying deep foundations. God hasten the day when the two Methodisms shall be one!

It is clear that the Russian work of both Methodist churches was viewed by those in the field holistically and not as separate agendas of separate churches.

In 1922 the church purchased a magnificent four-story building at Eliza-betas iela in Riga, Latvia. It became the Methodist headquarters of the Russian and Baltic Mission Conference, and after 1924 that of the BSMC and a symbol of the inclusive nature of Baltic Methodism. The American Methodist Episcopal Church, with a seating capacity of about five hundred and services in four languages, was on the first floor. English and French classes were offered weekdays free of charge. Superintendent Simons occupied the second floor. The Rev. John Witt, manager of the Methodist Child Welfare for the Baltic and Russian regions, resided on the third floor, and the fourth floor housed the Methodist Training Institute (or seminary).

On a trip to Latvia in 1922, Dr. George M. Fowles, treasurer of the Board of Foreign Missions of the Methodist Episcopal Church in New York, purchased for $5,000 a large building, formerly the so-called People's Temperance hall, in Liepaja, which was located on the harbor. It needed renovation, but the eight-hundred-seat auditorium provided excellent meeting space and a large ground floor for social services. It was here in this commodious Methodist building that the second session of the BSMC convened July 22-26, 1925.

The annual sessions of the BSMC tended to rotate between Riga, Latvia, and Tallinn, Estonia, and occasionally Kaunas, Lithuania. A complete set of records of all fifteen years of the BSMC does not exist, but some minutes and reports for the years 1924 (Tartu), 1925 (Liepaja), 1926 (Riga), 1927 (Riga), 1930 (Riga), 1931 (Tallinn), 1932 (Riga), 1933 (Tallinn), 1936 (Riga) are located in the Archives and History Center of The United Methodist Church at Drew University in Madison, New Jersey (USA). There were three districts within the BSMC: Lithuania, Latvia, and Estonia. The last appears to have had consistently the largest number of charges and churches. The Latvian District was second in size, and the Lithuanian District the smallest.

There is no question that the districts were experiencing growth throughout the period of the BSMC's existence, as reflected in the statistics of the conference minutes and the number of new churches being built and rental properties being acquired. For example, in 1931 in the Latvian District there were eleven appointments, but by 1939-40, in the BSMC, there were approximately thirty congregations with some three thousand members. Candidates for ordination of deacon and elder were presented at almost every annual conference, as were diaconal candidates for consecration.

The annual conference sessions were marked by an inclusive mixture of strong Wesleyan and biblical traditions, especially preaching of the Word, singing of Wesleyan hymns, and indigenous hymns in the various languages of the BSMC.

Pastor Richard Lupp has described the conference sessions as linguistically fascinating, for there were five official languages. He has also remarked that unlike most of the work in Lithuania and some of it in Latvia, where the worship was generally (though not exclusively) conducted in German, the Methodist work and worship in Estonia was almost always in the Estonian language.[46] There was also some Russian-language Methodist work in Latvia and Estonia.

The following items from the BSMC minutes are landmarks in the life of Methodism in Latvia. In 1931, under District Superintendent Fricis Timbers, Methodism was officially legalized as a church in Latvia. In 1934 the Methodist Church Law was issued by the Latvian government, and in 1938 the constitution of the Methodist Church in Latvia was approved, giving the Methodist Church equal rights with the Evangelical, Lutheran, and Greek Orthodox Churches.

At the BSMC of 1927, the decision was made to send two young Lithuanians to the seminary in Riga for study: Kostas Burbulys and Vilius Kvedaravičius.[47] When the Riga seminary was closed, Burbulys was transferred to the Methodist theological school at Frankfurt am Main, Germany, from which he was graduated in 1933. He returned immediately to Lithuania, and was assigned briefly to Traurage, a German-speaking Methodist congregation. After consultation with Bishop Wade, however, in which he expressed his desire to serve in a Lithuanian-speaking context, Burbulys was appointed to Šiauliai, where he conducted services in Lithuanian and German.[48]

At the time there was a distinct difference between the German and Lithuanian Methodist work in Lithuania. "All of the German congregations had their own church buildings and parsonages, but the Lithuanian congregations owned no property—they had to rent. This was expensive, and the Lithuanian congregations were small and poor."[49]

In 1928 Bishop Raymond J. Wade was appointed to the Northern European Area of the Methodist Episcopal Church, with residence in Stockholm. His episcopal area covered the following conferences: Baltic and Slavic, Denmark, Finland (2), Norway, Russia, Sweden. The first session of the BSMC was held August 1-5, 1924, in Tartu, Estonia. In the succeeding years, with one exception, the conference met annually until 1939, the year it was officially named an annual conference. Its last annual session was held July 18-23, 1939, in Tallinn, Estonia. It was to have met the following year in Kaunas, but the Soviets took over and made that impossible.

Diaconal work was carried on in Latvia by Deaconess Kristine Gettheim, who was the first woman licensed to preach in that country. Three women from Latvia and Lithuania, Mrs. Adolfs (Irma) Bergmanis and Mrs. Fricis Timbers (both from Latvia) and Mrs. Serge Mosienko (Lithuania), with Mrs. Raymond J. Wade, wife of the bishop, formed the Woman's Foreign Missionary Society.[50]

Following the pattern of Methodism to educate and inform, Methodist publishing houses were opened in Riga and in Tartu, and there began a series of publications, including hymnals, pamphlets, tracts, and literature for Sunday schools and youth. The following church papers or *Christian Advocates* were also published: *Kristigs Aizstavis* (Latvia), *Krikščionystes Sargas* (Lithuania), and *Kristlik Kaitsja* (Estonia).

From the World Service report of 1923 it is also clear that the work of the Methodist Church in the Baltic states was being implemented in a holistic Wesleyan sense, which involved the wedding of evangelistic and social work. There was extensive relief work by church World Service: food supplies were delivered throughout the Baltic region and Russia, orphanages for children were built and sustained. The report states: "Relief work, such as that carried on in Riga, where during the school year 900 students of the university had their only substantial meal each day in the Methodist Central Mission, has convinced the people of the practical nature of the Methodist program. The constituency of the church has more than tripled."[51]

Even with the dire needs of the people and the difficulties of diverse governments, cultures, and languages, the members of the BSMC had a vision beyond the Baltic region. Dr. George A. Simons reported in 1926 that the conference supported four mission day schools in China, Korea, and India.[52]

Within the BSMC Methodists engaged in some interdenominational endeavors with Lutherans, Baptists, Moravians, Orthodox, and Evangelical Church clergy and congregations, although the various districts (Estonian, Latvian, and Lithuanian) had their own specific national problems related to the established churches: Lutheran and Orthodox (Estonia and Latvia), and Roman Catholic (Lithuania).

Ecumenical Beginnings

Clearly the Methodist workers in the Baltic states and Russia sought to work wherever possible with clergy and laity of other denominations. The evidence of a spirit of Christian unity pervaded their theology of the church in thought and practice. Already in the 1930s there were foreshadowings of the ecumenical movement in a small but effective organization known as the Union of Believers in Latvia, which consisted of the following member churches: Evangelical, Lutheran, Greek Orthodox, Methodist, and Baptist. One finds the Lutheran Prefect of Liepaja present at the BSMC ordination service. In the quarterly bulletin *Methodism in Russia* (April-May-June 1924 issue), there is a photograph of the first Epworth League and Sunday School Convention of the Baltic States and Russia, combined with the Midyear Assembly of Preachers and Local Preachers. Directly in the center of the picture is a Russian Orthodox clergyman, the Rev. Pavel Gorskof.[53] On page nineteen of the same periodical, Dr. George Simons is pictured with him. The Rev. Gorskof was very active in temperance work, particularly at Dorpat University. It was at this university during this period that the theological faculty, primarily Lutheran in tradition, offered a prize for an essay on the subject "The Origin and Development of Methodist Societies in Estonia." It is also noteworthy that a Professor A. Bulgakoff of the Russian Orthodox Seminary in Kiev in 1887 published in Russian a two-volume work on the history of Methodism. His primary sources were Stevens, Southey, Lecky, Jacoby, et al.

In speaking of George Simons's ecumenical gifts, Leslie A. Marshall, editor of *The Riga Times*, remarked in his book *The Romance of a Tract and Its Sequel*, a volume about Simons and Methodist work in the Baltic states: "Ample evidence of his success in fostering relations with the leaders of the Russian Orthodox, the Lutheran and other Churches, was given in the numerous felicitations received and read at his recent anniversary in Riga."[54]

Mutual respect for other traditions, particularly the Russian Orthodox,[55] characterized the mission work of the Methodist Episcopal Church in the Baltic states and Russia and that of the Methodist Episcopal Church, South, in Siberia/Manchuria.

The Beginning of the End

In the early 1920s there was still considerable Methodist activity in Russia proper, centered around Saint Petersburg, and much has been written about the perspectives and activities of Bishops Nuelsen and Blake, the Rev. Julius Hecker, and others in this regard. In many ways Methodist leaders miscalculated the Russian political scene, as well as the political movements within the Russian Orthodox Church. And the 1924 General Conference of the Methodist Episcopal Church essentially closed the door on the Methodist Mission to Russia by refusing aid to the Russian Orthodox Church or to advance Methodist work in Russia.

The political turmoil within Russia, the atheistic posture of Communism, and the frustrating internal debate among Methodist leaders about how to respond to the Russian situation and Methodist mission there became a central focus of secular and church presses. As one reads the available materials, however, it is clear that in this process the Methodism of Lithuania and Latvia in the period from 1927 to 1944 has become forgotten history. Yet, during these years it was very much alive. For example, the records of the first German Central Conference, which was held in September 1936 under the leadership of Bishop Nuelsen, reveal that among the representatives of the Methodist Church from other European countries (e.g., Denmark, Norway, Sweden, Switzerland, Hungary, Yugoslavia) were guests from Latvia.[56]

With the advent of Soviet rule in the Baltic states there was a reign of terror, and many pastors and laity suffered persecution and death at the hands of merciless authorities. In Estonia District Superintendent Martin Prikask was imprisoned and executed, Jaan Jaagupsoo was mercilessly slain, Rudolfs Goldsmits was murdered in the streets of Agenskalns, and hosts of others were persecuted and some were forced to flee. The martyrs were numerous.

The stories of those who escaped the terror continue to inspire and amaze. Konstantin Wipp, an Estonian, "had been sent by the Russian captors to an island but managed to escape with two companions by boat to Sweden where he completed his education and served two pastorates [going] to the United States through the assistance of Overseas Relief and the assignment of a field by Bishop Wade."[57] Serge Mosienko, a Lithuanian and treasurer of the BSMC and the district superintendent of Lithuania, was pursued by the secret police, who tried to get him to furnish names of pastors and members, which he refused to do. After hiding in a barn overnight, the next day he escaped across the border into Germany with assistance from some acquaintances. His family joined him later in Germany. From there they left for the United States. Such stories can be multiplied time and again, not to mention those who senselessly went to their deaths.

The fact that in the face of the communist threat and liquidation of Methodism in Latvia and Lithuania most of the Methodist clergy and many of the laity were forced to flee to other countries gave the church little chance of survival in those Baltic states. Furthermore, with their final takeover in 1944 the Soviets forced the Latvian and Lithuanian Methodists to merge with other churches.

Destiny took a different turn in Estonia, where the authorities, generally speaking, did not dislodge Methodist clergy, who by and large were able to stand by their congregations, though not without grave suffering and persecution. Methodism's survival in Estonia may also have been due in part to the fact that the Estonian Methodist Church had become largely self-sustaining in the first half of the twentieth century.[58]

The Rev. Richard Lupp surmises that the Estonian Methodist Church was strengthened by a national and cultural identity, since most of its congregations worshiped and witnessed in the Estonian language.[59]

Lithuanian Methodism's demise was strongly tied to German repatriation. Nevertheless, the bravery and steadfastness in faith of the Methodists in the Baltic states in the face of communist persecution cannot be emphasized too strongly. As Methodism is now born again in Latvia and other regions of the Baltic, one must remember the sacrifice made by so many and the hope they give to all generations of Christians at the threshold of the twenty-first century.

The Last Appointments of the BSMC

The following list of appointments of the Baltic and Slavic Conference of 1939 enables one to grasp the extent of Methodist work in the Baltic states before the onslaught of the Soviets and before the demise of the Latvian and Lithuanian churches. The BSMC never convened again after 1939.

Estonia District
Martin Prikask, Superintendent
(Kuressaare, Estonia)

Avanduse and Circuit	Eduard Hark
Haapsalu and Circuit	Jaan Jaagupsoo
Kuressaare and Circuit	Martin Prikask
Lihula and Circuit	*To be supplied*
Narva	Konstantin Wipp
Paide	Voldemar Ojassoo

Pöide and Circuit	Vilhelm Õun
Rakvere and Circuit	Martin Kuigre
Pärnu and Circuit	Eduard Raud
Tallinn: First Church	Aleksander Kuum
Second Church and Kopli	*To be supplied*
Tapa and Circuit	Jaan Puskay
Tartu and Circuit	Ferdinand Tombo
Torgu and Circuit	Peeter Häng
Viljandi	Aleksei Poobus

Latvia District
Fricis Timbers, Superintendent
(Riga, Latvia)

Aizpute	Janis Geide
Grobina	*To be supplied*
Jekabpils	Vilhelms Volskis
Jelgava	Eduards Kaimins
Kandava	Karlis Beike
Kuldiga	Eduards Eidins
Liepaja: First Church	Voldemars Plavinskis
Second Church	Karlis Ernstsons
Ligatne	*To be supplied*
Matras	*To be supplied*
Nica	Karlis Iesalnieks
Riga: First Church (Akas iela)	Fricis Timbers
	Rudolfs Valdmanis
Second Church (Agenskaln)	Mikelis Svarcs
Third Church (Elizabetes Iela)	Rudolfs Krafts
Fourth Church (Bethany)	Adolfs Bergmanis
(and Russian work)	
Fifth Church (Philadelfia)	Rudolfs Goldsmits
(and German work)	Hans Soete
Rigas Melluzi (Riga Beach)	*To be supplied*
Ventspils	Adolfs Majorins
Ziemupe	Karlis Ernstons

Lithuania District
Sergei Mosienko, Superintendent
(Kaunas, Lithuania)

Biržai	Kostas Burbulys
Kaunas	Serge Mosienko

124

Kybartai	Alexander Röhrich
Pilviškai	Emil Blum
Šiauliai	Kostas Burbulys
Tauragė and Circuit	Richard Lupp
Marijampoė and Circuit	Oskar Kaufmann

Conferencewide Appointments

Adolfs Bergmanis, Connectional Correspondent and Correspondence Assistant to Mission Treasurer

Aleksander Kuum, Inspector of Bethesda, Deaconess Association

Aleksander Kuum, Martin Prikask, Voldemar Ojassoo, Richard Järv, Editors of the Estonian *Kristlik Kaitsja* (Christian Advocate)

Martin Kuigre, Treasurer for Estonia

Richard Lupp, President of Epworth League in Lithuania

Serge Mosienko, Richard Lupp, Editors of the Lithuanian *Krikščionistes Sargas* (Christian Advocate)

Serge Mosienko, Assistant Missions Treasurer for the Conference and Treasurer for Lithuania

Dr. George A. Simons, Chairman of the Jubilee Fund Commission

Hans Soete, Mission Treasurer, Bible and Temperance Evangelist for the Conference

Fricis Timbers, Eduards Kaimins, Karlis Beike, Editors of the Estonian *Kristlik Aizstavis* (Christian Advocate)

Ferdinand Tombo, President of Estonian Epworth League

Repatriation

The year 1941 brought the advent of a tremendous wave of repatriation of German citizens and people of German origin living abroad, who were summoned back to their homeland in time of war. Whereas the Russians had taken over most of the Baltic states in 1940, the Germans took them over in 1941 and initiated repatriation. This had a tremendous effect on Methodism in Lithuania and Latvia and upon Methodism in Germany.

The minutes of the Königsberg District of the Northeast German Annual Conference in 1941 and 1942, which were the last two sessions of that conference, include revealing information regarding Methodist clergy and laity from Lithuania and Latvia and repatriation to Germany.

At the beginning of and during World War II, some 46,000 people of German origin were repatriated to Germany. Many were from the Baltic states and other areas threatened by Russian takeover or where it had occurred. There were some five hundred Methodists who were resettled in the Königsberg District of the Northeast German Annual Conference.

In his 1941 district report, Karl Kreutzter records:

> With the Russian takeover of the former states of Estonia, Latvia, and Lithuania our blooming work there, our Methodist organization, came to an end. The pastors of Latvian and Estonian nationalities meanwhile have had to take up other professions: as bookkeepers, with the railroad, postal service or in banks. Our houses of worship were used by the Russians as dance halls and club houses. The Methodist work, above all in Lithuania, was founded by the German Methodists. Our hearts ache when we think that our church and congregations must end their service in this manner. A stormy wind is blowing across the earth.[60]

Pastor Serge Mosienko had fled to Germany in the fall of 1941, where the bishop appointed him to work with resettlement and problems related to the transfer of church property. Mosienko,[61] as did two other ethnic Lithuanian Methodist pastors (Emil Blum and Kostas Burbulys), eventually emigrated to the United States. There were six Lithuanian-German Methodist pastors repatriated to Germany: W. Blum, Alfred Hühn, Oskar Kaufmann, Arthur Leifert, Richard Lupp, and Alexander Röhrich.

Kreutzer reports further:

> The largest part of our brothers and sisters from Kowno [Kaunas] have been located in the camp at Scoldau and surrounding area. Brother Röhrich is their pastor. Two pastors by the name of Blum with a smaller group are located with the Prussian Stargard. The brothers and sisters from Kybarty [Kybartai] are located in Matzkau near Danzig and joined every Sunday with our congregation in Danzig. Pastor Richard Lupp is in Mecklenburg. . . . Some Methodists have been located in the area around Litzmannstadt[62] and are being cared for by our missionary deaconesses there.[63]

The next year (1942) Kreutzer's district report included the following pertinent information.

> Our Methodists from Lithuania are spread throughout Germany today and especially with us in the east. After various efforts the Rev. Richard Lupp succeeded in getting freed from the community camp in Zdunska wola and to take up residence in our available apartment in Litzmannstadt. He is trying to organize a diaspora service there. In Schröttersburg (southeast Prussia) a small refugee congregation has not been able to find a place of worship. Numbers of others who are resettling in Germany, even after a year and a half, are still in large community camps. One can understand why the desire for one's own home is so strong, when forty or fifty people, large and small, must live together.[64]

. . . .

Now our Lithuanian-Germans, who were intended for resettlement in the east should return to their homes. Since April 1 there is a resettlement service in Kaunas.[65] Soon the signal to return will be given. . . . Since the departure of the Lithuanian Methodists, our properties in Kaunas, Tauragė, Kybartai, Pilviškiai, etc. have been standing empty. If the members of our congregations return, they would be sent back. Our efforts in resettlement seem to have been for nothing. We must start all over again and are busy at the task of establishing the right goals in this matter.[66]

This was, of course, a vain hope, as Emma Robbert's account reveals. The German occupation of the Baltic states did not last. The Lithuanian Germans, if they returned home, remained only briefly, for the Russians came back in 1944 and Methodism in Lithuania and Latvia was at an end. Kostas Burbulys, a Methodist pastor who had been trained at the Methodist seminaries in Riga, Latvia, and Frankfurt, Germany, was the only Lithuanian Methodist pastor to stay behind when all of the others left. Burbulys finally fled on July 25, 1944, the day before the Russians came. In 1939, before the demise of Lithuanian Methodism, there had been about one thousand members with seven pastors, properties in five cities, two additional congregations and a number of fellowships. Two Latvian Methodist pastors also stayed behind and continued to minister for many years: Janis Geide, in either the Lutheran or Baptist Church, and Voldemars Plavinskis, who became a Lutheran minister.

The Northeast German Annual Conference was affected in other ways related to the final Russian surge and takeover of the Baltics in 1944–45. Two appointments in the conference lay very near the Lithuanian border: Insterburg (founded in 1921) and Eydtkuhnen (founded in 1929). They were a part of the Königsberg District and the two congregations closest to the German/Lithuanian border. "On January 21, 1945 after hard battles Insterburg was occupied by Russian troops. The city and Methodist congregation no longer exist. Today [1986] Insterburg has the Russian name Tchernjachowski."[67] The Russians made it a military center for the administration of Northeast Prussia.

Eydtkuhnen was a charge on the Insterburg circuit. A church was built there in 1929, and it attracted a substantial congregation. It was only about two hundred steps from the train station at Eydtkuhnen to the Lithuanian border.[68] Just across the border was the town of Kybartai, where there was a small but strong Methodist congregation. For many years there were numerous fruitful encounters between these two congregations.

Both of these towns were directly in the line of repatriation and the large movement of population and military, both German and Russian. The tensions created by this mobility and those resulting from the political turmoil of National Socialism and Communism made congregational life extremely difficult, particularly in Eydtkuhnen. The Russians totally destroyed the town in the fall of 1944. One must not forget that German Methodists likewise suffered greatly amid all the madness of war.

Paul Ernst Sommer has called the repatriation from Lithuania an odyssey.[69] What does he mean? Brought home, resettled, repatriated, persecuted, uprooted! Words such as these come to mind when one thinks of all these people endured. Yes, an odyssey! Life was a pendulum between disappointment and new beginnings.

Many of the Latvian and Lithuanian Methodist pastors eventually made their way to the United States. Some escaped to Germany and served there in the German Methodist Church. Most of the Latvian pastors were forced to flee, but few of them were of German origin, as was the case with Lithuanian Methodist pastors. Most of the Latvian pastors emigrated to the United States. Two pastors, Geide and Plavinskis, remained in Latvia and joined other churches. Many Latvian Methodist church members joined the Lutheran church, and many of the Lithuanian Methodists joined Pentecostal and Baptist churches. The Estonian Methodist pastors generally did not leave Estonia, although there were a few, such as Alexander Dennisson, Evald Leps, Aleksei Poobus, and Konstantin Wipp, who emigrated to the United States.

In 1946 Dr. Gaither P. Warfield, head of the Methodist Committee on Overseas Relief, and Bishop Wade made a trip through the refugee camps of Germany to look for expatriated Methodist pastors and their families. Dr. Warfield made the necessary arrangements with the government authorities, and Bishop Wade arranged for pastorates in Michigan, New York, Virginia, Massachusetts, Illinois, Wisconsin, Minnesota, Nebraska, Iowa, Missouri, and eventually some other states.[70] The BSMC families in the United States, which Bishop Wade listed in 1962,[71] were as follows:

The Rev. and Mrs. Adolfs Bergmanis
The Rev. and Mrs. Emil A. Blum
The Rev. and Mrs. Kostas Burbulys
The Rev. and Mrs. Kristaps Caune
The Rev. and Mrs. Eduards Eidins
The Rev. and Mrs. Karlis Ernstsons
The Rev. and Mrs. Ludwig Eskildsen
The Rev. and Mrs. Karlis Iesalnieks
The Rev. and Mrs. Janis Laupmanis
The Rev. Adolfs Majorins
The Rev. and Mrs. Serge Mosienko

The Rev. and Mrs. Aleksei Poobus
The Rev. and Mrs. Richard Skobe
The Rev. and Mrs. Fritz Springis
The Rev. and Mrs. Mikelis Svarcs
The Rev. and Mrs. Valdemars Teravskis
The Rev. and Mrs. Fricis Timbers
The Rev. and Mrs. Valdmanis
The Rev. Vilhelms Volskis
The Rev. and Mrs. Konstantin Wipp

At the "Reunion of Baltic and Slavic Refugee Pastors of the Methodist Church in the United States," organized by Bishop Wade in 1962 at Bay View, Michigan, greetings were received from the following Latvian and Lithuanian pastors living in Germany:

The Rev. W. Blum (East Germany)
The Rev. and Mrs. Alfred Hühn (West Germany)
The Rev. Oskar Kaufmann (West Germany)
The Rev. Arthur Leifert (West Germany)
The Rev. and Mrs. Richard Lupp (West Germany)
The Rev. Alexander Röhrich (West Germany)

The Methodists of the Baltic states demonstrated incredible strength and dedication. With independence after World War I, their newly won hope boded the transformation of shattered dreams and devastated lands into peace and fertile fields where one could worship freely. It was in this changing Baltic region that Methodism began to grow and bring spiritual renewal. The early and competent leadership of Dr. George A. Simons and Bishop John L. Nuelsen was a primary factor in its growth, and for eleven years, from 1928 until the final annual conference session of 1939, Bishop Raymond J. Wade provided exemplary pastoral and episcopal leadership. Twenty-two years would pass before a Methodist bishop could return to the Methodists of the Baltics, namely, when Bishop Odd Hagen visited Estonia, though unofficially, in September 1961.

CHAPTER 7

The Development of Estonian Methodism

[The two sections of this chapter were not intended when written to be a careful historical analysis of Estonian Methodism. Instead they are reports by two men who were intimately acquainted with the growth of Methodism in the Baltic region, particularly Estonia. Martin Prikask, who became superintendent of the Estonian District of the Baltic and Slavic Mission Conference, as well as a pastor in Tallinn, was associated with the Methodist movement in Estonia from its beginning. In the report-like telling of the story by Prikask and Puskay, also an Estonian Methodist pastor, one captures the sense of oral history and the local color and flavor of the moods, trends, difficulties, and successes of the time in which these men lived. Above all, they call to mind the *cloud of witnesses* who gave of themselves selflessly that others might hear the healing word of Christ's redemptive love and become a part of a caring community centered in that love. While the facts they record have veracity, it is the spirit of the mission and evangelism of early Methodism in the Baltic states, which endured the most trying of times, they convey that inspires anew and makes their reports worthy of our reading again and again. The Rev. Heigo Ritsbek places the Prikask and Puskay reports in perspective with a brief introduction.]

Estonian Methodism Prior to the Soviet Occupation (1907–1940)
Heigo Ritsbek

The story of Methodism in Estonia begins in 1907, when two friends, Vassili Täht and Karl Kuum—Estonians by nationality—arrived at the island of Saaremaa in Estonia and began evangelistic preaching there. Vassili Täht served the British and Foreign Bible Society. Karl Kuum was a simple farmer, and at the same time, a Moravian laypreacher. When on June 9, 1907, they arrived at Arensburg (now Kuressaare) on the island of Saaremaa and began evangelistic services, many people were converted. The first meetings were held at Mr. M. Trey's house.[1] They also held open-air meetings and up to three thousand people were present.[2] The first Methodist congregation was officially established at Arensburg on the island of Saaremaa on August 13, 1910, as Martin Prikask indicates in the section that follows.[3]

During this time, Estonia was a province of tsarist Russia. Everybody was considered to be a Lutheran, as the Lutheran Church enjoyed national church status. At the same time the Russian Orthodox Church also had many congregations in Estonia. This was partly the result of the local Russian government "Russification" policies and partly the result of the so-called "church-changing movement" in the 1840s, when hundreds and hundreds of Estonian peasants became Orthodox. These peasants believed that if they belonged to the same church as the tsar of the empire, they would be treated better by the local German nobility. Of course, their situation as Orthodox peasants remained the same as when they were Lutheran peasants. From the eighteenth century the Moravian Church existed in Estonia within the Lutheran Church as *ecclesiola in ecclesia*. A decade later the Seventh-Day Adventists and the Covenant Church in Estonia came into being.[4]

According to the Methodist monthly *Kristlik Kaitsja* (The Christian Advocate), it is very clear that Methodism came to Estonia because of "the lack of Christian life in the [Lutheran] Church."[5] Although this was not explicitly expressed, the same sentiment was probably expressed toward the Russian Orthodox Church, the other major church on the island of Saaremaa.

Reading *Kristlik Kaitsja*, one learns that the revival meetings with conversions, in which the converts were "turning away from sin," became the trademark of Estonian Methodism,[6] as did later the social ministry with soup kitchens, ministering to alcoholics and prostitutes ("The Blue Cross" movement), the temperance movement, and the ministry of deaconesses.[7] The Methodist churches had Sunday schools for children, which apparently were also a source for evangelism and mission. So the term "revival" referred to the worship services in the private homes or outside (later in the Methodist church buildings), where nominal Christians came to a committed life to Christ. "Revival week" indicated a longer period of such services. From the early Methodist periodicals it is not clear how these meetings were conducted, but probably they were very informal, with little (if any) fixed structure. It seems that the term "revival" was used more frequently during the first years of Estonian Methodism than later, when "revival" basically meant massive conversions.

The new so-called "free-churches," which emerged just before Estonia became an independent nation in 1918 and flourished during the first years of the new republic, acted on the basis of free choice: freedom to join any church, that is, membership based on the free will of people who joined these churches. One of these "free churches" was the Estonian Methodist Church (officially a mission of the Methodist Episcopal Church).

As there are no studies of the ways through which the new church members came into the Methodist Church in Estonia prior to the Soviet occupation, it is quite difficult to address this matter. However, as the *Kristlik Kaitsja* information sections from the years 1920 to 1940 are basically reports of the evangelistic rallies and the results of these events, it is possible to assume that at least the majority of the new members came from direct evangelistic activities of Estonian Methodism. The following comments from Martin Prikask and Jaan Puskay from a 1933 issue of *Kristlik Kaitsja* provide an interesting background to the development and spread of Methodism throughout Estonia.

The Development of the Estonian Methodist Church and Related Annual Conferences[8]
Martin Prikask

We will consider the establishment of the first congregation in Kuressaare as the beginning of Estonian Methodism. In 1907, Brother Vassili Täht arrived from Saint Petersburg to preach in Kuressaare. He was from Saaremaa, from the civil parish of Uuemoisa, the village of Leisi, and was in the service of the British and Foreign Bible Society. He was accompanied by brother Karl Kuum, who was from Tapa. They held lively and popularly attended meetings in various houses, and their sermons resulted in spiritual revivals, which I and my wife, along with many others, experienced.

Our meetings and prayer services were not appreciated by the local *Evangelischer* (Lutheran) Pastor Blossfeld, who began to reprimand us from the pulpit as "cliquish and fanatical." This, along with the general lack of spirituality, caused us eventually to seek a new home. Since our understanding of the biblical concept of Christian fellowship did not agree with the views of the Baptists and free churches (non-Lutherans) active in Saaremaa, we decided in the fall of 1908 to meet together to commemorate the death of our Lord in a private apartment in Kuressaare. This incident was in actuality the beginning of our congregation, although the church was formally established on August 13, 1910, when Dr. George A. Simons and Vassili Täht received three men and three women as the first members of the Estonian Methodist Church, in the house of Mrs. Vildenberg on Kohtu Street #2.

Until 1910 we did not have official ties to the Methodist Church, even though Dr. George A. Simons had visited Kuressaare already in 1909. The leaders of the believers' fellowship at the time were M. Trey and myself. Later we had to separate from M. Trey and his house, where we had hitherto held blissful meetings. In 1910, the Finnish Annual Conference was held in Saint Michael (Mikkeli), and on the conference agenda was an Estonian name: Brother Vassili Täht, who was appointed as preacher in Kuressaare.

Upon his arrival Brother Täht began his work in the city, whereas I evangelized more in the rural areas. Regardless of the persecution, our work advanced like the mustard seed planted in the Lord's field, watered with divine blessings. Soon vital congregations grew up throughout the large land. Because others have written about this, I will move on to give an overview of the annual conferences.

In 1911 at the Finnish Conference in Vaasa, a Russian mission was established. Attending at the time were Bishop W. Burt, Dr. George A. Simons, M. Prikask, V. Täht, A. Ivanov, H. Smorodin, and G. Durdis. Others attending the conference included L. Heinrich, A. Sistenen, and A. Karlson, who, however, did not remain in residence. Altogether the mission had nine members. At that conference I was assigned to Kuressaare, since brother Täht settled in Tallinn.

In the same year a study guide for preachers by Bishop Burt was published especially for use by the Russian Mission.

Already in July of 1912, the Russian Mission held its second conference independently in the first Methodist church built in Russia, namely, in Kaunas [Lithuania]. Bishop John L. Nuelsen presided. The conference consisted of twelve brothers: G. A. Simons, M. Prikask, L. Heinrich, V. Täht, H. P. Oksotksy, E. Rikker, P. Ludvig, A. Hühn, A. Karlson, G. Durdis, A. Tulihoovi, and K. Kuum.

Because many preachers also belonged to the Finnish Conference, they took part in two conferences. In 1913 the Finnish Conference was held in

Turku. Bishop Nuelsen presided and some members of the Russian Conference participated.

The Russian Mission held its third conference June 26-29 in the same year in Kybartai-Virbalis, with Bishop Nuelsen presiding. Virbalis was a border town in Russia where we built our first meeting hall. The conference was concluded with the marriage of Paul Ludvig and Alma Mikkonen, which was the first wedding in our family of preachers. Officiating at the ceremony were Dr. Simons and Dr. G. Jones. As a remembrance of the day, Dr. Jones presented the Sunday school with a harmonium.

The war began in 1914. The Finnish Conference was held in Helsinki on August 17 and a couple of brothers from the Russian Conference were in attendance. Most of the brothers had to enlist in the army. It was not even possible to attend the conference openly.

We came together for the Russian Conference on December 5 in Saint Petersburg County, in the village of Khandrovo, where a Russian Methodist prayer house had been built. Part of the conference was held at another prayer house in Sigolovo. The meetings were led by Dr. Simons.

That year was important for the Estonian Methodists, because in the same month the first prayer house for Estonians was dedicated in the Marinsk area in Siberia. I officiated at the dedication because the house was built by A. Karlson with funds from the mission.

In 1915 the Russian Mission held its conference on July 5, in Petrograd. Only a few members had come together because the war had pulled most into its grasp. Because we were without a bishop, the conference was led by Dr. Simons.

The Finnish Conference was held the same month in Gamlakarleby, under the direction of Dr. Simons. With great sadness we learned that brother A. Lukas had fallen in battle.

On August 5, 1916, some of us met together quietly in Petrograd. The war was devastating, and we were living under its oppression. The Finnish Conference was held in Ekenäs. Both meetings were led by Dr. Simons.

In 1917 the Russian Conference was held on May 21 in Petrograd, under the leadership of Dr. Simons. Those were eventful times. I had to leave Saaremaa and relocate in Tallinn. At the end of September I went to Russia and worked around Volosova until the end of the year. The same year the Finnish Conference had only one representative from the Russian Mission: Dr. Simons.

No Russian Conference was held in 1918. Dr. Simons left Russia in October. The Germans came from Saaremaa to the mainland. In January I was able to return to my homeland. I settled in Haapsalu, where on February 24 I established a Methodist congregation. At that time the membership consisted of twenty-four brothers and sixteen sisters. I managed to get to Kuressaare at the end of February. There I learned that, by German orders, our church building was being used as an elementary school. The members were scattered and the spiritual fervor had abated, but soon after my arrival the church was freed, and the congregation resumed its activities once again.

In 1919 the Estonian Methodists could not take part in the Finnish Conference, and the Russian Mission did not hold a conference.

The year 1920 is especially important to us, because at the conference held in Helsinki, August 11-16, it was decided that an independent annual conference would be established for the countries that had separated from Russia. Permission for this was given by the General Conference, meeting in Des Moines, Iowa (USA). This was the last joint conference between the Finns and the Estonians.

In the same year, with M. Prikask as editor in chief, the Estonian Methodist *Kristlik Kaitsja* (Christian Advocate) began publishing.

The year 1921 is a historic year for the Estonian Methodists. The first annual conference of the Methodist Church was held in Estonia. The conference was hosted by the Haapsalu congregation, and the meetings were led by Bishop John L. Nuelsen. Bishop Kukk of the Lutheran Church offered the castle-church for worship services during the conference, since the financial meeting took place in rented rooms. The conference was attended by foreign delegates, because representatives from three districts had come together: Russia, Karelia, Estonia-Latvia-Lithuania.

That year our family of preachers also grew. We were joined by H. Söte, J. Karlson, and E. Raud. M. Prikask was appointed superintendent of the Estonian District. The district superintendents of the Russian District and the Latvian-Lithuanian District were Hjalmar Salmi and H. Holzschuher, respectively. The same year some members were sent to school in Germany.

The 1922 conference was held July 26-31 in Riga, with Bishop Nuelsen presiding. The annual conference received the following as probationary members: E. Raud, F. Tombo, V. Meinvald, J. Tintse, A. Mikkov, and J. P. Karlson. At the same conference, Brother K. Kuum was ordained as the resident deacon. Mission secretaries were appointed in each country: M. Prikask in Estonia, H. Salmi in Russia, A. Freiburg in Latvia, and A. Hühn in Lithuania.

The annual conference of 1923 was held in Kaunas [Lithuania], August 1-5. Bishop Nuelsen presided. The roster of Estonian preachers increased by two, for the conference received Brothers J. Puskay and M. Krüger as probationary members. H. Söte was appointed editor of *Kristlik Kaitsja*.

Another historic year was 1924. The conference was held in Kuressaare and was renamed the Baltic and Slavic Mission Conference, with Bishop

A. Bast presiding. A. Kuum and A. Tõns were received as probationary members.

The 1925 conference was held July 22-26 in Liepaja under the direction of Bishop Richardson. The 1926 conference took place in Riga under the leadership of Bishop Nuelsen. In 1927 Bishop Edgar Blake led a conference in Riga, September 7-11. The same year the first nationwide Youth Conference was held in Tallinn during Pentecost.

In 1928 the conference was held in Tartu under the direction of Bishop Raymond J. Wade. From that time on neighbor-nations' capitals competed to host the conferences: 1929 in Tallinn, 1930 in Riga, 1931 in Tallinn, and 1932 in Riga. All of these conferences were led by our fatherly and dear bishop, Dr. Wade.

Tallinn has been chosen once again to host our Jubilee Conference. Our family of preachers has grown in the interim. We have been joined by: V. Ojassoo, A. Seck, J. Jakobson, P. Häng, V. Prii, and R. Järv. No longer with us are E. Valdmann and P. Gildemann. J. P. Karlson passed away earlier, and K. Kuum has gone on to eternal glory. Far away in Paraguay, Brother J. Karlson is sowing the seeds of the gospel.

My exhortation in this Jubilee year is—Onward in the Lord's name! Thousands of our neighbors are unsaved; the souls of thousands need illumination! Onward until the great Jubilee with our Lord, for which we expect renewed inspiration from this meeting. May the Lord continue to bless our dear church.

Historical Vignettes of Estonian Congregations[9]
Jaan Puskay

Looking back on the work that our Lord has done in Estonia through the Methodist Church, one must exclaim as the song says: "God's work is great!" The Almighty has revealed God's own self to us, as the following brief and compressed examples of our churches' history show.

The congregation in Kuressaare is our mother-congregation. Under God's guidance, Brothers V. Täht and K. Kuum went to Kuressaare to proclaim the gospel. This was on June 9, 1907. Presenting themselves as missionaries, they were directed from one group of believers to another. But none would accept them into their family. Finally, they were directed to Brother M. Trey's house, who received them and enabled them to preach God's Word in his own home. The sown Word found good soil, and a revival broke out and spread throughout Saaremaa and has lasted until the present.

Brother and Sister Prikask came to faith during the first meetings, which were initially held at Brother Trey's house. When it became apparent, however, that Brother Trey favored re-baptism, Brother Prikask along with his followers departed and began holding meetings at Sister M. Vildenberg's home. This movement developed into Methodism, and V. Täht was appointed as the first pastor in Tallinn and Kuressaare. In 1910 Brother M. Prikask was appointed as a local preacher, and in 1911 he was assigned as pastor in Kuressaare. Brother Prikask did not limit his work only to Kuressaare, but preached the gospel also in the farthest parts of Saaremaa.

God blessed Brother Prikask spiritually as well as financially, and in 1912 the congregation settled with great joy in its new church. Building the church required great faith and many prayers and sacrifices, but Brother Prikask did not give up, and as a result the Lord's work advanced. Nine years later the church needed to be expanded and an addition was built. Now the church is once again getting too small for us, and plans are under way for building a new stone church.

In addition to Brothers Täht and Prikask, the congregation in Kuressaare has been served by ten brothers and two sisters. The congregation makes its home in the city of Kuressaare, although most of its activity takes place in the rural areas, where in many places prayer halls can be found, even though most of our meetings take place in farm houses.

Pöide congregation. Brother Täht worked at the Pöide congregation for a time and many people came to faith. In 1924 an independent congregation was organized, and Brother A. Mikkov was appointed pastor. The congregation was without a pastor for awhile, until in 1930 Brother A. Tõns was appointed as pastor, and he continues to serve there today. Through the work of the Rev. Tõns, the congregation has grown from thirty to one hundred and forty members. Recently a new, large church and a parsonage were built. This cost 6,000 Kr. and they were built without any outside help.

Torgu congregation. The religious movement of Sõrve was established by Brother E. Raud, and the first meetings took place in January of 1921, in a schoolhouse in Mäebe and in the village of Hänga. We will hear of this congregation's further success from the chronicles of the Rev. K. Kuum.

In 1924 I was appointed as pastor of Torgu. In October 1924 I moved to my new work place in the village of Montu, into the home of Aado Lind, where my apartment was. We did not have meeting rooms at the time, but the organizing of a church was undertaken immediately. I found seven individuals who were members from the Torgu branch of the Kuressaare congregation. Space in Brother Lind's home became small and consideration was given to seeking a larger location. In October 1927 we concluded that a church was necessary and that we had to find resources in order to realize our goal. Financial support and outside help were not available, and all faith had to be

137

left in God's hands. Last summer (1926), we organized a lottery of which 12,000 cents remained in our account. This was our only capital.

In the interim we wrote to a sister in America and told her of our plans. She sent us $40. But we were still timid about beginning until a brother said to me secretly that he would assume the cost of building the rafters. I was quite shocked and cautioned him that we were not undertaking the building of a small church but rather one that was eight fathoms long and equally tall. But the brother remained steadfast in his decision. When the brothers were all conveniently together, I shared my secret with them and this inspired them to begin diligently working toward our goal. And although this job cost our brother 402 Kr., he nevertheless fulfilled his pledge faithfully. But this was not the end of this brother's charity, for he continued to support the church (total 1,000 Kr.). God bless this brother in the eternal kingdom—forever!

God opened the hearts of many others to support the church building. It is worth mentioning two sisters in particular, who both made donations totaling about 500 Kr. each. Others did their part also, some giving 100 Kr., some 50 Kr., so that we were able to dedicate our building on October 28, 1928. God has blessed our church by adding nearly twenty new members each year. Honor, thanksgiving, and praise in everything to the Father, Son, and Holy Ghost now and forever! Amen.

Brother K. Kuum became ill, and in 1932 Brother P. Häng, a schoolteacher, was appointed pastor. He labors there selflessly.

Tapa congregation. It is the oldest congregation on the mainland. Shortly after being saved, Brother K. Kuum settled in Tapa and began evangelizing. Although this work was fruitful and believers gathered around him, the congregation was not founded until 1912 under the direction of Dr. George A. Simons. There were ten founding members.

The Rev. K. Kuum labored in Tapa until 1921. Since then the congregation has been served by seven pastors and three vicars. The Rev. V. Ojassoo is there at present.

Until 1923 the meetings were held at Brother K. Kuum's house, then for about a year at Mr. Feldman's home. At the same time J. P. Karlson began building a church with external help, which was dedicated in 1924. From that time forward a couple of years can be considered the Tapa congregation's flowering period. Its most important branches are in Porkuni, Tammik, and Koeru.

The congregation has lost sixteen members through death, among them the founding members Brothers K. Kuum, J. Peial, Sisters Raamat, Nelke-Krappe, and Feierbach. Currently it has some seventy members and thirteen members in the Epworth League Association. In addition to this there is a Sunday school. Recently, thanks to the Rev. V. Ojasson's energetic efforts, the congregation received a burial place, which is the first Methodist cemetery in Estonia.

Haapsalu congregation. This congregation was founded on February 24, 1928, when twenty believers, four brothers and sixteen sisters, came together to commemorate the death of our Lord.

> On the basis of the gospel one arrived at the following understanding: only the sanctified can participate in the commemoration of our Lord's death, and God has ordained this only for the redeemed, but not for them that live in sin. We asked Brother Prikask, who lived in Haapsalu at the time, to distribute the body and blood of our Lord to us, which he kindly did.
> For over two years the meetings were held in Brother Mikkov's apartment, Ehte Street #7, under the name "Evangelical Meetings." But as the number of participants grew and the space became too small, the decision was made to join with the local Methodist church. That was on May 8, 1920. Posti Street #17 became the new location for meetings and the activities now took place under the name of the Methodist congregation.
> Even this place became too small and larger quarters were rented at Jaani Street #6, where the congregation worked from June 1, 1920 until July 23, 1922. The first Annual Conference of the Methodist Church in Estonia was also held in those rooms. Working in rented rooms is always problematical and as a result a thought occurred to us: "How wonderful it would be to have our own secure home." God opened the heart of our brother Dr. George A. Simons, who sought for us the monies needed to build a church. The church building began in 1921 under the direction of Brother J. Koplik. It cost 2,000,000 Mrk. and on July 23, 1922, the church was dedicated and the congregation settled into its new home.
> The Lord was continually near, blessing the congregation so that it grew and flowered. The membership had grown to the number seventy-seven, the youth group had forty-five members, and the Sunday School was started by Brother F. Tombo, who was their leader and carried a great burden for them.

The congregation in Haapsalu has been served by six pastors, and in addition to founding Pastor M. Kuigre's time in Haapsalu, this can be considered the church's fruitful period.

Uugla congregation. The Uugla congregation grew out of the Haapsalu congregation, and the work begun in Lihula was associated with the new congregation. To illustrate its blossoming time we will draw on a quotation from the *Kristlik Kaitsja* (Christian Advocate) of 1927: "In a short time a young congregation has developed from a few members. Our membership is a little over fifty, among them seventeen brothers. But we have many dear like-minded friends and followers."

Later the Uugla movement reached Palivere, where with the help of our dear departed friend Brother M. Sarnak, Brother Tõns built a beautiful prayer house, which was designed by Brother Tombo. We have hardly anything left of this movement except memories.

Lihula. The work in Lihula was begun by Sister Ida Joekallas, who had evangelized there with great love for many years. Four others have worked to assist this work, and Brother V. Meinvald has possibly done the most selfless work. Currently there is a small group of believers working there, whose labors for the Lord are not in vain.

The Haapsalu congregation has a few more branches, the furthest of them in Emmaste, under the care of Brother Altberg and others.

Rakvere congregation. This congregation was founded in 1920, and the first, who were affected by the reorganization, were members and followers of the Tapa congregation residing in Rakvere and the surrounding areas. The first organizing was entrusted to Brother M. Kuigre. Later Brother J. Karlson came from Finland and was subsequently appointed pastor of the congregation.

Pastor J. Karlson's energetic and steadfast work bore much fruit, not only in Rakvere but also in the surrounding areas. Soon the congregation was structured in Rakvere and a branch was developed in Kunda. Pastor J. Karlson was succeeded by Pastor H. Söte, who could serve the congregation for only one year, because the responsibilities of the children's home and editing *Kristlik Kaitsja* required him to be in Tallinn. After Pastor H. Söte, the congregation had various pastors until Pastor V. Ojasson.

At one time the congregation could have relocated from its rented quarters to its renovated house, but this did not suit Pastor Ojasson. A church building was initiated, and due to his perseverance and God's help, Pastor Ojasson was able to form ties with the community, with other congregations, and even in America through the help of our dear Bishop R. J. Wade. Thus on August 25, 1928, the new church was dedicated.

In the last few years membership has grown and the work has advanced. Pastor M. Kuigre is currently serving in Rakvere.

Pärnu congregation. The steps toward the congregation's founding go back to the first days of the World War, when Brother K. Kuum had strong ties with the believers in Pärnu. But reasons, which were neither dependent on Brother Kuum nor the Pärnu believers, prevented the founding of a congregation.

We will let an excerpt from the "Memoirs" of Pastor K. Kuum tell the story:

> Due to demands and wishes, I once again traveled to Pärnu. This was on July 20, 1921. With God's help I held seven meetings, which God graciously blessed. Many became children of God and set out on the new road of life.
>
> When the first Estonian Methodist church conference took place in Haapsalu, the believers in Pärnu sent a petition to the conference asking that someone be appointed there to set in order the founding of a congregation. I had been nominated in the petition. The Conference answered the petition and appointed me to go to Pärnu in order to begin the congregation and to preach the Word there.

My trip took place on August 24, 1921. There were some truly hungering souls and the Lord has greatly blessed this work. The meetings were begun immediately, almost every night in various meeting halls and private homes. On August 30, 1921 the first temporary council and body of representatives were elected at the home of Brother Kiinvaldt. The first members who requested a congregation were Edgar Bosch, Voldemar Ojassoo, August Kiinvaldt, Marie Kiinvaldt, Jüri Ojakäar, Riina Reiman and Anna Kuusik.

Brother E. Raud was appointed pastor of the congregation in 1924. Thanks to Pastor Raud's energetic work the finances of the church flourished. Branches were set up in Moisaküla, Abja, and Treimanni. In 1930 Pastor Raud was appointed to Kuressaare.

The Pärnu congregation has had the pleasure of hosting two Epworth League Association conferences and last winter a half-year conference. The membership in the congregation is over fifty, and in the Epworth League Association over thirty. Last winter the Sunday school roster had the names of nearly eighty children.

Tallinn congregation. Pastor M. Prikask was appointed as resident superintendent in Tallinn. Initially the work took place in rented rooms, but through the Lord's gracious leading real estate was acquired on Pärnu Road #19. Superintendent Prikask's own apartment is in this house, where he held meetings for small groups and received probationary members. Though these names do not appear in the books in Tallinn, it is likely that their names were noted in the Kuressaare register. Not until 1922, when Brother J. Tombo was appointed to Tallinn, was an independent congregation founded there.

During the Rev. Tombo's time the meetings were held in the house on the courtyard, and they were warm and cordial meetings. Later the work moved to the street-side house where the meetings continued until 1929, when the congregation relocated the church to Veerenni Street.

Information regarding the Rev. Täht's work in Tallinn is unavailable, but the work of the Rev. Tombo was very fruitful. Great crowds of people met together, there were great revivals, and the congregation grew. An Epworth League Association was founded, a choir was created, and a large Sunday School was functioning. The Rev. Tombo was assisted by Brothers J. Koddo, J. Oovel, and M. Koddo.

After many changes the congregation is now served by Superintendent Prikask and the Rev. Tombo. In the last year the congregation has grown by thirty members and the Epworth League Association by twenty members, the "Junior League" has twenty members, and an average number of seventy children attend Sunday school.

141

Nissi. The work in Nissi was at one time part of the Tallinn congregation and under the direction of Brother V. Meinvald. Many brothers and sisters have served it.

Kopli congregation. About the same time as the first congregation was founded, a Russian-German branch was begun in Tallinn. This group also worked a few years at Pärnu Road #19, until they settled in Kopli and concentrated mostly on work in Estonia. In addition to leading this congregation, the Rev. A. Seck assumed the responsibilities of leading the "Night Mission," which was started by the members of the first congregation. He continues to do so now. The Rev. Tombo serves Kopli at present and he is assisted by Brother H. Kruusi. The membership numbers thirty-five, Epworth League members fourteen, and over two hundred children are in the Sunday school.

Tartu First congregation. At the annual conference in 1923, the Rev. Karlson requested to be assigned to Tartu and the bishop fulfilled his request. An excerpt from the Tartu congregation's diary follows [as reported by the Rev. Karlson]:

> I arrived to work here on September 10, 1923. Until now we had not had our own hall in which to hold worship services, but today, on October 28, the hall rented on the second floor of Gildi Street #7 will be dedicated for our use. I have yearned for this day and now it is here.
>
> At present we must make a congregation out of three members, because we have no others. With great faith in our Lord Jesus we look toward the future, believing that our congregation will greatly increase. In this hope I undertake founding the congregation.
>
> The congregation was started with three members: the Rev. J. Karlson, Sister A. Karlson and Sister J. Aruväli. This small beginning was blessed by the Lord and two years later the congregation had grown to twenty-eight members with thirty-one probationary members, thirty-seven Epworth League Association members, and 195 children in the Sunday School.
>
> In the beginning the work in Tartu was far from easy. On the one hand, the newcomers were labeled as trouble-makers, separatists, sectarians and the people were discouraged from taking part in their meetings. On the other hand, the Methodists and their work was not considered complete.
>
> All this did not dishearten the Rev. Karlson. He continued valiantly to preach the gospel and fight against false teaching. Frequently leaving the narrow meeting halls, he went to the Police Square and elsewhere to proclaim the gospel to the masses. And his work in the Lord was not in vain.

At the conference in 1926, the Rev. A. Kuum was appointed as pastor in Tartu, and due to his faith and prayers, as well as his energetic efforts, the congregation bought a large stone house at Vallikraavi Street #18 for 5.5 million cents. Large donations from American believers made it possible to purchase this house, and the family of believers in our homeland did not merely remain as spectators but helped according to their means. Comments from an account of the acquisition of the house affirm that what they "asked in prayers was claimed in faith": "Faith and prayers had won. The times of testing still remain vivid in the memory of this congregation. They were the most difficult and at the same time most blessed times."

Currently the membership numbers over two hundred and the Epworth League Association over seventy, and nearly 150 children attend Sunday school. For nearly three years the congregation has sponsored a unique assistance program for the poor called *Ühisabi* (United Help), the technical activities of which are directed by Brother E. Suurhans. Many congregation members have assisted in this program out of great love. In conjunction with the congregation's *Ühisabi* work, a report flyer called *Kaastööline* (Fellow-worker) is published under the editorship of A. Kuum. This is the first of its kind appearing in Estonian churches.

Tartu Second congregation. This congregation began under the Blue Cross Association in Tartu, on March 1, 1931. The Blue Cross Evangelical Temperance Association of Tartu had functioned successfully since 1919, but due to many problems the work was in danger of coming to a standstill. Persistent workers like Brothers L. Raig, J. Künnapu, K. Kösta, A. Leismann, A. Eero, and many sisters did not want to accept the present situation and attempted to do everything possible in order to preserve the work and existence of the Blue Cross.

Finally associates were sought, and it was found that the Methodists had the most similar beliefs. A union was formed and the Rev. A. Kuum enabled Brother J. Jakobson to serve the Blue Cross. This kind of arrangement could not last for long because we were in dire need of laborers ourselves.

The association agreed unanimously at a meeting that the Blue Cross could function alongside the Methodist church, and it was decided that the two should labor as a team in the future. The Second congregation of Tartu was founded during the aforementioned time. Cooperation and agreement between the association and the church have been good. The Rev. J. Jakobson's selfless and diligent work has produced much fruit. There were eight founding members, and the number has now grown to eighteen, the Epworth League Association has twenty-one members, and the Blue Cross has about thirty members. In addition to this, a Christian high school group of eighteen works here also.

Viljandi congregation. In earlier times the Rev. K. Kuum visited Viljandi and led many to the Lord, but the official work was begun by the Rev. Liebner. After some reorganizing, which was undertaken in our church in 1928, Brother A. Seck was sent to work in Viljandi. The Rev. Seck worked here a few months, after which he was sent to Tallinn. He was succeeded by Brother P. Gildemann. Due to a critical change in 1931 the congregation was left without a pastor, until the Rev. V. Prii was released from the army and came to serve in Viljandi.

The congregation meets in rented rooms, and the financial difficulties are causing great strain. But the Lord has blessed our endeavors and the work continues. Brother Prii has much help from Brothers Meerits and Tuhk.

Finally, I would like to say: We believe that our house of faith has been built upon a rock and, if we remain on it, we will not fall, come "heavy rains," "raging seas," or "strong winds." When the Lord comes, God will reward our faithfulness.

CHAPTER 8

Estonian Methodism During the First Year Under the Plague of the Red Commissars[1] 1940–1941

Heigo Ritsbek

"Immediately before the outbreak of World War II, Nazi Germany and Soviet Russia signed the Non-Aggression Pact of August 23, 1939, generally referred to as the Molotov-Ribbentrop Pact. This treaty contained secret provisions for dividing Eastern Europe into spheres of influence."[2] This pact is considered by many as one of the reasons for the onset of World War II. For Estonia, the Pact had terrible results. On June 17, 1940, Estonia was occupied by the Soviet Union. The Soviet secret police began to imprison and execute the population.

> The first mass deportation from Estonia to Soviet slave camps started on the night of June 13, 1941. Overnight, more than 10,000 people, including children and the elderly (or almost 1 percent of the population), were herded into overloaded box cars and taken away to remote areas in northern Russia and Siberia. These journeys often lasted several weeks under inhuman conditions, during which time a large number of deportees perished. Additionally, 1,741 people were later found in mass graves in Estonia. After the start of the Russian-German war on June 21, 1941, some 30,000 more Estonians were deported by the Soviets under the guise of conscription or were forced to leave Estonia to do slave labor. All told, some 60,000 Estonians were arrested, murdered or deported during the first Soviet occupation 1940-1941.[3]

It is clear that under such circumstances, the Methodist Church in Estonia, which was founded by the missionary activities of the Methodist Episcopal Church in the United States of America, suffered very much. There were twenty-one Methodist congregations with 1,600 full members in Estonia in 1940 when the Soviets came.[4] Among the first victims of the Soviet mass terror in the Methodist clergy was Martin Prikask (b. 1877), the

145

superintendent of the Methodist Church in Estonia. He became the first Methodist martyr in Estonia.[5]

The Rev. Martin Prikask was arrested on July 1, 1941, at the parsonage of Kuressaare Methodist Church on the island of Saaremaa.[6] He was taken by boat to Tallinn, the capital of Estonia. The first interrogation protocol in the KGB file is dated July 19, 1941, and this is "the only interrogation protocol which is in [the] Estonian language" in his KGB file.[7]

The first interrogation was conducted by an Estonian, the Pärnu county KGB chief Kikkas.[8] His first questions pertained to family name, time and place of birth, education, etc. Then the question was asked: "You had a house at Kuressaare; what income did you get from this?" The answer from Prikask is recorded in the file:[9] "About 10-12 'Kroons' (Estonian currency) a month." The next question was "Was this house nationalized?"[10] Answer: "No, but it was taken away by the army." Then the KGB officer asked for data concerning Prikask's wife and said, "Tell about your life!" Prikask's answer was recorded in the protocol as follows:

> In 1900 I went to serve in the tsarist army. I was in the "musical company" in Petersburg. Later I was sent to Vassili Island (a part of Sankt Petersburg). I finished this school with a degree of "fourth level cadett master." In 1906 I left the army. Then I settled at Kuressaare, got "6 bushel land" from the nobleman and this was my income. Four years I owned a grocery store, during my free-time I was a preacher.

Question: "Where did you preach?"
Answer: "In private homes, community houses and in the country-side. Later I joined the Methodist Church."
Question: "Did you get salary?"
Answer: "I was supported voluntarily, later I worked as a bookkeeper."
Question: "To which political organizations did you belong?"
Answer: "I did not participate in any of them, not in the National Guard, not in the Political Organization of Estonia, not in the national-socialist union, only in the Red Cross." [11]

This protocol as well as the following information is known to us because of the efforts of the chairman of the Board of Kuressaare United Methodist Church, Mr. Arvi Lindmäe. Lindmäe copied a protocol of a "witness" by somebody called Mr. Nellis Vladimir. We know that Nellis Vladimir worked at this time as the chief of the KGB jail at Kuressaare, and so he had to be a KGB worker himself. During the Nazi occupation he was executed.[12] The protocol is dated August 2, 1941. He said that he knew Martin Prikask for more than twenty years. Nellis Vladimir said that Martin Prikask "served as a pastor in the so-called Methodist sect. He collected money from them, to whom he promised the heavenly kingdom. Sometimes he preached and continued to collect the money to the bank. He Martin Prikask organized reactionary movements and mobilized members to the National Guard."[13]

There are several other "witnesses" in this file, whom Lindmäe indicated were mostly absurd and fallacious.[14] However, to the amazement of Lindmäe, on every sheet of these confessions, there was the genuine signature of the Rev. Martin Prikask. Lindmäe asked from the chief of the KGB at Kuressaare how it was possible that Martin Prikask signed such absurd "confessions." The answer from the KGB officer was that these were times when there were lots of possibilities to press a person to sign such "documents."[15] We do not have documented or other evidence of torture regarding the Rev. Martin Prikask, but it is quite possible that he was tortured, at least mentally, until he signed the so-called confessions.

There are some witnesses to the fact that Martin Prikask preached the gospel during his imprisonment to the people who were in the same prison cell with him.[16]

In the secret file there is the sentence of the "court," signed by a first-lieutenant Tihhomirov, dated March 19, 1942. There are three points:

1. In the beginning of December 1940, during a conversation with his neighbor, citizen Prikask was not satisfied with the Soviet power because of the lack of food.
2. Before the elections to the Supreme Soviet Prikask did anti-Soviet agitation to citizen Kodar and was not satisfied with the Communist power.
3. At the end of August 1941 on a train Prikask glorified German technology and disparaged the Soviet army. Being a Methodist preacher he owned a personal church, organized a Christian political party and had three private homes. During the years 1940-1941 he systematically did anti-Soviet agitation against the Soviet Union using the religious background, etc. He is extremely dangerous to the Soviet power. I suggest he receive the highest punishment—to execute him by shooting and to confiscate all his property.

March 19, 1942
First-lieutenant Tihhomirov[17]

Then we have another sentence to death:

August 12, 1942—sentenced to death.
Special Commission of the Peoples Commissariat of the Interior Ministry of the Soviet Union.
Prikask, Martin, father's name Rits—to execute by shooting.

This is signed by the name Ivanov. And then there is another line: "September 9, 1942 the sentence was fulfilled."[18] We know that the Rev. Martin Prikask was executed September 9, 1942, at Aleksandrovka village in the Irkutsk oblast.[19]

At the same time that the Rev. Martin Prikask was arrested two other Methodist ministers from Saaremaa, the Rev. Peeter Häng from Torgu Methodist Church and the Rev. Vassili Prii from Korkvere Methodist Church, were also arrested. They did not come back from the Soviet Gulag just like their superintendent.[20] As mentioned earlier, Superintendent Martin Prikask did not want to escape, but as he foresaw the possibility of his arrest, he appointed a young man, Mr. Orest Aavik, as his successor as pastor of the Kuressaare Methodist Church.[21] Several times the Soviet authorities wanted to confiscate this church building. Once they almost succeeded in doing this, but because of the bold action by Mr. Orest Aavik, the church remained the house of prayer.[22] It serves to the present as the Kuressaare United Methodist Church.

The fourth minister of Estonian Methodism who became a martyr during the first year of the Soviet occupation is the Rev. Jaan Jaagupsoo. From 1933 he served the Haapsalu Methodist Church, which has probably the most beautiful Estonian Methodist church building. When in July 1941 the Soviets illegally announced the conscription of Estonians into the Red Army, following their occupation of Estonia, the Rev. Jaan Jaagupsoo was among those hiding in the forests. This was the time when the Soviets officially organized the so-called "destroying battalions" that burned down the villages, killed the people, raped the women, and in several documented cases, nailed the children to trees, and caused other acts of horror.

In July 1941, when the Rev. Jaan Jaagupsoo was captured by some Soviet soldiers from one of these "destroying battalions," his eyes were kicked out and he was dropped into a dry well. All this torture was observed by the wife of Pastor Jaagupsoo who found her husband dead when she reached him. One only can imagine the terrifying situation the next Sunday morning at Haapsalu Methodist Church when they realized what had happened to their pastor.[23] So from thirteen active ordained Methodist ministers in Estonia in 1940, four lost their lives during the first year of the Soviet occupation. When we see the other Christian churches and denominations in Estonia, then these losses were even smaller, for example, than the Lutheran Church and the Orthodox Church had to suffer. In these two denominations nearly 90 percent of pastors and priests were killed or deported.[24]

When Estonia, Latvia, and Lithuania were incorporated into the Soviet Union in August, 1940, the Soviet authorities had formulated plans concerning the religious organizations. They accepted the existence of the

Russian Orthodox Church, the Baptist Church, and in the Baltic settings the Lutheran and Roman Catholic Churches. The Seventh-Day Adventists, quite unlike mainline Protestantism, were somehow tolerated. No other denominations were to be allowed to exist. The Salvation Army, the Moravians, and some other religious organizations were closed. The Methodist churches in Latvia and Lithuania were liquidated. How did the Methodist Church in Estonia survive?

When the superintendent of the Methodist Church in Estonia, Martin Prikask, was arrested and deported to Siberia, the remaining pastors elected the Rev. Martin Kuigre, who had been pastor of the Rakvere Methodist Church since 1932, as the superintendent. It is not known where this meeting occurred nor whether there were other candidates considered for the post of the superintendent.

When the Soviets began to implement their religious laws, the Rev. Martin Kuigre was invited to a meeting with the Minister of Religious Affairs in Estonia. It is not known whether anyone else, besides the Rev. Jaan Puskay, the pastor of Tapa Methodist Church, was present.

> The minister made a suggestion to Superintendent Kuigre for the Methodists in Estonia to join the Lutheran Church, mentioning that these two denominations [both] have infant baptism. Superintendent Kuigre answered that although both [Lutheran and Methodist] churches have infant baptism, there is a great difference in the substance of this and it is impossible to merge. Then the minister of Religious Affairs said: "If you will not join the Lutheran Church, then the Methodist Church will be closed." After this statement Superintendent M. Kuigre said with great seriousness, "If the Methodist Church will be closed, we will continue to function secretly." After a long pause the minister of Religious Affairs answered: "Okay, but give me some kind of constitution." Superintendent M. Kuigre answered: "We have a written book—the *Discipline*—and we will continue to function based on it." Then Pastor Puskay mentioned that he gave his personal copy of the *Discipline of the Methodist Church* to the minister of Religious Affairs.[25]

Aleksander Kuum, the Rev. Hugo Oengo, and others testify that the KGB and other Soviet organizations tried their best to liquidate Methodism in Estonia as they did in Lithuania and in Latvia. Quite interesting is a KGB interrogation of the Rev. Aleksander Kuum, one of the pastors of Tallinn Methodist Church. He was asked what difference it would make if the authorities were to close the Methodist Church or the Methodist ministers were to do it themselves, whereupon they would become Baptist ministers. The Rev. Kuum answered that there was a great difference: "When you will give me a rope and ask me to hang myself up, I will be responsible before the Lord. But if you hang me up, you will be responsible to the Lord." The question still remains how Methodism remained in Estonia as an institution. There can be several answers, but I think that the most important consideration is the boldness of the Estonian Methodist clergy. They refused to compromise and for some reason the Soviets did not use force.

During the first year of the Soviet occupation in Estonia (1940-1941) no Methodist churches were confiscated, despite the evidence that attempts were made, as in the case of the Kuressaare Methodist Church.

We do not know exactly what was the loss in membership in the Estonian Methodist Church during the first year of the Soviet occupation. However, it is clear that it lost more than one third of its clergy. It lost numerous laypersons also. This was only the first incidence of suffering under the Red Commissars. After relatively relaxed German occupation (1941-1944), the Soviets came back and the persecution resumed.

CHAPTER 9

Methodism in the Soviet Union Since World War II[1]

Mark Elliott

Background

Methodism progressed through the northwestern portions of the Russian Empire beginning in Finland (from 1861), then to Saint Petersburg (from 1889), to Lithuania (from 1893),[2] to Latvia (from 1904), and to Estonia (from 1907) by means of Swedish, Finnish, German, and American mission activity.[3]

Methodism made its way to Estonia through the influence of an American missionary in Saint Petersburg. An energetic bachelor, Indiana native, and graduate of Drew University, the Rev. George Simons was the unlikely New World connection between the capital of the Russian Empire and its nearest Baltic possession. Upon his arrival in Saint Petersburg in 1907, Simons made the acquaintance of an Estonian, Vassili Täht, who shortly became a member of the ethnically mixed Methodist congregation of Saint Petersburg, which held Sunday services in succession in German, English, Russian, Swedish, Finnish, and Estonian.[4] Täht quickly joined forces that same year with an Estonian friend, Karl Kuum, a Moravian laypastor, soon to turn Methodist. The two of them began house and open-air preaching on the large island of Saaremaa, Estonia, with reports of thousands in attendance.[5]

In 1908, in the wake of these meetings, converts formed the first Methodist congregation in Estonia at Kuressaare, Saaremaa, officially recognized as a Methodist church in 1910. The Kuressaare sanctuary, erected in 1912, is the oldest in Estonia and still is in use.[6]

On the eve of World War II, Methodism in an independent Estonia counted sixteen hundred full members, an additional fifteen hundred youth and children, twenty-six churches and Sunday schools, fifteen pastors, and a monthly periodical, *Kristlik Kaitsja* (Christian Advocate).[7] In 1945, in the wake of two Soviet occupations, two deportations, Red Army- and Nazi-forced conscriptions, large-scale westward flight, and battle casualties, what remained of the thirty-one hundred members and adherents were some seven hundred Methodists in twelve churches. Church membership in the capital of Tallinn declined from some three hundred in 1939 to 175 in 1945, with only forty still active.[8] One-third of the Estonian Methodist clergy were killed in Soviet prisons or died in Siberian labor camps, including Superintendent Martin Prikask.[9] Furthermore, the dismemberment of Methodism on Soviet soil in the 1920s and 1930s was followed after 1945 by the banning of the denomination in the newly annexed territories of Latvia, Lithuania, and Western Ukraine.[10]

Postwar Growth

Nevertheless, growth against great odds characterizes Estonian Methodism throughout most of the postwar years. Membership in Tallinn's Merepuiestee Street Church, which has been the largest Methodist congregation in Europe since the early 1960s, peaked in 1971 with 1,166 full members, while the denomination as a whole recorded its high mark to date in 1974 with an Estonian membership of 2,363.[11]

In accounting for the survival—indeed expansion—of Estonian Methodism under Soviet rule, a strong, highly committed leadership cannot be overemphasized. Whereas only 77 of 250 Lutheran clergy remained in Estonia at the end of World War II, and whereas the majority of Methodist ministers in Latvia and Lithuania fled westward before the advancing Red Army, most Estonian Methodist preachers remained at their posts.[12]

Of twenty-eight former Baltic Methodist ministers attending a 1962 reunion in Bay View, Michigan, or sending greetings to the gathering, only two were Estonian (Alex Poobus and Konstantin Wipp).[13] Only one other Methodist minister, Eduard Raud, is known to have left Estonia during the war.[14] As of 1940 Estonian Methodism was self-supporting, whereas Latvia and Lithuanian Methodists still received financial support from the United States. Whether or not greater Estonian self-sufficiency contributed to a given minister's decision to stay with his flock, one can only speculate.[15] The survival of Estonian Methodism, with its remnant of some seven hundred members in twelve churches in 1945, appears all the more remarkable when it is noted that Estonia's Moravian Brethren, with more than one hundred churches as of 1940, saw all of their congregations closed by Soviet authorities following the war.[16]

Symbolic of the fortitude of Estonian Methodism was its unofficial patriarch, the Rev. Alexander Kuum (1899–1989). Son of the 1907 Saaremaa evangelist, the Rev. Kuum served many years as pastor of the Tallinn Methodist Church (1938–52 and 1956–70) and as Methodist superintendent (1962–74). The night of March 9-10, 1944, a Russian bombing raid on Tallinn destroyed the twelve-hundred-seat Methodist sanctuary. Returning from the countryside, Kuum was crushed to find only charred embers where the church had stood. Digging through the ashes he salved a metal piece from the baptismal font that still read, "Suffer the little children to come unto me." Taking heart, he determined to start his church anew with his own six children and the few remaining members who had not fled or been killed in the war.[17]

Decades later Kuum shared the passion of his heart at a 1971 meeting of the Methodist World Conference in Denver, Colorado: "We Methodists in Estonia have one goal—to work for God in the Methodist way. Our aim is to save souls. We hold our hands high to receive God's power for we can't do without Him in these turbulent times."[18] Western pastors, college and seminary professors, and bishops all have been humbled in the presence of the quiet, steel-like but joyous faith of Alexander Kuum, who counted even Siberian imprisonment (1952–56) a blessing.[19]

The Rev. Hugo Oengo (1907–78), Kuum's successor as superintendent (1974–78), by all accounts brought exceptional gifts to his difficult job: a professor at the Tallinn Technical University, a member of the Estonian Academy of Sciences, and one of Estonia's foremost construction engineers. Evacuated to Sverdlovsk in the Urals on the eve of the German invasion and a worker on major Estonian projects for the Russians after the war, he ultimately lost his job due to his outspoken witness. Like Kuum, Oengo had a reputation as a powerful evangelist with a special burden for the preaching of sanctification and healing.[20]

The quiet humility, gentle manner, and spiritual depth of the Rev. Olav Pärnamets (1937–), Oengo's successor as superintendent (1979–), consistently have won Estonian Methodism committed friends and helpers from the West. Pastor of Tallinn's Merepuiestee Street Methodist Church since 1970, the Rev. Pärnamets holds to the conviction that motivated the Rev. Kuum and the Rev. Oengo before him: that prayer, evangelism, and openness to revival are essential to the spiritual vitality of the church.[21]

Several Russian sources point to leadership through twelve-member class meetings as a factor explaining Methodist vitality. In 1979 the journal of Moscow's Institute of Scientific Atheism went so far as to argue that, "The existence of the classes and the fairly flexible and capable management of them is one of the main reasons for the vitality and activity of the Estonian Methodist Church."[22] Such small-group accountability indeed would be beneficial, Methodist leaders agree, but it has not been a feature of the denomination's life in Estonia, since it was rooted out by Soviet authorities under Stalin.[23]

In addition to strong leadership, Estonian Methodism's growth may stem in part from *comparatively* restrained Soviet interference in church life. For all its trials under Soviet rule, the denomination has had to endure a relatively tolerable regimen compared to most churches in the USSR. Admittedly, the Stalinist years proved harrowing, with mass deportations of more than one hundred thousand members of the nation's professional, spiritual, cultural, and political elite in 1940, 1945–46, and 1949.[24] Nevertheless, from the late 1950s on, de-Stalinization introduced an unwritten *modus vivendi* between Moscow and the Baltic states: In return for Baltic efficiency, industry, and political submission, Moscow was willing to concede a somewhat looser leash, especially in regard to cultural life and foreign contacts.

Several factors contributed to the compromise. In the case of Estonia, the Russians found it quite difficult to penetrate the culture or comprehend the language.[25] Estonian Methodists, in contrast to Baptists and Adventists, have had the added advantage of not having to take orders from a non-Estonian, Moscow-based denominational leadership ever susceptible to political pressures.

Geography also has worked to Estonia's advantage. Tallinn is a mere forty miles across the Gulf of Finland from Helsinki and is a port of entry for large numbers of Scandinavian and other Western tourists. The Tallinn Methodist congregation, within sight of a major Intourist hotel and within walking distance of the port of entry for innumerable Western ferry passengers, undoubtedly has benefited from knowing and being known by large numbers of Western Christians who have worshiped with them. Because of the similarity of the languages and the proximity, Finnish television has been an Estonian mainstay for years. The Tallinn vicinity is the only part of the Soviet Union able to receive Western television broadcasts.[26]

The Estonian Methodist Church holds membership in the Northern European Central Conference of The United Methodist Church. The presiding bishop from 1970 to 1989 was the Rev. Ole Borgen, a Norwegian residing in Stockholm, Sweden. He first met with Estonian Methodists in 1972 and averaged biannual visits throughout his episcopacy. The bishop feels he was able to provide a measure of protection to his Estonian charges through (1) constant contact, (2) the unspoken possibility of bad publicity in the West if authorities were overbearing with Methodists, and (3) his avoidance of the twin pitfalls of heavy public criticism of Moscow or gratuitous praise of the Soviet system.

In 1989, Rein Ristlaan, the newly appointed head of the Estonian Council of Religious Affairs (CRA), told Borgen directly that Moscow did not like having an outside bishop over Estonian Methodists. Soviet authorities nevertheless grudgingly have acquiesced to Methodist connectionalism, much to the long-term benefit of the Estonian churches.[27]

Finally, Estonian Methodist leaders have proved comparatively resilient in the face of state harassment. Estonian Methodist pastor Heigo Ritsbek characterizes Alexander Kuum as "a good diplomat—a good ice breaker. Kuum was fearless and made jokes of it when he was threatened by the KGB."[28] The Rev. Oengo, like Kuum, knew Russian life firsthand. Schooled in the language and culture of his Slavic overlords, Oengo was not easily manipulated. According to his bishop, "He knew how to handle the Russians."[29]

The current superintendent, The Rev. Olav Pärnamets, experienced his first KGB interrogation as a teenager in the early 1950s at the time òf Alexander Kuum's arrest. Well before *glasnost* the Rev. Pärnamets encouraged important unsanctioned activities, such as Sunday schools led by his wife, even as he endured repeated KGB and CRA blandishments. The Rev. Heigo Ritsbek, by no means a stranger to state pressures, put it succinctly: "In Estonia we had practically no underground churches, but all churches had some underground ministries."[30] And Estonian Methodist leaders have had a tradition of testing the limits of what the state will tolerate.

In addition to strong leadership and comparatively restrained state interference, Methodism grew in the postwar era due to the church's emphasis on evangelism. The period of greatest expansion appears to have occurred in the mid to late 1950s. Between 1953 and 1962 the Tallinn Methodist Church more than tripled its size from just over three hundred members in 1953 to one thousand in 1962. Also, over a longer time frame, the very small congregations in the rest of the country doubled their ranks from 530 total members in 1945 to 1,048 by 1964.[31] The return of Alexander Kuum from Siberian imprisonment in 1956 appears to have been the primary human catalyst for growth. Many saw a reflection of the divine in this pastor's love and lack of malice. "I have no bitterness," he told a Western visitor years later. "It was for me a time of discovery, deeper truth, even though it was a time of suffering."[32] On Kuum's first Sunday back in the Merepuiestee Street pulpit that same spirit must have communicated to his congregation. It proved to be an emotional reunion, with everyone present standing to honor their shepherd. After the service many followed Kuum to his home for a time of hymn singing and continued rejoicing.

A revival soon broke out in the Tallinn church, which saw many converts added to the membership.[33] The same phenomenon also occurred in 1956 in the Kuressaare Church following special services led by Hugo Oengo.[34]

Such regularly scheduled revival weeks, usually led by an invited guest pastor, have been a longstanding feature of Estonian Methodist life.[35] A remarkably sympathetic Soviet analysis of Methodist growth, written well before Gorbachev, attributes much of the church's success to these "revival weeks" and other forms of active missionary recruitment.[36]

Another factor that likely has contributed to Estonian Methodists' growth is the church's strong commitment to basic Christian beliefs coupled with unusual flexibility in worship and tolerance for a range of views on what are considered secondary issues. They, for example, confound their Baptist and Lutheran friends by baptizing adults, as do the former, and children, as do the latter. Similarly, the majority of Methodist pastors have no personal experience with *glossolalia* (speaking in tongues), but at the same time they have included believers of Pentecostal persuasion within their fellowships since at least the 1940s.[37]

The most dramatic example of Estonian Methodism's openness to new forms of worship concerns its outreach to youth beginning in the late 1960s through contemporary rock music. As background it is important to note that Estonians are enthusiastic lovers of music, it being perhaps the ultimate expression of the national culture. Methodists, no less than other Estonians, share this passion. Only two decades after the war, for example, the Merepuiestee Street Church boasted five different choirs, an orchestra, and a trumpet ensemble.[38]

According to Bishop Borgen, new musical expressions were a fruit of a revival among Methodists in the late 1960s, which in turn contributed to the spread of the revival, especially among unchurched young people.[39] Also, performances of Western Christian groups such as *Living Sound, The Reach Out Singers*, and *The Continental Singers* inspired imitation and led to Western gifts to young Methodist and Baptist musicians of a wide range of equipment, including synthesizers, amplifiers, speakers, drums, and electric guitars.[40]

Jaanus Kärner of the Tallinn Methodist Church formed the first Christian rock group in the Soviet Union in 1969. Kärner's *Selah* helped spawn other Estonian ensembles such as *Ezra*, and also Valeri Barinov's *Trumpet Call* in Leningrad, better known in the West than the others because of its success in securing a commercial recording in Nashville.[41]

The impact this new sound had on the Methodist Church and the youth in Tallinn is best described in the words of the Rev. Heigo Ritsbek, an eyewitness:

God sent another mighty movement of His Spirit . . . during [the] seventies. . . . Many young people began to attend the services at Tallinn Methodist Church on Thursdays, where through the music of the first gospel rock group in Eastern Europe the youth from Estonia and even from Russia were able to understand the message of Jesus for the first time in their lives. It was the message they had never heard before. All these Thursday evening worship services with the musical group *Selah* were jam-packed. It was a very moving experience to pray every evening with so many young people who committed their lives to Jesus.[42]

By 1975 the Tallinn Methodist Church was meeting for worship seven times weekly with an average attendance of almost five hundred persons per service. Typically, four sermons in each meeting were interspersed by music from (now) twelve choral and instrumental groups performing traditional, folk and gospel rock arrangements.[43]

Methodist "peace rallies" (1977–81) and youth camps (1980–) serve as final examples of the denomination's imagination and flexibility in reaching young people—and its boldness in testing the limits of official toleration. Organized by the Rev. Heigo Ritsbek, these energetic youth-oriented events proved very successful, which in turn led to repeated and debilitating clashes with authorities. Herbert Murd, leader of *Ezra* and co-laborer with Ritsbek in various youth ministries, was arrested twice, in 1980 and 1981, serving difficult, one-year prison sentences on each occasion. Tragically, the ordeal destroyed not only Murd's marriage, but all his ties with the church; of late he has been working as a secular concert organizer. The Rev. Ritsbek was subjected to innumerable police interrogations and was denied visas to attend Methodist meetings abroad on forty occasions. He finally emigrated to the United States with his family in February 1989.[44]

Finally, Methodism has experienced growth because of the moral and material support it has received from Christians in the West. Indeed, from the death of Stalin to the present, perhaps the most formative development for the denomination has been the end of its isolation. Estonian Methodism has emerged from its virtual quarantine in the 1940s and 1950s.

With the dismantling of all Methodist work in Latvia and Lithuania, even the existence of the Estonian church was in question for some time. "For quite a while," notes a U.S. United Methodist Church official, "the churches . . . were out of contact with Methodist leadership in Sweden and in this country."[45] In 1952, the same year Alexander Kuum was banished to Siberia, proceedings of a Soviet peace conference held at Holy Trinity-Saint Sergius Monastery included a rare acknowledgment of the continued existence of Estonian Methodism. In addition to a predictably fawning tribute to Stalin and Soviet peace policy by Estonian Methodist pastor Ferdinand Tombo, the conference volume, published in English, also noted that the Rev. Martin Kuigre, superintendent of the Estonian Methodist Church, had attended.[46]

Dr. Harry Denman, director of the Board of Evangelism of The Methodist Church, visited Tallinn in 1956, the first known postwar contact of the Estonian church with a Methodist from the United States.[47] An especially dramatic break in Estonian Methodism's lonely vigil came in September 1962 with a visit from Bishop Odd Hagen of the Northern European Central Conference of the Methodist Church, the first bishop to visit Estonia in twenty-two years. "The situation," he reported, "is easier than it was under Stalin—but difficulties are many."[48] The previous April, the Estonian's second annual conference in more than two decades elected as its superintendent Alexander Kuum, no stranger to difficulties.

In 1965 Estonian Methodists received their first-ever visit from a U.S. Methodist bishop, Richard Raines, and in 1966, their second, as they hosted Bishop Ralph Ward. The 1960s also saw perhaps Estonian Methodism's most acclaimed guest ever, Corrie ten Boom of *Hiding Place* fame. But in terms of systematic sustenance and encouragement in the 1960s, the most important Western "breathing hole," to use Bishop Borgen's expression, was growing numbers of Finnish Methodist and Pentecostal visitors using the relatively easy access of the Gulf of Finland ferry between Helsinki and Tallinn.[49] In the 1970s and 1980s the number of contacts with Scandinavian, West European, and U.S. church and parachurch representatives, as well as with increasing numbers of Western Christian tourists, absolutely exploded.

In the opposite direction, Soviet authorities permitted Superintendent Alexander Kuum his first postwar trip abroad to attend the Second World Christian Peace Conference in Prague, Czechoslovakia, in 1964. Subsequently Kuum was able to travel to Sweden and Finland in 1966, to Finland again in 1967, and to the United Methodist Annual Conference in Plauen, East Germany, in 1972. Superintendent Kuum's participation in the 1968 United Methodist General Conference in Dallas, Texas, was the first-ever visit of a Methodist from the Soviet Union to the United States.[50] In August 1971, the Rev. Kuum also attended the World Methodist Conference meeting in Denver, Colorado. The superintendent addressed the gathering, with Bishop Borgen serving as translator.[51]

The Rev. Hugo Oengo likewise managed a number of official visits to European Methodist meetings in his tenure as superintendent (1974–78), including trips to Finland, Sweden, Norway, East Germany, Switzerland, and England.[52] Finally, the present superintendent, Olav Pärnamets, has traveled extensively. Since 1975, in addition to various Northern European Conference meetings in Sweden, Denmark, and Finland, he has attended one U.S. General Conference (1988), three sessions of the Conference of European Churches (1979, 1987, 1989), two U.S. Methodist Board of Discipleship New World Missions (1978 and 1990), the Second Lausanne Conference on World Evangelization (1989), and four meetings of the World Methodist Council (1978, 1981, 1985, and 1986).

Evaluating the relative importance and effectiveness of Estonian Methodism's various Western contacts is fraught with difficulty, in good measure because the players are legion. But a second judgment comes easily to anyone conversant with the subject: that is, that the development of East-West ties has been a major—likely, *the* major—influence on the corporate life and morale of postwar Estonian Methodism. Especially for the past two decades, most major aspects of the church's life—for good and ill—bear the imprint of Western influence. To say this is not to belittle the Estonian Methodist achievement in the Soviet era. Actually, Estonian Methodism consciously and judiciously chose to encourage Western ties for its own protection.[53]

Ties with Western Christians

The most important East-West relationship has been that between Estonian Methodists and The United Methodist Northern European Central Conference, especially its bishop and its small contingent of Swedish- and Finnish-speaking Methodists from Finland. The relative ease and regularity of Finnish Methodist contacts and Bishop Borgen's forthright yet carefully nuanced relationship with the Estonian Council of Religious Affairs cannot be overestimated.[54]

The collective ministries of a host of parachurch groups rank second in significance. By no means can all such organizations be listed. But among others, important contributions were made by the Finnish-based staff of Youth with a Mission; touring Christian rock groups, especially *Living Sound* (Terry Law), *Reach Out Singers,* and *Continental Singers;* I Care Ministries (Scott Wesley Brown); Slaviska Missionen (Rauli Lehtonen); Estonian Christian Ministries (Endel Meiusi); Campus Crusade for Christ (Jaan Heimets); Biblical Education by Extension (Charlie Warner); and Issachar (George Otis and Steve Weber).

Throughout the postwar years, Scandinavian Christians have taken a disproportionately greater interest in fellow believers in the Baltic states than have other Western Christians. Geographic proximity (meaning lower travel costs), cultural and historic ties, linguistic affinity (in the case of Estonian and Finnish), and the dynamic and comparatively large Pentecostal churches of the Nordic region, all help explain Scandinavia's importance to Estonian Methodism.[55]

United States tour groups, many including Christians from The United Methodist Church and other denominations, have been an encouragement and help to Estonian Methodists, even as these visitors have been encouraged by participation in worship in Estonia. By this means evangelically minded Estonian Methodism first made contact with Asbury College, Asbury Theological Seminary, and the Good News movement—all of Wilmore, Kentucky, and all strongly identified with the evangelical camp within United Methodism.

Olav Pärnamets learned English with a dream in mind of one day studying at Asbury Theological Seminary. That possibility seems, now, to have passed, but with the 1989–90 academic year Heigo Ritsbek did become the first Estonian Methodist to commence studies at Asbury Seminary. Estonian Methodism's predilection for the Asbury institutions and the like-minded Good News movement proved a pleasant if unexpected surprise in March 1981 as the writer, at that time an Asbury College professor, led a tour group to Estonia.[56]

In March 1981, an Asbury College tour group under this writer's direction, and including Dr. and Mrs. Harold Kuhn (now retired professor of philosophy of religion at Asbury Theological Seminary and retired professor of German at Asbury College, respectively), worshiped with Estonian Methodists for the first time. This initial Asbury connection ultimately spawned a variety of helps for Estonian Methodism emanating not only from the college and seminary but also from a number of Wesleyan parachurch bodies: the Estonian Methodist Fund, the Ed Robb Evangelistic Association, the Francis Asbury Society, and Missionary World Service and Evangelism. Most recently the thirty-six-member Asbury College Concert Choir, under the direction of Dr. Don Donaldson, performed in the Merepuiestee Street Methodist and Oleviste Baptist Churches in Tallinn in May 1990.

The Asbury institution's most significant contribution to Estonian Methodism to date would appear to be an ongoing series of pastors workshops led by faculty from Asbury Theological Seminary. In December 1985, Dr. Robert Mulholland, professor of New Testament, accepted this author's invitation to travel to Estonia for work with Methodist pastors. His lectures on Acts and Revelation, subjects requested by the Rev. Pärnamets, were received with eagerness and rapt attention by more than one hundred pastors and laypersons. Now provost of Asbury Seminary, Dr. Mulholland is in an ideal position to facilitate the continuation of these pastors' workshops. In August 1988, Dr. Steve O'Malley, professor of church history and historical theology, gave lectures to assembled Estonian Methodists on historic Christian teachings as framed in the Apostle's Creed. Finally, in August 1989, Dr. and Mrs. David Seamands traveled to Estonia. Dr. Seamands, professor of pastoral ministry and author of a number of best-selling books including *Healing for Damaged Emotions*, led fellow Methodist ministers in Russian-occupied Estonia down the difficult but liberating path of forgiveness of one's enemies. One would have to be hard-hearted indeed not to be moved by the gripping trip reports of this trio of professors.[57]

Since 1978 many British Methodists have come to a rich appreciation for Estonian Methodism through trips organized by the Rev. David Bridge. In addition to sizable groups escorted to Estonia, in 1988 the Rev. Bridge managed an unprecedented visit to a newly registered Methodist church in a previously off-limits border village in Western Ukraine. (In Tallinn in 1982, the Rev. Bridge had witnessed a moving service of ordination for the Rev. Ivan Vuksta, pastor of this small, ethnically diverse congregation in Kamenitsa, Transcarpathia, annexed by the Soviet Union from Czechoslovakia after World War II.)[58]

Ten U.S. Methodist bishops (Richard Raines, Ralph Ward, Jack Tuell, Finis Crutchfield, Paul Washburn, Marjorie Matthews, Paul Milhouse, Lance Webb, Edward Tullis, and C. P. Minnick) have visited Estonia, as well as representatives of U.S. United Methodist boards and agencies (Harry Denman, Eddie Fox, William Ellington, Ezra Earl Jones, Mary Sue Robinson, Carl Soule, Robert McClean, and Maxie Dunnam). While some United Methodist officials from the United States have had a powerful spiritual impact upon Estonian Methodists, Bishop Webb being a revered example, other American representatives caused consternation within Estonian Methodist ranks by espousing pro-Socialist, even pro-Marxist sentiments and by questioning various tenets of historic Christian and Wesleyan doctrine.[59]

Additional Western groups that have established ties with Estonian Methodism include the World Methodist Council (Estonian visits by General Secretary Dr. Joe Hale, Dr. Alan Walker, and Dr. Maxie Dunnam), the Estonian emigré community (including the Rev. Evald Leps and Endel Meiusi), and the ecumenical movement (World Council of Churches and the U.S. National Council of Churches).

Membership Decline

In contrast to the postwar growth into the 1970s, between 1974 and 1990 Estonian Methodist membership fell from 2,363 to 1,783, a decline of 25 percent. Similarly, the size of Tallinn's Merepuiestee Street Church, which numbered 1,166 in 1971, stood at 880 in January 1990.[60] Painfully conscious of the downturn and earnestly praying for renewal is the Rev. Olav Pärnamets. During an August 1985 visit to England he reflected with remarkable candor on the situation, seeing unfortunate similarities in the English and Estonian experiences:

> We have to go back to our founder to the sources where all is clear and powerful, so that when we want to go forward, as we must, we have to go very much deeper than we are at the moment. . . . My feeling is that we in both Estonia and Britain do not have the hearts to save souls, to preach the Gospel with the life-changing love and power as John Wesley and others did in their generation. . . . The Lord wants to give us revival but sometimes we have become so lukewarm and formalistic and lifeless, so that when the Lord sends revival we do not recognize it.

A final line epitomizes the Rev. Pärnamets's understanding of the solution: "But we are not a hopeless people—God can do it again when we pray."[61]

One-time visitors rarely perceive a need for renewal in this Estonian church; in fact, just the opposite. Enriched by the perseverance, friendliness, and deep faith of these Methodists, the vast majority of Western guests depart blessed and oblivious to the spiritual concerns voiced by the Rev. Pärnamets. However, a number of longer-term Western observers quite sympathetic to Estonian Methodism have detected smaller crowds and waning vitality in recent years.[62] In any case, the statistics for the past two decades are such that, sadly, Estonian Methodism is misplaced as the opening chapter in Lorna and Michael Bourdeaux's study, *Ten Growing Soviet Churches*.

The Rev. Pärnamets is to be commended for so squarely facing the difficult problem of membership decline and, as he puts it, lukewarmness. Evaluating the causes in human terms, likewise, is a painful exercise for one sympathetic to the church and its leaders. But historical research worthy of the name will have it no other way.

In demographic terms, funerals were frequent in the 1970s and 1980s for many of the mostly middle-aged converts of the revival years of the 1950s. Whereas the Tallinn Methodist Church conducted an average of twenty funerals for members per year in the 1960s, the number of funerals per year in the 1980s rose to fifty.[63] On the other hand, in the 1970s and 1980s many young people attended and even joined the Methodist Church—but they did not necessarily remain. Quite a few joined the Baptist Church; recently quite a few have emigrated to the West; and, also recently, quite a few have joined a strongly nationalistic Pentecostal movement, Word of Life.

While it is true that Christian rock music in the Soviet Union started in the Estonian Methodist Church and that Alexander Kuum and Hugo Oengo favored it for its appeal to youth, other Methodists, including former Moravians, opposed it. By the time the Rev. Pärnamets was reconciled to

162

Jaanus Kärner and the *Selah* sound in 1977, many young people already had departed the fold. Heigo Ritsbek estimates that 40 percent of the youth who joined Tallinn's Oleviste Baptist Church in 1976 were converted in Methodist meetings.[64]

Emigration to the West in the 1980s, as well, has taken its toll. Some seventy former members of the Tallinn Methodist Church now live in the United States, as do approximately sixty from the Russian congregation and ten from the Estonian congregation. Between July 1988 and July 1989 alone, thirty Russian-speaking Methodist families departed for the West.[65]

The loss of members to the Word of Life movement in the late 1980s also weakened Estonian Methodism. Imported books and *samizdat* (privately reproduced and distributed literature) advocating "health and wealth" prosperity theology have been circulating in the Baltic states for decades. Generously funded by its advocates, especially in the United States and Scandinavia, this "theology of success," with which Estonia's Word of Life Church identifies, teaches that a true Christian will (a) possess health and wealth; and (b) profess the baptism of the Holy Spirit accompanied by *glossolalia* (speaking in tongues) and healing miracles. Prosperity theology holds that believers who do not possess the above signs of grace "are not Christians at all, or are Christians weak in faith or are living in sin." A radical offshoot of the Charismatic movement, various aspects of "health and wealth" teaching derive from American preachers Kenneth E. Hagin (especially influential in Scandinavia and the Baltic states), Kenneth Copeland, Robert H. Schuller, and Norman Vincent Peale, and Scandinavians Ulf Ekman (Sweden) and Hans Braterud (Norway).[66] In addition, the Estonian Word of Life Church aggressively advocates national independence and has criticized Methodist and Baptist leaders unwilling to take public positions on political issues.[67]

On several occasions Scandinavian guest preachers urged Word of Life teachings on Methodist gatherings without the blessing of the church's leadership. "Health and wealth" theology spread within Methodist ranks to the point that serious friction emerged in a church not known for its material aspirations, politics, or doctrinaire theology. Finally, in 1987, more than one hundred young advocates of Kenneth Hagin's teachings left the Methodist Church (mostly adherents, rather than members), while a larger departure from the Oleviste Baptist Church occurred at the same time over the same issue. Many young people, including musicians, left the Tallinn Methodist Church, causing the Rev. Pärnamets, the Rev. Ritsbek, and the congregation genuine grief.[68]

The Rev. Hans Växby, the Northern European Central Conference's new bishop as of 1989, has taken steps to regularize the channeling of Western aid to Estonian Methodists. On January 22, 1990, Växby appointed a

Helsinki-based Estonian support group, including one representative each from the Finnish-speaking and the Swedish-speaking annual conferences of Finland; an Estonian living in Finland; the Rev. Pärnamets; the bishop and, as chairman, the Rev. Håkan Sandström, a Swedish-speaking Finn with a long history of assistance to Estonian Methodism. "The intention with the group," Bishop Växby relates, "is to coordinate all help to Estonia as well as all information and exchange programs with Methodists within the [Northern European] Central Conference (Denmark, Finland, Norway, and Sweden), with other Central Conferences, United Methodists all over the world, British Methodism and other Methodist Churches and with individuals and congregations of other denominations."[69]

One of the specific charges of the support group is to coordinate Western visits with Estonian Methodists. Some such liaison is needed given the extraordinarily large volume of visitors the Tallinn Methodist Church in particular is obliged to host. Heigo Ritsbek, who for years bore the brunt of translating duties, admits, "We had no normal church life. How could you . . . with five hundred foreign guests in a year?"[70]

The practice of having the vast majority of Western guests preach also would appear to have been a mixed blessing. British Methodist David Bridge, who delivered his fair share of sermons in Estonia, has written to the present writer with second thoughts concerning the phenomenon: "As you have experienced yourself, visitors are frequently invited to preach in the church. While this is a nice thing in small doses, the growing number of visitors must have meant that the worship and teaching life of the church has been seriously disrupted. Again not all visitors are of equal value and a few seem to have done real harm."[71]

The church's leadership would see foreign guests introducing divisive Word of Life teachings as one example. A second would be culturally insensitive sermons by some United Methodists theologically and politically far afield from the strongly evangelical Estonian Methodists. Such messages delivered by Western preachers, nicknamed "Leftodists," agitated the membership sufficiently that the Tallinn Methodist pastors on occasion have refrained from announcing some upcoming U.S. Methodist visitors beforehand.[72]

Disruptive messages aside, which in any case would appear to be less numerous than edifying ones, the sheer volume of visitors leading in worship would seem to inhibit any continuity in teaching from Estonian pastors. Why the Rev. Pärnamets directs, and why leaders before him directed, foreign guests into the pulpit as a matter of course is an interesting question. Traditional Estonian hospitality must play a part. In addition, a psychological reaction to decades of fearsome isolation may be at work.[73] In 1987, when asked by representatives of a parachurch ministry, "what was the most important thing we could do for him [the Rev. Pärnamets], we were impressed with his period of silent consideration of the question and greatly touched by his reply: 'Maintaining fellowship of the entire Body of Christ, visiting and praying so that we know that we are not alone.' "[74]

Throughout the Rev. Pärnamets's tenure the superintendent and his church have been an exceptional blessing to a host of Western sojourners. Teenagers and bishops alike have come away, and still come away, moved by the worship and witness of this far-flung outpost of Methodism. The Rev. Eddie Fox of the United Methodist Board of Discipleship speaks for many in recounting his time among Estonian Methodists: "I have never experienced such intensity of worship of Jesus Christ. As the elements for holy communion were served, many persons openly wept for joy."[75] But perhaps the most telling testimonial comes from the pages of the Soviet Academy of Science journal, *Voprosy nauchnogo ateisma (Problems of Scientific Atheism)*, in a 1979 analysis of factors contributing to Methodist growth and vitality, not the least of which this Marxist piece lists as the centrality of prayer and the congregation's obvious dependence upon it during worship.[76] Not surprisingly, Lorna and Michael Bourdeaux, from the vantage point of 1986, characterize this article as "one of the liveliest and most attractive accounts of Christian life ever to have appeared in a Soviet source."[77]

1980s: Signs of Hope

For all the concern over membership decline since the 1970s, *glasnost* in the 1980s has provided Estonian Methodism with any number of hopeful signs. In December 1988–January 1989, Endel Meiusi of Estonian Christian Ministries, with the assistance of the International Bible Society, imported twenty thousand copies of a revised translation of the Estonian Bible. This shipment, forming the largest legal distribution of Estonian Bibles since the Soviet wartime takeover, was printed in Finland and shipped to Tallinn. Weighing some 26 tons, the Scriptures were distributed in proportion to membership to the Lutherans, Evangelical Christians-Baptists, Orthodox, Methodists (two thousand copies), and Pentecostals.[78]

Subsequent, even larger shipments of Estonian Scriptures bring total imports for 1988–90 to two hundred thousand. Estonian Methodists now have sufficient Scriptures for their membership, with an additional supply for use in outreach to nonbelievers.[79] At the same time that Estonian Methodists were the beneficiaries of donated Scriptures, the membership managed a 1989 contribution of six thousand rubles from its modest resources for Armenian earthquake relief.[80]

Work with children and young people also has taken on renewed vitality of late. Sunday schools, begun without state permission in 1972, but unofficially tolerated for years, came under new restrictions in the mid-1980s. Today, in contrast, the work is open and growing, at present in Tallinn numbering one hundred Estonian and seventy Russian children. As Urve Pärnamets, founder of the Methodist Sunday schools put it, "Now in Sunday school I see ten pairs of new eyes I haven't seen before and they listen well. So we have a big field of work."[81] The Rev. Üllas Tankler also relates a burgeoning Sunday school ministry in his Pärnu congregation.[82]

In the summer of 1988 young people from the Tallinn Methodist and Oleviste Baptist Churches inaugurated a first-ever youth evangelism campaign in connection with an annual festival in the city's historic Old Town.[83] The next summer the Tallinn Methodist Youth Choir began a women's prison ministry which has seen scores of inmates lives transformed.[84]

In Pärnu in March 1989, and soon after in Tallinn, Methodists and Baptists launched a joint children's foundation. Through an interdenominational children's choir, funds are being raised for aid to orphans.[85] In June 1989 the Tallinn Methodist Church held a confirmation service for twenty-four young people, while the denomination's annual summer camp in July had 250 participants.[86] In 1989 the Pärnu Methodist Church was able to donate Bibles to each of the city's thirteen schools.[87] Finally, in August 1989 an Estonian organizing committee, including Methodists, worked with Youth for Christ, Outreach for Christ International, Scott Wesley Brown, and others to sponsor a gospel festival including four days of concerts by some one hundred Western and Estonian Christian musicians. Held in the six-thousand-seat Lenin Palace of Culture and Sports, more than thirteen hundred persons made public, Christian commitments. A large number of Methodists of all ages sat together. A visiting David Seamands heard them repeat, "We're here. We know it's happening, but we can't believe it. We've prayed for it so long!"[88]

While Estonian Methodism still considers education for pastors a major need, a number of developments in the 1980s have at least made short-term contributions to that end: pastors' workshops led by Asbury Theological Seminary faculty (1986–), Youth with a Mission Schools of Evangelism (1986–), and Biblical Education by Extension (late 1980s–). In 1987 The Rev. Üllas Tankler, pastor of the Pärnu Methodist Church, left for the Methodist Seminary at Bad Klosterlausnitz, East Germany, becoming the first Estonian Methodist since World War II to study abroad. More recently, in September-November 1989, The Rev. Toomas Pajusoo from Tallinn studied at the Free Church Bible College, Santala, Finland. (Heigo Ritsbek, studying at Asbury Theological Seminary from September 1989, emigrated to the United States in February 1989 with little expectation of returning to

Estonia. Should Estonia regain its independence in the next several years, the Rev. Ritsbek likely would return.)[89]

Church planting and church building in the 1980s also have boosted the morale of Estonian Methodism: dedication of a new church building in Narva (1987); dedication of a newly renovated Orthodox chapel for a newly registered Methodist congregation at Kärsa (February 1990); permission granted for Methodist congregations in Tallinn and Pärnu to build their own sanctuaries after decades of renting from Seventh-Day Adventists (1989); registration of a Methodist congregation in Syktyvkar, Komi [A.S.S.R., U.S.F.S.R.] (1988); and the possibility of Methodist registration for a fellowship of believers in Yakutsk, Siberia.[90] After World War II, the Rev. Endel Rang from the Tapa Methodist Church spent time in a Siberian labor camp. For many years he has returned at least once a year to minister to several small fellowships he helped to establish. Estonian authorities have given permission for Methodists to establish a building fund with a hard-currency bank account. Western contributions now may go directly toward the construction of the Tallinn Methodist Church.

Bishop Hans Växby's deep sympathy for and active interest in Estonian Methodism continues a pattern ably set by Bishop Ole Borgen before him. Since his April 1989 election to head the Northern European Central Conference, Bishop Växby has visited Estonia twice, with another trip planned to survey the prospects for Methodism in such seemingly improbable Soviet regions as Komi and Siberia. Especially heartening has been the bishop's timely appointment of an Estonian support group. This may be interpreted as a response to the clear need for more systematic liaison between Estonian Methodism and its Western sympathizers.

Conclusion

In the era of *glasnost*, churchgoing actually is becoming popular and patriotic in Estonia. But as Sunday school founder Urve Pärnamets has put it, "Our nation needs more than just going to church."[91] Increasing freedom of expression in Estonia can also, within the church, give rise to a new problem of nominalism. As Estonia and its Methodist Church revel in new liberties and opportunities, Bishop Borgen's recent caution should be taken seriously: "They [Estonian Methodists] will find it is much more difficult to be a Christian in good times than in bad times." A saying of the bishop's father puts it even more succinctly: "It takes a strong back to carry good days."[92] Whether the days be good or bad, there still is no reason to accept F. I. Federenko's 1965 prediction that any time now, "one should anticipate [the] complete disappearance of Methodism from the Soviet Union."[93]

CHAPTER 10

Methodism Renewed but Never Abandoned

S T Kimbrough, Jr.

The breakdown of the walls of communism from Berlin to Moscow and throughout what was once the Soviet Union during the last decade of the twentieth century has created a flood tide of religious activity in the lands east of central Europe. Up until a few years ago this would have been unthinkable. For most of this century we have heard story upon story, report upon report of religious and political oppression in such horrifying proportions that people of the *free* world have been awestruck to the point of paralysis or circumventing political systems that prohibited the right to practice one's religion freely.

Suddenly the door to the east has been opened by liberating political and economic developments, which have the world still reeling. Religious communities within the CIS (Commonwealth of Independent States), countries of the former Soviet Union, and those in lands once dominated by it, are encountering freedom and frustration in ways they could not have anticipated before 1990. The extremely complex history of the Russian Orthodox Church during the twentieth century has yet to be fully written, especially in ways that will enable understanding of internal and external relationships. In the light of such history and contemporary contexts, we must come to new understandings of one another and put aside old assumptions and prejudices.

In the late nineteenth century there were diverse missionary efforts to bring new direction to Christian life and community in many parts of the old Russian Empire. The Orthodox Church was riddled with strife, and its intimate relationship to the Russian monarchy proved time and again to be a stumbling block to its effectiveness. Historically the oscillation between Patriarchy and Holy Synod complicated governance of the church, and the priests and other leaders used the illiteracy of many segments of the population, particularly with regard to the Old Slavic language of liturgy, to manipulate the people. Western churches began to conceive Orthodoxy as essentially nonevangelical in its overall thrust. Some Roman Catholic Church officials expressed hope that their church might one day replace Orthodoxy, a hope voiced for Methodism by some bishops at the turn of the century.

Why would Methodists have thought that religious life and community centered in a Wesleyan approach to Christian faith would have found a favorable response in the lands where Russian Orthodoxy was dominant? This is a question that missiologists and church historians will continue to explore. But when one observes the missionary outreach of the Methodist Episcopal Church and the Methodist Episcopal Church, South, as well as the *Evangelische Gemeinschaft* (Evangelical Church) in the lands of northern and eastern Europe beginning in the 1860s, it is clear that their early efforts represented a holistic Wesleyan response to human need, Christ, and the church. They were marked by mutual respect for Russian Orthodoxy and other churches. These missionary efforts were strongly evangelistic, seeking to enable people to make decisions to become servants of Christ as a part of a gospel community, and powerfully humanitarian. Such decisions meant integration into community where the faithful were involved in the quest for education (both biblical and secular studies), prayer, the inner witness of the Spirit, praising God in song, sound preaching of the Word, sacramental life, and social outreach. These were not emphases that could be casually included or excluded in the missionary efforts: they were mutual imperatives, as they had been with the Wesleys. The early Methodist and Evangelical Church work in the Baltic states and parts of Russia[1] sought to implement these mutual imperatives. Such a holistic approach to the church's outreach did not characterize Russian Orthodoxy at the turn of the century. Hence, Methodism entered the world of the old Russian Empire where there was a tremendous vacuum of holistic gospel community. This is what it sought to create through a life and ministry that bypassed no human need, spiritual or physical.

The religious world of the former Soviet states cannot be oversimplified in either ecumenical or evangelical circles by assumptions that distort the truth of history. The assumption underlying some current missionary outreach is that the Russians are/were atheistic Communists desperately in need of Christian salvation from the west. Such a view disregards the long history of Christian churches and witness in that part of the world (and is a total distortion of the meaning of Communist Party membership and its ideologies). Similarly, the assumption that the Russian Orthodox Church has been the dominant religious force in the life of the former Soviet states, now often improperly designated "Russia" by some, ignores the religious diversity of these states, perpetuates a Moscow-oriented view of life for this part of the world that is illusory, and does not take into account the rich ethnic, cultural, and religious diversity of the vast countries of the CIS. There are many significant populations of non-Russian Orthodox religious persuasion, particularly Moslem and Jewish, as well as significant Christian communities such as Armenian, Georgian, and Ukrainian, where there is no unanimity of Orthodoxy.

Without question, the Russian Orthodox Church has been a dominant Christian force in many of the regions of the former Soviet Union for more than ten centuries, but The Roman Catholic Church and Protestant denominations such as Lutheran (*Evangelisch*), Baptist, and Moravian also have significant histories in many parts of the former Soviet Union and neighboring states. One cannot and must not forget, however, the suffering of Russian Orthodoxy throughout the Bolshevik Revolution and the years of Communist domination, or the importance of its move into the world ecumenical community by joining the World Council of Churches in 1961. Its history, however, is not unilinear but one filled with dynamic and tumultuous cultural, social, and political relationships with religious communities, peoples, and governments.

The Past

Methodist Beginnings in Russia

The first Methodist venture in Russia proper came through the Swedish Methodist, B. A. Carlson, who preached in Saint Petersburg in 1889, the year a small Methodist congregation was formed there. The first known Methodist outreach among Russians, however, goes back to 1860, when F. W. Flocken of the Bulgaria Mission in Schumla went to minister to the Russians in Tultcha on the Danube. He baptized four Russian children and received the first convert, Gabriel Elieff. The first Russian Methodist chapel was built there in 1868. Though Flocken had the support of local religious groups, such as the Molokan and Lipovan sects, there was such bitter opposition from the rest of the population that he was forced to flee and the chapel was abandoned. Contrary to the views of mission historians and popular opinion about the early missionary efforts of the Methodist Church in the Baltic states, which were then a part of the old Russian Empire, *the first Methodist congregation in the Baltic states, namely in Kaunas, Lithuania (1900), was not the direct result of Methodist missions.*[2] At its inception it had nothing to do with Methodism and was begun by an independent indigenous group of German-speaking Lithuanians. When it discovered, quite coincidentally, that its evangelical emphases of prayer, Bible study, proclamation, witness, and abstinence from alcohol were akin to Methodist emphases, it invited Methodist pastor Heinrich Ramke from Königsberg, Germany, to visit Kaunas and discuss Methodism and the possibility of the group's joining the Methodist Church. It voted to affiliate with the church, and the following year, 1901, Bishop John L. Nuelsen sent word of conference approval. Hence, an independent, indigenous religious movement, which grew up on the soil of the old Russian Empire, found its identity and home in Methodism. Its first pastor, Georg Durdis, was appointed by the Northeast German Methodist Annual Conference in 1905.

It should also be noted that the first Latvian-or Lettish-speaking Methodist congregation in Latvia (Liepaja, 1921) was also not the result of Methodist missions per se. Rather, an independent, indigenous congregation of Moravians led by their pastor, Alfred Freiburg, made the unanimous decision to join en masse (125 members) the Methodist denomination. Freiburg had studied diligently the works of Wesley and other Methodist sources provided him by Dr. George A. Simons, then superintendent of the Methodist Episcopal Church mission in Saint Petersburg, and others. Here are distinct indigenous religious movements on soil, once a part of the old Russian Empire, which can by no means be understood as missional attempts to proselytize the Russian Orthodox. In fact, the members of the group of Christians in Kaunas, Lithuania, who decided to become Methodist were baptized and confirmed Lutherans.[3]

Foreshadowings of an Ecumenical Spirit

Foreshadowings of a decidedly *ecumenical spirit* pervaded the early missionary efforts of the Methodist Episcopal Church, the Methodist Episcopal Church, South, and the Evangelical Church in the Baltic states, Russia, and Siberia/Manchuria. The World Service report of the Methodist Episcopal Church in 1923 states succinctly one vital aspect of its vision in the Baltics and Russia at the time: "Every indication . . . shows that Methodism is to render its greatest service, by helping to revive vital religion within the Russian Orthodox Church."[4] Along with a clear vision of the opportunity for a holistic, Wesleyan witness in the old Russian Empire, there was a deep desire to work with the Russian Orthodox and other churches. The deep respect for Orthodoxy, as reflected in the practices of such missionary efforts, is eloquently expressed in an article that was published in a Russian newspaper, *Russky Golos*, in Harbin, Manchuria, and quoted in the September 1923 issue of *The Missionary Voice*, a publication of the Board of Missions of the Methodist Episcopal Church, South:[5]

The Methodist Mission, headed by Mr. H. W. Jenkins, arrived in Harbin a year and a half ago. They have now completed the building of the Mission residence located in an attractive building on Telinskaya Street. The house contains flats, classrooms and all kinds of equipment.

The opening of the Institute gathered many persons quite unknown to Harbin. In a short speech Mr. Erwin gave the audience some facts in regard to the beginnings of Methodism. Mr. Pöysti, also a Methodist preacher, a Finn by birth, but speaking beautiful Russian, spoke of the activities of the Methodists in Europe. Mr. Jenkins emphasized the fact that the Methodists do not wish to hinder other religions and explained why no lessons will be given in the Institute on Saturdays. This has caused some comment, but he explained that the arrangement was due not to the observance of the Jewish Sabbath, but to a desire to enable the Orthodox people to attend the evening church service on Saturdays.

Clearly the Methodist and Evangelical Church mission workers in the Baltic states and Russia also sought to work wherever possible with clergy and laity of other denominations. The evidence of a spirit of Christian unity pervaded their theology of the church in thought and practice.[6]

Without question, the Methodist Episcopal Church became entangled in the political and religious life of the Russian Orthodox Church in the 1920s. Its support of the "Living Church" movement, a reform movement that in the end was embarrassed by its seizure of power from Patriarch Tikhon, became problematical within Methodist and Russian Orthodox circles. With the demise of the Russian monarchy, the Russian Orthodox Church found itself in constant conflict with the Bolsheviks. The church was severely limited and persecuted by the government, which saw religion as a remnant of the monarchy to be eliminated. When Patriarch Tikhon was arrested by the authorities for criticism of and resistance to the government, he granted permission to a group of Renovators, clergy who hoped for radical changes and called themselves the "Living Church," to occupy the chancery of the church. However, the "Living Church" movement failed to establish itself as the dominant religious body in Russia. When Tikhon was released from prison in 1924, he emerged as the leader once again of the Russian Orthodox Church. This placed the Methodist Episcopal Church in an embarrassing and difficult situation. Nevertheless, there were leaders like Bishops Nuelsen and Blake who had a vision of cooperative ministry with Russian Orthodoxy and who actively sought support among Methodists for the Russian Orthodox Church, such as funding to reopen a theological seminary closed by the Bolsheviks. The support and mutual commitment of early Russian Methodism and Methodist leaders was not forgotten. At Patriarch Tikhon's death, the new head of the Holy Synod of the Russian Orthodox Church, Metropolitan Seraphim of Moscow, wrote to Bishop John Nuelsen as follows:

The services rendered by Bishops Blake and Nuelsen and by Drs. Hartman and Hecker and by American Methodists and other Christian friends will go down in the history of the Orthodox Church as one of the brightest pages in that dark and trying time of the church.[7]

Of course, by 1927 the fate of Methodist work in Saint Petersburg and Siberia/Manchuria was sealed, and except for the work sustained throughout the Communist domination in Estonia and a few other isolated places, Methodism was destined for liquidation from the life of Russian-speaking people. Sister Anna Eklund managed to keep the work in Saint Petersburg alive until 1931, when she was forced to flee.

The Present

What are we to say today to the new efforts of the United Methodist Church Russia Initiative and outreach to the people in lands where Russian Orthodoxy is the largest singular Christian church, or in lands once under the domination of the Soviet Union, some of which are largely non-Christian? How are those efforts to be judged? Obviously, one needs to examine the past carefully to understand the successes and failures of those who undertook the mission of Methodists in this part of the world at the turn of the century and during the first quarter of the twentieth century. The attempts at close cooperative efforts with the Russian Orthodox Church in the past also need careful scrutiny for the building of new and sound relationships with that communion. There is a need for in-depth study of episcopal leadership in the early days of the Russian missions of the first part of this century to help shape current episcopal direction. Foundational ecumenical efforts must be the basis of all work in these countries and a careful study of the meaning of mission for a church that would stand firmly within a Wesleyan tradition as it enters the new century. Throughout the current official United Methodist Russia Initiative there has been ongoing consultation with officials of the Russian Orthodox Church and the Orthodox Church in America.

1989

It is most interesting that the first new seeds of Methodism sown on Russian soil, and actually before the formal breakdown of Communism, were planted by an indigenous Russian named Vladislav Spektorov of Samara, Russia. In 1989, while in Estonia, he had attended a Russian-speaking United Methodist congregation in Tallinn. As a result of this contact and experience, Spektorov became a Christian.

He later traveled back to Tallinn for a brief training course and then returned to his native Samara and began distributing literature encouraging others to make Christian commitments. Soon he had formed a small group of believers, which began meeting in homes. This was the beginning of the Samara United Methodist Church, which was officially established in 1991. The congregation has been nurtured particularly by the Russian-speaking congregation from Tallinn.

> The church is formally organized with thirty-five members and a Sunday worship attendance averaging 120. . . . The congregation meets in a Lutheran church building on Sundays and in a public meeting place during the week. It is registered with the government under the Estonian church registry. . . . Members are now serving in a hospital and a prison. With financial assistance from foreign contributors, the church also sponsors a free lunch program in a local restaurant for pensioners and others in need.[8]

1990

The first United Methodist contacts from the United States, which began in what is now Russia as signs of the Communist breakdown surfaced, were established by Mr. Chang Son Kum, a Korean-American United Methodist layman in Moscow, and Mr. Young Cheul Kwon. Through their efforts a prayer group was organized on June 3, 1990, which gave rise to the establishment of the first United Methodist Church in Moscow. During the same month the Rev. Dea Hee Kim[9] traveled to Moscow to conduct the first worship service of a Korean-American United Methodist group in Russia. On December 28, 1990, with Dr. Randolph Nugent, general secretary of the General Board of Global Ministries (GBGM), present and Bishop C. Dale White presiding, the Rev. Young Cheul Cho was assigned as a missionary from the New York Annual Conference to serve as pastor to the Moscow congregation, which was officially registered as the "Russian-American Korean Union of the Methodist Church."[10] The congregation, which serves Koreans, Korean-Russians, and Russians, meets in a rented space of the Trade Union Congress building. Meanwhile, other contacts had been initiated by the Rev. Dwight Ramsey, then pastor of Broadmoor United Methodist Church in Shreveport, Louisiana. In July 1990 he traveled to Sverdlovsk (Ekaterinburg) on a peace exchange and took Bibles in Russian translation with him. Through his efforts, interest in a congregation grew in Ekaterinburg. By October of that year a United Methodist church was legally registered in the city.

The initial activities of Mr. Kum and the Rev. Ramsey were not initiated by official action of The United Methodist Church or any of its agencies. But as they sought to share their commitment to Christ and the church with those whom they encountered in Russia, it was affirmed within the United

Methodist tradition, of which they were a part. Hence, they renewed the vision of Methodist work, which had begun in Russia more than a century ago; work that had been suspended by Communist rule but not forgotten.

1991

When Bishop J. Woodrow Hearn, then president of GBGM and General Secretary Randolph Nugent made an exploratory visit in January 1991 to the former Soviet Union, they could not have anticipated what would transpire in the following months. Through the arrangements of Suzanne Stafford, a United Methodist laywoman with the Soviet Peace Foundation, a secular relief organization in Russia, Hearn and Nugent traveled to the USSR. During their stay they met with representatives of governmental agencies, the Russian Orthodox Church, and the Soviet Peace Fund. Through visits to hospitals, clinics, homes and centers for the elderly, and observance of the hardships of daily life, they encountered the tremendous needs of the Russian people for food, medical care, and the development of political, economical, industrial, and human resources amid governmental and economic turmoil, poverty, and unemployment.

On January 5 the Rev. Young Cheul Cho arrived from the United States to assume work as pastor of the congregation, Moscow United Methodist Church, founded by the Korean Americans.

By February 1991 the Rev. Dwight Ramsey had made another trip to Ekaterinburg. The interest in an established United Methodist congregation had grown to such an extent, that in August of that year Bishops Hans Växby of the Northern Europe Central Conference, whose residence is in Helsinki, Finland, and William B. Oden of the Louisiana Area of the U.S. South Central Jurisdiction traveled to Russia. In Ekaterinburg they consecrated Lydia Istomina, a trained educator, as a local preacher to serve the congregation, which was established in partnership with the Broadmoor United Methodist Church of Shreveport, Louisiana.

> Her ministry has attracted members of the academic and technical communities. The church perceives its mission to be the creation of a new society through the Christian faith. The church offers a holistic ministry sponsoring a school for hearing impaired children, a veterans club, health services, alcoholic treatment and food/relief ministries to the general population. The church has 600 members. It serves 200 persons through a prison ministry. The congregation meets in a former communist party building.[11]

In April 1991 Bishop Hearn and Dr. Nugent made an extensive report of their January 1991 trip to the spring meeting of GBGM in New York City. The directors of the Board at this meeting approved an allocation of $216,000 from the Program Development Fund to implement a Russia initiative. It was also recommended that a Joint Commission on Humanitarian Aid have the oversight of and responsibility for the initiative's policies, strategies, objectives, and provision of resources. The commission's members would consist of three representatives from The United Methodist Church and the Soviet Peace Fund, with cooperation from the Russian Orthodox Church. Its primary task was to oversee distribution of medical assistance, food, and other supplies, as well as to help facilitate the education and training of clergy. In June 1991 a meeting was held in Vienna, Austria, with representatives of the Russian Orthodox Church, the Soviet Peace Fund, the United Methodist General Boards of Global Ministries and Discipleship, and United Methodist Communications (UMCom). Joint agreements were signed by the United Methodist boards, UMCom, and the Soviet Peace Fund, which outlined cooperative work to be undertaken in the areas of humanitarian aid, medical work, and communications. GBGM, on behalf of The United Methodist Church, and the Soviet Peace Fund signed an agreement regarding the formation of the Joint Commission on Humanitarian Aid. Although the Russian Orthodox Church never officially entered such an agreement, it has cooperated where possible in achieving the goals of the commission.

In August 1991 the Rev. Ramsey made an additional trip to Ekaterinburg and was accompanied by Bishops Växby and Oden, Dr. Spurgeon Dunham, then editor of *The United Methodist Reporter*, as well as educators and physicians primarily from the Broadmoor United Methodist Church in Shreveport. In the broad sense of Wesleyan outreach to the whole person and community, they explored possibilities of service in education, medicine, and other areas.

At an October meeting of the European College of Bishops of The United Methodist Church, it was proposed that Bishop Rüdiger Minor of Dresden, Germany, be assigned to direct the Russia Initiative of the church. When the Council of Bishops of The United Methodist Church convened during the same month, it approved this proposal. Bishop Minor's responsibilities were outlined as follows:[12]

    a. Visit all annual conferences bordering former Soviet republics to assess and cultivate programs of missionary outreach to Russians and other former Soviet nationalities within and beyond their borders.

    b. Visit all groups and congregations identified in the former Soviet republics which have an identifiable relationship to the United Methodist Church.

    c. Identify places and potential for new United Methodist ministries.

    d. Cultivate ecumenical and bilateral church partnerships to facilitate new ministries.

    e. Develop plans for theological training and leadership development for responding to needs of emerging congregations and church structures.

   f. Develop reports and recommend project development strategies for sup-
      porting bodies in The United Methodist Church.
   g. Engage in interpretation and information sharing with United Methodist
      Church constituencies in Europe and the USA.

At the fall 1991 meeting (October) of GBGM the directors approved the shipment to Russia of food through the United Methodist Committee on Relief (UMCOR) and medical supplies and services through the Health and Welfare Ministries program department. Also in October 1991, this department helped negotiate a series of partner relationships between United Methodist-related hospitals in the United States and hospitals in the Commonwealth of Independent States. The first partnership was formed between the Methodist Health Systems of Memphis (Tennessee) and the Moscow-based Scientific Research Institute of Pediatric Hematology. The Memphis-based system committed itself to establishing appropriate training opportunities for the Institute's physicians within its own hospitals or allied hospitals, exchanging clinical care personnel on a short-term basis, increasing the supply of medicines and equipment available to the Institute, and helping the Institute develop appropriate standards of care, services, and procedures to maximize patient well-being.

The second partner relationship was formed between the Methodist Hospital of Indiana, Inc., and Moscow's largest trauma care facility, Hospital #7. The U.S. and Russian physicians of these facilities have visited each others' hospitals, and the Indiana hospital has developed a trauma training program to enable Russian physicians to become trainers of other physicians and has prepared training manuals in Russian.

The third partner relationship is between Riverside Methodist Hospital in Columbus (Ohio) and Zaoksky Regional Hospital in Russia's Tula District, sixty miles south of Moscow. Riverside's surgical staff conducts training on site in Zaoksky for the Russian physicians. The program includes training on basic diagnostic equipment supplied by UMCOR, and more advanced surgical training to meet the needs of the Zaoksky surgeons. Working cooperatively with GBGM Health and Welfare Ministries, Riverside has developed a system for selecting and sending equipment to Zaoksky.

These hospitals and the *fel'dsher* (first aid) stations associated with them, along with the Novozybkov Central Regional Hospital and other hospitals, polyclinics, and first aid stations in the Bryansk Region of Russia, which suffered severely from the Chernobyl Nuclear Plant accident, received $4.8 million worth of medicines in a cooperative effort between the Health and Welfare Ministries program department and UMCOR to bring much needed medicines into the CIS. Health and Welfare Ministries and UMCOR have also worked cooperatively to identify hospitals in Russia, Uzbekistan, and

Kazakhstan, which needed bandages and sterile supplies. Hospitals in Nukus, Uzbekistan, which treat families affected by the Aral Sea catastrophe, have been surveyed, and partner relationships are also being established.

The Health and Welfare Ministries program department has also examined the needs of nursing homes, special orphanages for children with physically and mentally challenging conditions, and orphanages for teenagers in Samara in southern Russia. There are United Methodist-related child care agencies and retirement and long-term care programs eager to work with the Samara institutions in support of the United Methodist Church that has been established there. On October 31, 1991, Dr. R. Bruce Weaver, then interim associate general secretary of UMCOR and the Rev. Dean Hancock, UMCOR staff member, attended a meeting in Geneva, Switzerland, and negotiated an agreement with a Moscow ecumenical committee formed by the World Council of Churches (WCC) for the distribution of humanitarian aid in the Moscow region of the former Soviet Union. On November 7, 1991, the following communiqué to Mr. Klaus Posser of CICARWS of the WCC, Geneva, Switzerland, was signed by Archbishop Sergii of Sonechnogarsk of the Russian Orthodox Church and Dr. R. Bruce Weaver of UMCOR:

> There was a meeting between the delegation of the Russian Orthodox Church, headed by Archbishop Sergii of Sonechnogarsk, Chairman of the Department of Charity and Social Service, the delegation of the United Methodist Committee on Relief, headed by Dr. R. Bruce Weaver, and the representative of CICARWS, Mr. Miroslav Matrenczyk, on the subject of humanitarian relief for Moscow and the Moscow region.
>
> It was taken into consideration that UMCOR was the Lead Agency for providing relief in this area. An ecumenical committee for the fulfillment of the project was established with the following participants:
>
> CICAWRS [relief organization of the WCC]
> UMCOR
> Russian Orthodox Church
> Union of Orthodox Brotherhood
> All Union Council of Christian Baptist [Churches]
> Lutheran Community of Moscow
> Community of Georgian Orthodox Church of Moscow
> Armenian Moscow Diocese
>
>
> Signed,
> Archbishop Sergii Sonechnogarskii,
> Russian Orthodox Church
> Dr. R. Bruce Weaver,
> United Methodist Committee on Relief
> Nov. 7, 1991[13]
>

Humanitarian aid to other areas was designated as follows: Saint Petersburg (Finnchurch Aid), Siberia (Norwegian Church Aid), Volgograd/Armenia (Deutsches Diakonisches Werk), Ukraine (Hungarian Interchurch Aid and HEKS).

In November 1991 the Rev. Adam Kuczma, former superintendent of the United Methodist Church in Poland, was recruited by Dr. Weaver and the Rev. Robert J. Harman, deputy general secretary of the World Division of GBGM, to direct the 1991–92 Russia Winter Food distribution program. Through his fluent command of the Russian language, the Rev. Kuczma was able to relate to the Russian partners, monitor the warehouse processing of the food, and visit persons and organizations/institutions that received the aid. He also reported weekly to Dr. Weaver, who served as coordinator of the relief to Russia as the interim associate general secretary of UMCOR. During the winter of 1991 UMCOR became a primary channel of aid to Russia, or more specifically, to Moscow and its immediate surrounding area. Through initial arrangements with Norwegian Church Aid, UMCOR sent some 4,160 boxes of food to Moscow. The first shipment arrived in Moscow during December 1991, and the first distribution took place on December 17. Each box contained flour, sugar, macaroni, rice, canned meat, dehydrated milk and fruit juice, and solid chocolate bars. Distribution in Moscow, Kromask, Sverdlovsk, Dobrinsk, and other towns near Moscow was implemented through the prior arrangement with the Russian, Armenian, and Georgian Orthodox churches, as well as the Baptist Alliance, Korean Methodist Church and Koreans of The United Methodist Church, and the Russian Lutheran Church. It was determined that distribution would be made to persons in need without regard to religious affiliation. A warehouse in Moscow was secured for processing all goods. Distribution was extremely well managed, and both general and specific needs were met. For example, the Soviet Peace Fund distributed 126 of its initially allotted 195 boxes to the Association of Help to Families with Invalid Children. Hospitals, orphanages, homes for the elderly, families, single mothers with children, and others received food and medical supplies through the ecumenical coalition, led by the Russian Orthodox Church as agreed. UMCOR has an ongoing food and medical supply relief program to Russia and has established an Advance Special with the title "Soviet Food/Medical Crisis,"[14] to which United Methodists generously have responded with tons of boxed food and financial support. Every bishop, district superintendent, pastor, and congregation has been contacted and informed of the need.

Finally, two other occurrences during the fall of 1991 should be noted. First, through the auspices of the Soviet Peace Fund, Chris Hena, a young Russian-speaking Liberian woman who was a medical student for six years in the Russian city of Krasnodar, some 150 miles from the border of what was Soviet Georgia, was appointed by GBGM as a missionary to Moscow.

Second, on November 13, 1991, Moscow United Theological Seminary was founded by the Rev. Young Cheul Cho and his congregation. It offers courses in Korean language and culture, and lay, pastoral, and missionary training. Its faculty represents many denominations including: United Methodist, Korean Methodist, United Presbyterian, Russian Baptist, and Russian Orthodox.

1992

Bishop Rüdiger Minor's appointment to direct the United Methodist Russia Initiative became effective on January 1, 1992, and during that month he made his first official episcopal visit to the CIS, January 12-23. His time was spent primarily in Moscow, where he established contact with GBGM missionary Chris Hena, who is working to coordinate hospital partnerships and to cultivate small group ministries with students from the neighborhood school in Sonsova, where she lives. She also assists with services at a children's neuro-psychological clinic and leads Bible studies with patients, staff, and parents.[15]

Bishop Minor also established contacts with the Korean United Methodist Church in Moscow, the Union Council of Evangelical Christian-Baptist [Churches], the U.S. and German Embassy officials, the Rev. Dwight Ramsey, who was returning to the United States, and Pastor Lydia Istomina of the United Methodist Church in Ekaterinburg. In the arena of humanitarian aid, Bishop Minor met with the Rev. Kuczma, UMCOR representative in Moscow, representatives of the Soviet Peace Foundation and the Orthodox Brotherhood "Faith," and a number of individuals working with handicapped children, such as the director of Sanitorium #65. Bishop Minor reported:

> The most visible Methodist work in the city of Moscow is the Korean Church. . . . This church is working with Koreans and Russians and ministers especially to those Russian Koreans who have been living for generations in Russia (or the Soviet Union) and lost their contacts to the national culture as well as their native tongue. The church has started a Korean language school that teaches to speak as well as read and write in Korean. There were about 120 students in five classes when I was visiting there, among them several Russians. The worship service is in Korean with simultaneous translation into Russian. . . . There are in the Russian Federation presently four Korean congregations, and three more in the CIS: in Ukraine, Kazakhstan, and Uzbekistan.[16]

On January 22, 1992, the second UMCOR shipment of food arrived at the Moscow warehouse. On this occasion Dr. Kuczma gratefully joined in a service of blessing and thanksgiving conducted by a Russian Orthodox priest.

By March 3, 1992, the UMCOR Hotline reported that more than 300 tons of food were en route or had been delivered to Moscow. By March 20 of the same year, UMCOR had overseen the shipment of 26,000 boxes of essential foodstuffs. As of July 1992 more than 100,000 boxes of food had been delivered, totaling four million pounds, with an estimated value of $4,000,000. Goods for shipment from the United States were processed through a central warehouse in New Windsor, Maryland and from there on to the Port of Baltimore. Thereafter they proceeded to New York, Antwerp (Belgium), and Saint Petersburg.

These UMCOR efforts were accompanied and followed by a series of meetings between leaders of the Russian Orthodox and United Methodist Churches, which have had continual contact through the World Council of Churches since 1961, when the Russian Orthodox Church became a member of that body. Closer contact has been developed between the two churches since 1991. It has been fostered also through the Joint Commission on Humanitarian Aid. Most recently the relationships have developed further through the Office of the Patriarch and the Russian Orthodox Church's Department of External Affairs, as well as through two new departments of the church: the Department of Charity and the Department of Christian Education and Catechism.

Interest in the Russia Initiative has also been expressed from other regions of United Methodism. Estonia was the one country where a significant number of Methodist churches survived during the reign of Communism. It has many close ties to Russia and many Russian-speaking citizens. In March 1992 Bishop Växby led a seminar on Methodism and mission among Russians sponsored by the Estonian United Methodist Church. Also at that time Bishop Minor met with two groups of Christians in Saint Petersburg.

The report of Bishop Minor's third trip, namely, to Estonia, Russia, and Poland illustrates that, even with the importance of the U.S. United Methodist Russia Initiative, "European Annual Conferences have remained in contact with a small number of Methodist congregations throughout the period of communist control. New work has been initiated independently from United Methodists in the United States."[17]

This is exemplified particularly in Ukraine. The United Methodist Church in Poland is attempting to identify former Methodist congregations that were merged with the Baptist denomination, which had been a Protestant body recognized by the Soviet government. In the region of Sub-Carpathia (Uzhgorod and Kaminica), the Methodist church was founded by the Czechoslovakia Annual Conference in the 1920s and the first church was acquired in 1929.

> [Methodist] work in Kaminica was started by independent efforts in 1934. After some association with the church in Uzhgorod, the members decided to affiliate with the Methodist Church in 1935. Evangelistic efforts have extended the work to the communities of Huta, Petroc and Jenkovce. In 1940 the area fell to the control of Hungary. Slovaks left the area and the church in Uzgorod was re-populated with Hungarians. When it came under Russian occupation after World War II, the members were forced to become Baptists, the officially recognized Protestant work in the region. The Methodist pastor disagreed with this action and held together a small group of Methodists meeting in homes. In 1964, leaders in the congregations at Kaminica and Uzgorod learned about the Methodist work in Estonia. Contact was made and pastoral training made possible in Tallinn. More aggressive efforts to organize formally and register the congregations under Russian authority met with resistance. In 1989, contact was established with the Hungary Annual Conference.
> The church in Kaminica has thirty-five registered members. Sixty persons attend services held on Friday evenings and Sundays in a newly constructed residence of Ivan Vakusta, who was ordained a deacon in November 1968 by the Bishop of the Northern Europe Central Conference.
> The church in Uzhgorod has been re-established with twenty-five members. Through cooperation of the Czechoslovakia and Hungary annual conferences attempts are being made to restore the church property.[18]

The roots of the Wesleyan tradition in the Baltic countries and Ukraine are strong. It is there that Methodism survived Bolshevik and Communist domination. Now the Estonian United Methodist Church is renewing its relationships in northwestern Russia and Latvia. It has some Russian-speaking congregations within its own annual conference and has founded, as already noted, a new congregation in Samara, Russia. Bishop Hans Växby is also cooperating with the United Methodist Russia Initiative in reestablishing Methodist contacts in the Baltic states and Russia. For example, he is assisting with the return of former Methodist church properties in Latvia and Lithuania to The United Methodist Church.

As the political situation in the former Soviet Union changed, GBGM saw the opportunity "to renew mission suspended but never abandoned."[19] The spring of 1992 brought the legal registration of two more United Methodist churches in Russia: the First United Methodist Church of Moscow and the First United Methodist Church of Saint Petersburg. The Moscow church was registered with the city by friends and representatives of the United Methodist Church in Ekaterinburg. It was organized by musician, Ludmila Pavlovna Garbuzova, who is now serving it as a lay pastor. The congregation began meeting in January 1992 in a local school.

There are two United Methodist churches in Saint Petersburg:[20] First United Methodist Church, which was established in 1992, and Bethany United Methodist Church, which was begun in 1993 and whose first pastor is the Rev. Oksana Petrova.

At their spring meeting (1992) in Stamford, Connecticut, the directors of GBGM approved the establishment of a United Methodist "mission" in Russia. In accordance with the provisions of *The Book of Discipline*, this action was presented to and approved by the Council of Bishops. The European College of Bishops then recommended the appointment of a bishop to oversee the new work. For the first time since 1927, when the Methodist Episcopal Church was forced to withdraw from Saint Petersburg, the 1992 General Conference officially authorized United Methodist work in the CIS, at the outset primarily in Russia. In June 1992 Dr. R. Bruce Weaver was engaged by the World Division of GBGM to become the coordinator of New Mission Development in the Commonwealth of Independent States. The task was to relate to all United Methodist Church groups from the United States participating in the Russia Initiative and to provide consultation and resources for their further participation. Hence, a program was organized that includes: 1) Partner Churches within Russian communities (involving both evangelism and humanitarian services); 2) Volunteers in Mission groups for locations in Russia; 3) supplemental salaries by U.S. churches for persons serving Russian United Methodist congregations; and 4) recruitment of churches to provide funds for Christian education, leadership training programs, and theological training for Russian pastors.

As a part of the effort to develop Partner Churches, representatives of two congregations, St. Luke's United Methodist Church of Oklahoma City and the United Methodist Church of Morristown, New Jersey, were invited by the Rev. Robert Harman to participate in a prototype partnership program now directed by Dr. Bruce Weaver. They went to the cities of Kerch (Crimea, Ukraine) and Ulyanovsk (Russia). On the first Saturday in July 1992, seventy-five Russians gathered in the Hall of Culture in Kerch with the U.S. Partner Church representatives from Morristown and formally expressed their desire to establish a United Methodist church. Dr. W. James White, then pastor of the United Methodist Church of Morristown and now GBGM area secretary for Europe reports, "I returned to Kerch in August 1992 to ascertain their intentions regarding the formation of a United Methodist Church—they agreed that they would continue to meet as a church fellowship, and have done so ever since that time. They have been nurtured in this process by the Morristown United Methodist Church."[21] As a result of the interest that emerged in the formation of a United Methodist church in Ulyanovsk, the Rev. Brian Kent and Mrs.

Lorena Kent were commissioned as United Methodist missionaries and assigned to Ulyanovsk.

Another United Methodist church was established in Ukraine, namely, in the city of Sevastopol, in August 1992 by the Rev. Dwight Ramsey. It is now served by the Rev. Andrei Pupko.

On August 15-17, 1992, a new chapter in United Methodist mission history began. During those three days representatives from newly forming United Methodist congregations in the CIS gathered in Moscow for the first formal meeting of the newly established United Methodist Episcopal area in the CIS, now known as the area of Eurasia. Others attending included Russian Orthodox priest, Father Ioann Ekonomtsev, chair of the department of religious education of the Moscow Patriarchate, pastors from Estonia and Latvia and elsewhere in Europe, and some forty United Methodists from the United States. These persons gathered to celebrate Bishop Rüdiger R. Minor's assumption of episcopal duties of the Eurasia Area and the "mission renewed but never abandoned."

The events were hosted by the Rev. Young Cheul Cho, missionary from the New York Annual Conference, and his congregation of the Russian-Korean Moscow United Methodist Church. The meetings were held in the auditorium of the Union Academy of Social Work, which is the regular place of worship for the congregation, with the following bishops presiding and addressing the various sessions of the garthering: Heinrich Bolleter (Zürich, Switzerland, Central and Southern Europe area), Rüdiger R. Minor (Moscow and Dresden, Eurasia area), William Oden (Baton Rouge, Louisiana), Dan O. Solomon (Oklahoma City, Oklahoma), Hans Växby (Helsinki, Finland, Northern Europe area), and Joseph Yeakel (Washington, D.C., president of the Council of Bishops). Also during August two United Methodist leaders, Bishop Melvin G. Talbert, secretary of the Council of Bishops, and Dr. Bruce W. Robbins, general secretary of the General Commission on Christian Unity and Interreligious Concerns, attended a meeting of the Central Committee of the World Council of Churches with delegates of the Russian Orthodox Church. To settle some differences the desire was expressed to bring a delegation from both churches together in Moscow for consultation. In December 1992 an invitation was received for a January 1993 meeting in Moscow with the Patriarch of the Russian Orthodox Church. The United Methodist Church delegation to this meeting included: Bishop Melvin G. Talbert, Bishop Joseph H. Yeakel (president of the Council of Bishops), Bishop Rüdiger Minor (the Eurasia Area), Dr. Randolph Nugent (general secretary of GBGM), Dr. Bruce W. Robbins, and the Rev. Robert J. Harman (deputy general secretary of the World Division of GBGM). Father Leonid Kishkovsky, a former president of the National

Council of Churches of Christ in the USA and a member of the Orthodox Church in America, was an adviser to the United Methodist delegation.

During the fall of 1992, through the sponsorship of the Mission Education and Cultivation Department of GBGM, a United Methodist radio program was initiated on Open Radio, which potentially reaches some 75 million people in western Russia and bordering states. In 1993–94 the broadcast was expanded to Soviet Radio Channel One. The program, which is under the supervision of Bishop Minor, includes sacred music, Bible study, worship, personal witness, and an emphasis on Christian unity.

In October 1992 seven missionaries, recruited and funded by the Korean American Mission to Russia, were commissioned by GBGM. In November 1992 the Health and Welfare Program Department of GBGM formed its first partnership between U.S. and Russian health care institutions, namely the Methodist Hospital of Indiana, Inc. and Hospital #7 in Moscow.

During 1992 the Moscow United Methodist Church (Korean-American) also established three new congregations: Western United Methodist Church, founded by Andrei Kim on April 26, 1992; Moscow Northern United Methodist Church, founded by Vallery Ho on September 5, 1992; and Moscow United Methodist Church, founded by Son Gue Lee on October 10, 1992.

Also in 1992 the World Evangelism Committee of the World Methodist Council, under the leadership of Dr. Eddie Fox, began a program known as "Connecting Congregations," through which it seeks to link congregations of the Methodist/Wesleyan tradition throughout the world in global witness to Christ. The program originated during May in Czechoslovakia in connection with eight new congregations. As of July 1994, Dr. Fox reported eleven Connecting Congregations in Latvia (4), Estonia (6), and Russia (1). In Latvia they are located in Riga (two congregations are connected with First United Methodist Church, Maryville, Tennessee),[22] Liepaja (Metropolitan United Methodist Church, Detroit, Michigan), Matras (First United Methodist Church, Pine Bluff, Arizona). In Estonia there are three Russian-speaking congregations in Tallinn, Paldiski (First United Methodist Church, Marietta, Georgia), Kunda (Wesley Methodist Church, Singapore), and Keila (First United Methodist Church, Peoria, Illinois). There are three Estonian-speaking congregations: Kohtla-Jarva (Mt. Bethel United Methodist Church, Marietta, Georgia), Rusmae (Forest United Methodist Church, Forest, Massachusetts), and Karsa/Ahja (First United Methodist Church, Bartlesville, Oklahoma). There is one congregation in Russia: Pskov (Christ Church United Methodist, Memphis, Tennessee).

1993[23]

The meeting to which the Patriarch of the Russian Orthodox Church had invited United Methodist Church leaders was held January 21-22, 1993, in Moscow. There were many subjects of discussion, such as humanitarian aid, United Methodist presence in Russia, development of congregations, mission, and evangelism. There was no consensus on these matters, and it should be noted that not all actions of The United Methodist Church and its Russia Initiative have met with Russian Orthodox Church approval. It was agreed, however, that both church bodies commit themselves to further dialogue. To that end, a working committee was appointed to continue the discussions of issues and questions that had been raised during this meeting and previous ones. The most significant result is that these two churches, which understand themselves to be part of the one Church of Jesus Christ, agreed to the continuance of dialogue.

A project known as the "Blagovest 'Good News' Village," approved by UMCOR in January 1993, illustrates one way in which United Methodist and Russian Orthodox Churches may share in cooperative ministry in the present and future. In Blagovest, a village in the countryside south of Moscow, the local church has been returned to the Orthodox Church by the Russian government. The "Good News" Village is a concept of outreach being developed by the Russian Orthodox Church. Its primary purpose is to "provide good, medical care and housing for low income, elderly 'pensioners' who are currently living alone and physically unable to provide for themselves."[24] UMCOR made an initial grant of $30,000 to this program.

In other parts of Russia UMCOR is helping develop a "Prisoners Aid Program," soup kitchens, cottage industries, and quality care for children, women, and other persons-at-risk who are hospitalized, institutionalized, or otherwise in need.

In the spring of 1993 UMCOR also approved a grant of $30,000 over three years for the support of the establishment of a Russian Orthodox university located on Arbat Street in Moscow.

During the summer of 1993, plans were developed for United Methodist Volunteers in Mission teams to participate in projects of the Russia Initiative.

During August 1993 the Women's Division of GBGM sent a staff team of women to Russia to explore diverse possibilities of outreach. Ms. Joyce Sohl, deputy general secretary of the Women's Division, accompanied the team and outlined the fourfold purpose as follows:[25]

1. To determine ways that the World and Women's Divisions can assist in meeting the needs of women, children, and youth in the newly established worshipping communities;
2. To meet with women of the Russian Orthodox Church to gain understanding of their concerns and needs;
3. To ascertain the changing role of women in the Russian society;
4. To meet women active in various segments of society.

The team's visit illuminated a variety of complex issues facing women in Russia today and established contacts with several different groups of women. As a result, Sohl reports that "Assistance has been given to the Russian Orthodox women regarding the formation of a women's organization within their church."[26] The Women's Division is also seeking ways to bring clergy and laity of The United Methodist Church together with Russian Orthodox women and women of various secular organizations to focus on concerns of women and to examine the networking of service ministries to women and children throughout the country. Grants have already been made to several organizations that work with women and children in the area of Saint Petersburg. The Women's Division is also seeking ways to assist the women now serving United Methodist churches in Russia as laypastors with their pursuit of education and to establish relationships with other women in ministry.

In December 1993 another delegation of United Methodist leaders visited Russia. It included Dr. Randolph Nugent, Bishop J. Woodrow Hearn, the Rev. Dwight Ramsey, and Dr. Kenneth Lutgen. Two meetings were of particular significance. First, Patriarch Aleksy II of the Russian Orthodox Church invited Dr. Nugent to a private meeting in his home at Peradelkina. They discussed a number of matters of mutual interest to the two churches, particularly the desire to join in mission in the eastern part of the country and to work on a concept of continued dialogue that would be cordial and beneficial to both communions. Second, Hearn, Ramsey, and Lutgen were invited to meet with Mrs. Boris Yeltsin, wife of the president of Russia.

Also during 1993 the Moscow United Methodist Church established two more congregations: Perovskaya United Methodist Church (November 13, 1993), founded by Andrei Kim, and the Chinese United Methodist Church (November 15, 1993). Susanna Cho began a special work with children on November 6, 1993. During the winter of 1993, through UMCOR, United Methodists provided winter coats for Armenia (125,000 coats valued at $1.7 million).

1994

United Methodism's presence in Russia and Ukraine today reflects a Wesleyan response to human need, spiritual and physical. As of 1994 there are twenty-two United Methodist churches in Russia and two in Ukraine.

Russia

Ekaterinburg	First United Methodist Church, (est. 1990)
	Pastor, Lydia Istomina
	United Methodist Church "Return" (est. 1994)
	Pastor, Elena Stepanova
Lytkarino	Lytkarino United Methodist Church
	Pastor, Vladimir Makarov
Moscow	Russian-American-Korean United Methodist Church (est. 1991)
	Pastor, Young Cheul Cho
	Moscow Northern United Methodist Church (est. 1992)
	Pastor: Vallery Ho
	Solntsevo United Methodist Church (est. 1992)
	Pastor: Andrei Hmyrov
	Vnukovo United Methodist Church (est. 1992)
	Pastor: Dmitri Lee
	Perovo United Methodist Church (est. 1993)
	Pastor: Andrei Kim
	Chinese United Methodist Church (est. 1993)
	Pastor: to be appointed
	First United Methodist Church, Moscow (est. 1992)
	Pastor: Ludmila Garbuzova
	Moscow United Methodist Church (est. 1993)
	Pastor: Yo Han Choi
	Calvary United Methodist Church (est. 1993)
	Pastor: Park Sun E
	Olympic United Methodist Church (est. 1993)
	Pastor: Nak In Sung
Pskov	United Methodist Church, Pskov (est. 1992)
	Pastor: Nelly Mamanova
Samara	Samara United Methodist Church (est. 1991)
	Pastor: Vladislav Spektorov

Saint Petersburg	First United Methodist Church (est. 1992) Pastor: William Lovelace Holy Trinity United Methodist Church (est. 1993) Pastor: Oksana Petrova Bethany United Methodist Church, Saint Petersburg-Pushkin (est. 1992) Pastor: Andrei Pupko Mary and Martha United Methodist Church Pastor: Andrei Pupko
Ulyanovsk	Ulyanovsk United Methodist Church (est. 1994) Pastor: to be appointed
Voronesh	Voronesh United Methodist Church Pastor: Vyacheslav Kim
Yuzno-Sakhalinsk	Sakhaline United Methodist Church Pastor: Rev. Kyang Seuk (Paul) Choi Mrs. Eun-Kyung Choi
Ukraine	
Kerch	Kerch United Methodist Church (est. 1994) Pastor: to be appointed
Sevastopol	Sevastopol United Methodist Church (est. 1992) Pastor: Ivan Koslov

(The United Methodist churches in Uzhgorod and Kaminica, though in Ukraine, are affiliated with the Hungarian Annual Conference and hence are not under the episcopal jurisdiction of the bishop of Eurasia.)

There are also fellowships relating to United Methodism in the following cities: Chapayevsk, Kerch (Crimea, Ukraine), Moscow, Nabereshniye Chelny, Otradny, Podolsk, Pyshma, Syzran, Ulyanovsk.

The following United Methodist missionaries are stationed in Russia:

Moscow

The Rev. Young Cheul Cho, Mrs. Susanna Cho, The Rev. Yo Han Choi, Ms. Chris Hena, Ms. Sun Lae Kim, Ms. Seung Ye Park, Mr. Nak In Sung, The Rev. William Warnock, Mrs. Grace Warnock

Saint Petersburg

The Rev. William Lovelace

Ulyanovsk

The Rev. Brian Kent, Mrs. Lorena Kent

In September 1994 the Patriarch of Moscow and All Russia, Aleksy II, made a historic visit to Alaska, marking the bicentennial of the Orthodox Church in Alaska. On September 19 he was awarded an honorary degree of Doctor of Divinity by Alaska Pacific University, a United Methodist-related institution. The president of the university, Dr. F. Thomas Trotter, paid this tribute to the Patriarch in conferring the degree:

> Your Holiness, Aleksy II, Patriarch of Moscow and All Russia, you have come to celebrate the bicentennial of the arrival of the first Christian missionaries to Alaska. You are the descendent of those priests who first came to Alaska and the spiritual leader of over 60 million Orthodox Christians living in Russia, Ukraine, and other parts of the world. After completing your theological studies at the Leningrad Theological Seminary, you returned to your home republic of Estonia in 1961, you became active in the Department of External Church Relations for the Moscow Patriarchate where you published 180 articles on theological, historical, and ecumenical issues. In 1986, you became Metropolitan of Leningrad and Novgorod, and were enthroned as Patriarch of Moscow and All Russia in 1990. You have courageously led your people into a time of dramatic change in your country, discouraging violence in the August 1991, coup, encouraging democratic institutions, reopening religious schools, establishing an Orthodox-Christian youth movement, and opening relationships with other Christian communities around the world. Alaska Pacific University has historic ties with the United Methodist Church and cherishes its active relationship with other religious bodies, especially the Russian Orthodox community in Alaska. On your historic visit to Alaska, we remember those faithful ties and honor them as we honor you with the degree of Doctor of Divinity (*honoris causa*).[27]

The Patriarch replied: "I accept this honor from Alaska Pacific University not for myself, but for the whole Russian Orthodox Church who brought education and the gospel to Alaska."[28] This historic honoring of the leader of the Russian Orthodox Church by a United Methodist-related institution of higher learning signals the continuing ecumenical ties fostered by Orthodoxy and United Methodism.

Before making some concluding comments on the importance of United Methodist and Russian Orthodox dialogue for the future, it is essential to survey briefly the reestablishment of Methodism in Latvia, which was once a part of the old Russian Empire and for half a century under the domination of the Soviet Union, the outreach of GBGM's Health and Welfare Ministries Program Department in Kazakhstan, and the work of the Korean Methodist Church in the CIS.

The Rebirth of Methodism in Latvia and Lithuania

Latvia

The birth and demise of Methodism in Latvia is intimately bound to the twentieth century history of the old Russian Empire and the Soviet Union. After its liquidation in 1946/1947 by the Soviets, it lay dormant for more than forty years. Latvia had a brief respite of independence (as did Methodism) between the world wars, but during the Second World War it was conquered first by the Soviets, then by the Germans, and once again by the Soviets and absorbed into the Soviet Union. Believing that Methodists had served as agents of the CIA of the United States, the new Communist regime forced any remaining Methodists to join the Lutheran Church and confiscated all church property. Latvia received its independence once again under Mikhail Gorbachev in 1990, which has enabled the rebirth of Methodism. The story of that rebirth begins with Agnes Plavinskis, the widow of a former Latvian Methodist pastor of the Baltic and Slavic Mission Conference. Mrs. Plavinskis was living in Liepaja, Latvia, and in 1989 she wrote to Mr. Fritz Hervarth, an expatriate Latvian living in Massachusetts who once served as a youth pastor and choir director at the "Friendship in the Gospel" Methodist Church in Riga. He was to have been ordained by Bishop Raymond Wade at the Baltic and Slavic Annual Conference in July 1940, but the Soviet invasion in June prevented the bishop's entry into the country. As the Riga church could no longer afford two pastors, in January 1941 Hervarth became an assistant to the pastor of the Landze Lutheran Church in Zura, Latvia, a position he held until he was arrested by the Gestapo for hiding Jews. He was soon freed, however, and fled to Sweden where he became a pastor of a Mission church until 1948, when he and some companions made a daring voyage by sailboat to the United States. With the turn of political events in 1990, Hervarth returned to Latvia for the first time in forty-eight years. The following year he made another trip and met with Mrs. Plavinskis and a Lutheran pastor by the name of the Rev. Arys Viksna and encouraged them to work for the rebirth of Methodism in Latvia.

At the July 8, 1990, meeting of the annual conference in Tallinn, Estonia, the Latvian United Methodist Church was officially reconstituted with two pastors, the Rev. James Sturitis, a former pastor of the underground Pentecostal church, and the Rev. Arys Viksna, and representatives of two congregations as the founding members. Latvian Methodism had been officially reborn. In September 1990 Hervarth was contacted by the Rev. James Sturitis, who expressed his commitment to the revival of the Latvian United Methodist Church. Shortly thereafter the government agreed to return church property taken by the Communists in 1946 to the legal owners, if proof of ownership could be provided. Hervarth was able to designate specific previously owned Methodist Church properties in Latvia. He asked Sturitis to contact a lawyer in Riga and provided money for initial legal expenses to begin the process of returning the properties. Thereafter he contacted the United Methodist Church in South Yarmouth, Massachusetts, which is near his home and where the Rev. Roger A. Davis is pastor, requesting additional assistance. The Rev. Davis and the congregation financially and spiritually supported Hervarth and others to help them reclaim the Methodist properties. It is important to note that the legal documents regarding these properties had been preserved by the district superintendent of Latvia, Fricis Timbers, when he fled the country in 1940 in the face of the Soviet takeover. He carried them in a cloth bag during six years of flight until 1946, when he personally placed them in the hands of Bishop Paul N. Garber in Zurich, Switzerland. Thus the mission agency of The Methodist Church became the repository for these valuable documents. In March 1992 the original ownership certificates were sent to Hervarth, verifying that three properties were formerly owned by the Foreign Mission Board of the Methodist Episcopal Church before the Communists had taken them. GBGM was contacted immediately, and through a meeting of the Rev. Robert Harman and Bishop Hans Växby it was agreed that GBGM would assume the legal costs for processing the return of the properties. During the same month Hervarth received word that a Methodist congregation had been initiated once again in Liepaja, of which Mrs. Plavinskis is a member.

On March 23, 1992, Bishop Rüdiger Minor traveled to Riga, Latvia, accompanied by the Rev. and Mrs. Sturitis, and met with Mr. Janis Timpa of the Religious Organizations of the Latvian Ministry of Justice and Archbishop Karlis Gailitis of the Lutheran Church in Latvia to examine the situation of the Methodist properties. They visited three properties in Riga that were previously owned by the Methodist Church. The properties were located on Elizabeth, Akas, and Slokas streets. The Elizabeth Street property, a four-story building that once housed the Methodist Seminary, a Methodist congregation, and two dwellings for staff, was filled with apartments and families. The Akas Street property had been turned into a sports center and in the center of the sanctuary stood a boxing ring. A United Methodist congregation of a few former Methodists and new persons[29] has been reestablished and is meeting in a room of the Akas Street building, which had been outfitted for gymnastics during the Communist period. The pastor is Andris Vainovskis. The Slokas Street property was built by the Latvian Methodist Church in the 1930s, and hence was not a property owned by the Foreign Mission Board of the Methodist Episcopal Church.

When the Soviets forced remaining Methodist pastors and congregations to become Lutherans, the pastor and most of the remaining members of the Methodist church on Slokas Street became Lutheran. Today, however, the building has been restored to the United Methodist Church and is being served by the Rev. Milda Vainovskis. These congregations in Riga and one in Liepaja are now a part of the newly formed Latvian District of the Estonia Provisional Annual Conference.

No one anticipated that before the end of the twentieth century God would raise a Latvian Methodist remnant out of the rubble of the defeat and the despair of Communist domination. But now the voice and embrace of Christ's redemption and healing can once again be heard and felt through the few who remain and who have never lost the vision of Holy Scripture and of the Wesleys: that life can be reclaimed and renewed through God's love—love that goes in search of and seeks justice for all human beings and all creation at all costs, even death upon a cross.

There is an important climax to this story of Methodism's rebirth in Latvia. In deep appreciation and acknowledgment of all that Fritz Hervarth had done to enable the renewal of Methodism in his homeland, Bishop Hans Växby expressed the desire to effect the Methodist ordination Hervarth had been denied by the Soviet takeover of Latvia. The Rev. Roger A. Davis has provided this account of what transpired.

> In April, Fritz and I spoke with Bishop Hans Växby on the phone. He was most gracious and appreciative of all that Fritz had done. He spoke of the esteem with which the Latvian Methodists held him. Because of all Fritz had done, he said that he would be glad to ordain [him], but he could not do so unless Fritz was a member of the Methodist Church. Asked whether Fritz becoming a member of our church would meet the requirement, the Bishop said it would.
>
> On the day of Pentecost, with the words of the prophet Joel ringing in our ears, in which God declares, "that I will pour out my Spirit upon all flesh, and your sons and your daughters shall prophesy, and your young men shall see visions, and your old men shall dream dreams," Fritz became a member of the South Yarmouth United Methodist Church [South Yarmouth, Massachusetts]. It was an emotional service.
>
> On June 19th, at the Southern New England Annual Conference, meeting in Springfield, Massachusetts, in another emotional service, described as an "historic ordination," a dream came true as Bishop Skeete, as a courtesy to Bishop Växby of Northern Europe, ordained Fritz as an elder in the Estonia Provisional Annual Conference of the United Methodist Church. Could there be any doubt that God is faithful?[30]

Lithuania

During the period November 5-10, 1994 Dr. S T Kimbrough, Jr., Executive Secretary of Mission Evangelism of the GBGM, Dr. James White, Executive Secretary for Europe of the World Division of GBGM, The Rev. Arthur Leifert, who was born in Lithuania and was an active member of the Methodist Episcopal Church in Tauragė, Lithuania and entered the Methodist seminary at Frankfurt, Germany from the Baltic and Slavic Missionary Conference, traveled to Lithuania to explore the former sites of Methodist churches, to meet with archival officials regarding research of church documents and history, properties, and members, and to meet with remaining Methodists in Lithuania.

They visited the sites of former Methodist congregations in Kaunas, Piviškiai, Kybartai, Tauragė, Šiauliai, Biržai, and Vilnius and found the following properties: the church and two parsonages in Kaunas, the church in Pilviškiai, and the parsonage in Tauragė. There were no Methodist properties in Šiauliai, Biržai, and Vilnius. The church buildings in Tauragė and Kybartai no longer exist.

In Tauragė they were welcomed by Bishop Jonas Kalvanus, the Lutheran bishop, who entertained them in his home and who spoke with great affection about the relationship of Lutherans and Methodists. He expressed hope that Methodism would return to Lithuania soon. In Tauragė they also visited a former member of the Methodist Episcopal Church, Else Bendikienė, who has not been able to worship in a Methodist church for over fifty-five years. They also visited the former Methodist Episcopal Church parsonage in Tauragė.

In Pilviškiai they found the former Methodist Episcopal Church which is still standing in the Šiančiai section of the city. It is in very bad repair but is still used as a sport center for table tennis and gymnastics. The two parsonages which were also owned by the church are still standing and are used as dwellings, though in terrible condition.

In Šiauliai through the assistance of Mr. Algimantes Serafinavičius the GBGM team visited the house which once belonged to Rev. Kostas Burbulys, who was a Methodist Episcopal minister in that city. The congregation met in his home. The property was returned to him within the last three years and has been donated to a Baptist congregation. Mr. Serfinavičius, who was baptized by the Methodist Episcopal minister of Šiauliai, Rev. Burbulys, still lives in that city and is very anxious to assist United Methodism to return to Lithuania in general and to Šiauliai in particular.

In Biržai Kimbrough, White, and Leifert visited the building on Kestucio St. 3, where a Methodist congregation once rented space and held its services. They met with relatives of Rev. Burbulys in Biržai and with a former member of the church there, Maryte Kezelytė.

In Kaunas and Vilnius Dr. Kimbrough began the process of historical research related to the Methodist Episcopal Church in Lithuania from 1900 to 1944. He and his colleagues were most graciously received and were provided some initial documents discovered by the National Archives in Vilnius.

In Vilnius they also visited the Children's University Hospital and explored possibilities of how The United Methodist Church might assist with needs of this medical facility and other health care institutions in Lithuania.

After consultations in Helsinki, Finland between Bishop Hans Växby of the Northern European Central Conference of The United Methodist Church and GBGM staff (Dr. Randolph Nugent, General Secretary, Dr. James White, and Dr. S T Kimbrough, Jr.), a second exploratory trip was made to Lithuania from February 8 to 14, 1994 by Kimbrough, White, and Ms. Cathie Lyons, Deputy General Secretary of the Health and Welfare Program Department of GBGM.

They examined the possibilities for assistance and outreach in Vilnius with the Children's University Hospital and State Children's Home #1. Visits were made to both facilities and extensive conversations held with officials.

Dr. Kimbrough's further research turned up numerous documents which provided careful descriptions of all former Methodist properties and their addresses. An important letter of April 12, 1906 from the Ministry of Internal Affairs of the Department of Foreign Religions in St. Petersburg was found which authorized the Methodist Episcopal Church in Kaunas to hold services and which acknowledged the receipt of the request to build a church.

The documents illustrate that the Methodist Episcopal Church was a bona fide and legally recognized church in Lithuania in the early part of the twentieth century and that the Russian imperial government through its offices in St. Petersburg approved the holding of Methodist Episcopal worship services, organization of congregations, and the building of churches.

A third trip to Lithuania was made from May 16 to 19, 1995 by The Rev. Robert Harman, Dr. S T Kimbrough, Jr., and lawyer, Mr. Timothy Jaroch, to investigate reclamation of former Methodist properties. Sites of former churches and parsonages in Tauragė, Pilviškiai, and Kaunas were visited.

On May 18 Harman and Kimbrough had the unique privilege of bringing together a small group of former members of the Kaunas church, who have remained there throughout the Soviet period to the present: Atonina

Suliakienė, Liongina Bungardienė, and Irene Tylienė. Another member, Mr. Honoratus Owaldas, was not able to join the group, due to other commitments that day. They rejoiced over the possibility of the renewal of their congregation and the reestablishment of Methodism in Lithuania.

Meetings with the vice-mayor of Kaunas and other government officials revealed the process to be followed for registration of United Methodist congregations in Lithuania and for the reclamation of property.

Methodists in Lithuania have been denied their places of worship and existence as a religious body for over fifty years, but Methodism is now being renewed through the faithful who have remained in Kaunas and in other cities of Lithuania throughout the Soviet period.

Outreach in Kazakhstan

The Health and Welfare Ministries program department began work in the Semipalatinsk Region of eastern Kazakhstan in April 1993. The region served for forty years as the primary nuclear testing area for the Soviet Union. From August 1949, beginning with the atomic bomb, through 1989 some 563 nuclear weapons were tested in the Semipalatinsk Region. More than a million people there and in neighboring areas of Russia have been repeatedly exposed to radiation.There has been repeated radiation exposure to over a million people there and in neighboring areas of Russia.

This tragedy has produced overwhelming needs in the arenas of health care and medicine. In the Seminpalatinsk Region hospitals have received more than $250,000 worth of medicines from The United Methodist Church through the Health and Welfare Ministries of GBGM. Cathie Lyons, associate general secretary of the Health and Welfare Ministries Program Department, reports as follows:[31]

> The focus of the Department's/GBGM's work presently includes: working with orphanages and special schools caring for children and youth who have been affected by the nuclear testing. The Ayaguz Orphanage House for Mentally Retarded Children serves 320 severely affected children and youth. The majority of these children were born into families which lived in the villages adjacent to the test areas. Flat bed carts were delivered to Ayaguz in December 1993 for use by children who are unable to sit in wheelchairs. Medicines were delivered to Ayaguz in February 1994 and in the summer of 1994 a team of specialists in developmental pediatrics and the care of children and youth with severe mental retardation worked with the staff of Ayaguz to exchange information and knowledge.
>
> In June 1994 partner relationships were formed between United Methodist-related child care agencies in the United States and similar programs in the Semipalatinsk Region. The Baby Fold in Normal, Illinois and Orphanage #3 in Semipalatinsk City both serve children in need from shortly after birth

to age seven and have much to learn from and share with one another. Flat Rock Home for Children and Adults in Flat Rock, Ohio, which serves mentally retarded and/or developmentally disabled children, youth and adults has entered a relationship with the Ayaguz Orphanage for Mentally Retarded Children. Conversations are underway regarding the possibility of finding partner agencies among United Methodist child care and retirement and long term care programs to work with the Semipalatinsk Special School for the Deaf and the city's Nursing Home which provides ongoing care for the children from the Ayaguz facility after they have reached age 18. Hearing aids by the Siemens Company were presented to the School for the Deaf in December.

United Methodist hospitals and dentists in the United States have donated renovated hospital and dental equipment to the Health and Welfare Ministries Program Department. It has been shipped to the Semipalatinsk Region, where U.S. facilities will sponsor on-site training in the use and maintenance of the equipment. This has enabled the establishment of a pediatric dental program and the upgrading of a dental room in a psychiatric facility.

Lyons reports further:[32]

> The Department is responding to a request from Dr. Boris Gusev, Director of the Kazakh Scientific-Research Institute for Radiation Medicine and Ecology, for opportunities for scientific exchange between USA scientists and physicians in the field of radiation medicine and ecology and the physicians at the Institute. A series of three events was held in 1994 which enabled exchanges of personnel and information. Drs. Bakhyt Tumenova, Boris Gusev, and Zhaksibay Zhumadilov traveled to the United States in April and October of 1994 for dialogue with USA scientists and physicians. In the summer of 1994 a team of USA scientists travelled to Semipalatinsk to work with physicians at the Kazakh Scientific-Research Institute for Radiation Medicine and Ecology and the Kazakh Medical Institute.
>
> GBGM's work in this Central Asia Republic is providing opportunities for United Methodist professionals through the Health and Welfare Ministries Program Department to work directly with Muslim professionals of the Semipalatinsk Region in helping and healing ministries. The welcome and hospitality which have been extended to United Methodist teams in this region by the Muslim doctors and child care workers is a witness to interfaith cooperation through ministries of mutual concern extended to communities which bear a heavy burden of illness and other problems associated with the four decades of nuclear testing.

Just as Methodist workers in Saint Petersburg more than a half century ago supplied aid to state hospitals and child care facilities, so today United Methodist missional outreach remains faithful to a Wesleyan holistic witness that bypasses no human need. Cathie Lyons summarized this witness eloquently in the following words.

197

I confess that I feel most comfortable with mission evangelism when it is intimately related to health ministries for, indeed, I do not believe the two can be separated. In Russia and the other republics of the former Soviet Union, health workers and hospitals are embracing the Health and Welfare Ministries of GBGM and the United Methodist Church with open arms and deeply grateful hearts. I believe we have much to learn from Russian health workers and from the people of the former USSR. It is indeed a place where one can recognize the crucified and risen Christ in persons, many of whom have known the fear of persecution and the practice of state-imprisoned atheism for a lifetime.[33]

The Korean Methodist Church in Countries of the Former Soviet Union

In January 1988 the Rev. Sundo Kim, senior pastor of the Kwang Lim Methodist Church in Seoul, Korea, traveled to Moscow with his wife and representatives of his congregation where they met with Mr. Mikhail Kang, a Korean-Russian resident of Moscow, government officials, and leaders of the Russian Orthodox Church. From the time of this visit in 1988 to 1991, two additional trips were made to investigate the establishment of a mission center in Moscow. On March 14, 1991, a contract was finalized providing a twenty-five year lease for the use of land and an existing building located at Koptevskaya Street 30A in Moscow. The building was designated for use as a mission, cultural, and trade center. It would provide international trade services and cultural training, and religious education would be permitted.

When it became obvious that efforts to renovate the aged building were futile, it was demolished and plans for a new building were procured. The ground-breaking ceremony for the Kwang Lim Mission Center took place on September 10, 1991. The Kwang Lim Methodist Church in Seoul, for which the center is named, sent its first missionary, Mr. Eun Chul Yun, to Moscow on January 29, 1993.

The Kwang Lim Methodist Church has also extended its missionary outreach to Estonia. After a 1992 trip to Moscow, Dr. and Mrs. Sundo Kim returned to Korea by way of Estonia, where they encountered many needs among the United Methodists. As a result of contacts made at the time, in September 1993 the Rev. Olaf Pärnamets and the Rev. Toomas Pajusoo, pastor and associate pastor, respectively, of the Tallinn United Methodist Church in Tallinn, Estonia, visited Seoul, Korea, where they met with Dr. Kim and officials of the mission societies of the Kwang Lim Methodist Church and presented plans for a Baltic Mission Center. Its purpose is to train ministers and laity for the work of United Methodism in the Baltic countries. On September 18, 1993, the mission societies of the Kwang Lim

Methodist Church (Men's Mission Society, Women's Mission Society) committed $1 million over a two-year period for the center, which is to be a two-story building with facilities for worship, classrooms, offices, and a library.

At present the Korean Methodist churches have twenty-one missionaries in countries of the former Soviet Union:

Russia

The Rev. Joong Kyu Kim, the Rev. Chang Gook Oh, Mr. Nak In Sung, the Rev. Hae Kun Kim, the Rev. Ji Yeol Yoo, the Rev. Kwang Ok Kim, Mr. Jin Ho Lim, the Rev. Wung Ik Hwang, Ms. Pil Yeo Park, the Rev. Sun Il Kim, the Rev. Sung Chan Choi, the Rev. Dong Geon Lee, the Rev. Hack Chul Cho, the Rev.Seong Soo Kim, the Rev. Eun Cheol Yoon, the Rev. Heung Gi Hong, the Rev. Jong Hoon Park

Kazakhstan

Mr. Chang Sup Song, Mr. Tae Hong Jung, the Rev. In Kee Lee

Uzbekistan

The Rev. Dong Wook Won

At the Korea Annual Conference, which met in Seoul in September 1920, Bishop Lambuth appointed the Rev. Chai Duk Chung as the first Korean Methodist missionary to serve on Russian soil at the Siberia-Manchuria Mission of the Methodist Episcopal Church, South, in Vladivostok. Hence, the Korean Methodist Church and American Korean United Methodist missional outreach in Russia and other countries of the CIS today represent "Methodism renewed but never abandoned!"

The Future of United Methodist and Russian Orthodox Dialogue

A primary concern for United Methodist and Russian Orthodox dialogue in the future will be the quest for an ecumenical theology that moves beyond mere conciliation to unity in Christ. If this is done seriously, it will be no mean task, and one that will involve an engaged, ongoing dialogue, especially in the following areas of concern.

First, ecumenical discussions of the last three decades have made crystal clear that churches of the Orthodox and Roman Catholic traditions understand the unity that exists within them to be God's will fully present and active in their own church life. While Konrad Reiser suggests that the Holy Trinity may become the new paradigm for shared life in the community of the faithful,[34] which could replace the hope for organic union of the church, a vital question remains as to what extent the churches are willing to stand under the corrective judgment of Holy Scripture and its revelation of God's light in Jesus Christ as to what constitutes the Body of Christ, the church. Second, an ecumenical theology of integrity must also address the question of mutual commitment (covenant) and unity in the body and blood of Jesus Christ (i.e., the Eucharist or Holy Communion). To what extent are Christians and the churches to which they belong willing to commit themselves to full communion in the Eucharist (i.e., full and mutual communion for all)?

Finally, a new day will dawn in ecumenical theology when United Methodism, Russian Orthodoxy, and all Christian churches seriously address judgment and redemption not merely in terms of self-perpetuation of ecclesial traditions and human action of the oppressed against oppressor but as God's action in Jesus Christ. Lesslie Newbigin cautions that "There is almost a total neglect of the missionary factor in the ecumenical movement."[35] Therefore, if churches of the United Methodist and Orthodox traditions are committed to an ecumenical theology, they must ask: Can a church with a total amnesia of the missional and evangelistic work of the church exist with integrity? What does the ecumenical option of "faith offered to all" mean for United Methodism and Orthodoxy?

These questions and issues, which are raised anew by the Russia Initiative of United Methodism, are at the heart of a vibrant, dynamic, and developing ecumenical theology. Responses to them will not be easy, and no one should expect quick answers. What is vital is that dialogue continues and that the heart of these matters is addressed.

Some may aver that United Methodism should not be in the CIS today. It should not *invade* the territory of Russian Orthodoxy. However, United Methodism does not need to justify its presence in terms of authentic, historical witness. It has been there before, motivated by beckoning human need and the call to offer the option of life lived out as a mandate of sacrificial love, which draws people together into community—a community of love and justice as revealed in Christ. As Donald Carl Malone has stated, "There was no need for Methodists to move into Russia for they were already there before the revolution, and although the Methodist mission was not large, it was strong enough to endure the revolution and famine."[36] Furthermore, Methodism did survive in Estonia and two Ukranian communities throughout the Bolshevik Revolution and Soviet domination amid severe suffering and oppression, as did the Russian Orthodox Church throughout the former Soviet Union. While Estonian Methodism may have been small, when compared with the size of Russian Orthodoxy, it was constant, faithful, and relentlessly persevering.

It should be added that to think of Russia and other countries of the former Soviet Union in terms of a monolithic church is to ignore the fact that millions of Russians and citizens of other countries of the CIS have no religion at all after seven decades of Bolshevik and Communist domination. Furthermore, there has been an *invasion* of these countries by western evangelicals, many of whom have little or no interest in relating to Russian Orthodoxy. Therefore, one should not be surprised at the various attempts within the Russian Parliament to limit the activity of foreign religious groups and churches. United Methodism, as a sacramental and evangelical church and member of the World Council of Churches, is committed to working with the Orthodox Church of Russia and elsewhere. Hence, it represents a sacramental, evangelical, and theological option in the context of the CIS countries that many evangelical groups and churches do not.

United Methodism must not be in Russia or any part of the CIS in order to seduce the Russian Orthodox. It is committed to a spirit of ecumenical outreach with other communions, including Orthodoxy, other denominations, and people of other living faiths. The foundations of such a spirit of mutual commitment were laid by Methodists and the *Evangelische Gemeinschaft* in the Baltic states and Russia almost a century ago. This must be the spirit of the current Russia Initiative, for the action of the General Conference of The United Methodist Church in 1992 essentially resumes the work begun over a century ago in what was then the Russian Empire. The current United Methodist bishop of Eurasia, Rüdiger R. Minor, captures this spirit in a 1992 report, when he says: "Faith development should take the first place, and we should not be sorry, if people who found living faith in a Methodist group would carry this faith into their Orthodox church."[37] And he reiterates in the same report the spirit of Christian unity implicit in United Methodist outreach:

> In this situation we need dialogue with the Russian Orthodox Church about the meaning of mission and partnership. The proposed theological conversations between Orthodox and Methodist Churches on a worldwide level can support this dialogue. The same is true for studies that are done between the churches in Europe who seek ways for a common witness to the gospel. This, again, is an area where people seek for a shift of paradigms. Neither the paradigm of treating Russia as a place for church planting like a new suburb of an American city is acceptable, nor the paradigm of treating the whole of Russia as the property of the Orthodox Church. As Methodists we should stick to our ecumenical obligation and not become weary of seeking and offering partnership in mission. We should insist on ecumenical partnership in all programs of humanitarian help. We should look for possibilities of joint efforts, for example in the fields of education, communication, and publishing. We will always look for good partnership with all churches

in Russia. Even now in some of the cities, where the UMC works, it is the only one that develops good relationships with Orthodox, as well as Protestant churches. But most of all we should challenge others and be challenged by our own tradition to be "a company of men and women having the form and seeking the power of godliness, united in order to pray together, to receive the word of exhortation, and to watch over another in love, that they may help each other work out their salvation."[38] (The General Rules of The United Methodist Church, par. 68, *The Book of Discipline*)

United Methodism is willing to look anew at the meaning of mission and evangelism and a world very different from the west but where human needs are alike, and yet, not alike. It is willing to explore new avenues of building community by the implementation of the biblical vision of reality. In that world of reality the call to be a servant of Jesus Christ is a call to loving, sacrificial service, a call to peace, harmony, and justice, a call to redemption from the evils of a world that perpetuates hatred, war, and discord. When this vision shapes missional outreach, love is *the* priority of priorities in life and service, the kind of love encountered in Jesus Christ. That love can be lived out viably with mutual respect for all people, cultures, religions, and nations, for it does not seek to nullify one's creatureliness with all the uniqueness each person comes into and journeys through this world. Instead that love affirms such uniqueness, for it comes from God.

Wesleyan Outreach and Evangelization in the Future

As churches of the Wesleyan tradition, such as the United Methodist, look toward a new century and reach out toward the east again with helpful hearts and hands, they will have to evaluate with great care their developed patterns of mission and evangelism over against Scripture, the Wesleyan tradition, contemporary contexts, and ecumenical spirit. *Evangelism* is not a word used by the Wesleys in their efforts to create gospel community centered in Jesus Christ. And one must face the fact that the word has come to be equated with North American revivalism or at least revivalistic types of evangelism. The Wesleyan pattern of outreach indeed involved confrontation with oneself before God as one in need of the redemptive love expressed in Jesus Christ. However, John Wesley did not equate decision and salvation per se. In 1745 he stated very clearly his understanding of salvation.

> By salvation I mean, not barely (according to the vulgar notion) deliverance, from hell, or going to heaven, but a present deliverance from sin, a restoration of the soul to its primitive health, its original purity; a recovery of the divine nature; the renewal of our souls after the image of God in right-

eousness and true holiness, in justice, mercy and truth. This implies all holy and heavenly tempers, and by consequence all holiness of conversation.[39]

John and Charles Wesley, as Anglican priests and founders of the Methodist movement within the Church of England, called all within the church and outside it, who would follow, to a life of holy living that was a total response to the gospel, that is, commitment to Jesus Christ is not a final experience, it is an initiating experience into gospel community where concern for the whole life of all is primary. Hence, those who follow in this tradition seek wholeness wherever they find brokenness, healing and justice where they find pain and suffering. It was in this spirit that the first Methodist missionaries went to the lands of the old Russian Empire. It is in this spirit that they go again now. One does not go with presumption or with a sense of superiority or dominance, but with a sense of humility that God is able to use human beings as vessels of healing and redemption, as frail as they may be.

People called Methodists may need to be freed from the trappings of certain understandings of the word *evangelism,* many of which are decidedly contrary to the Wesleyan tradition. *Evangelization* may be a far better word for this tradition, for it implies process and may help foster the understanding that awakening to one's lostness and need is initiation into discipleship, a lifelong quest. The Wesleys did not construct an equation as follows: *decision = salvation* or *salvation = decision.* They understood faith and practice as the lifelong process and pilgrimage of those who would follow Jesus Christ, which requires a tremendous investment of self in growth and nurture and in service to God and others. It is not surprising from this perspective that John Wesley in his later years, when asked by some preachers to share something about his own Christian experience, quoted a stanza from a hymn of his brother Charles:

Jesus, confirm my heart's desire
  To work, and speak, and think for thee,
Still let me guard the holy fire,
  And still stir up thy gift in me,

Ready for all thy perfect will
  My acts of faith and love repeat,
'Till death thy endless mercies seal,
  And make my sacrifice complete.[40]

Any Methodist work, United Methodist or other, in the CIS or elsewhere must have integration into gospel community, into a discipling process, and into sacramental life as the goals of evangelization. It was in this way that John and Charles Wesley reached out to the hungering, destitute, poverty-stricken, and wealthy masses of England. John Wesley's quotation from his brother's hymn describes the posture of one who seeks perfect love, who is constantly open to the possibility of the realization of God's will, who is ready to act in faith and to repeat acts of love. Into such discipleship one is initiated when awakening faith comes through encounter with Christ's self-giving love, and it results in constant engagement of self in thought, word, deed, and openness to the gift of the Spirit. It was within the Hebrew and Greek scriptures that the Wesleys discovered this kind of missional outreach. When a church or any part of it transforms *the Wesleyan understanding of witness and initiation into Christ's discipleship into revivalistic numericalism,* and outreach goals into membership multiplication and self-perpetuation of the church, one is indeed far removed from the Wesleys' approach to Christian witness and service.

It is in the spirit of the holistic gospel outreach of the Wesleys that United Methodism is in Russia today. Its primary interest is not merely the perpetuation of churches of the "Methodist" tradition, as much as this evangelical and sacramental fellowship within the Body of Christ is valued by its adherents. It seeks to foster a gospel community of love and healing service that is not limited by denominational boundaries. It is the redemptive love of Christ, self-giving and sacrificial love for others, that affirms and establishes such community. Where the Russian Orthodox Church and other communions can be strengthened by United Methodist engagement in any form, this can only contribute to the wholeness of Christ's church, for United Methodism is committed to the unity of the church.

What shall we say then to the work of The United Methodist Church today in Russia and the Baltic states, to its outreach in the countries now designated CIS, which were once a part of the Soviet Union, or in countries that were once under its domination? Ecumenical insensitivity would be senseless, such as a disregard for the Russian Orthodox Church and other churches of these countries. Some would plead: "Evangelize, evangelize, evangelize!" Others cry out: "Humanitarian aid only!" For those in the Wesleyan tradition, however, such sharp separation of the missional tasks is uncommon. Human beings are whole creations with holistic needs and gifts. The needs and gifts of the spirit, mind, and heart are not separate from those of the body. It is self-understood for those who stand in this tradition that the spirit of the Hebrew affirmation, "You shall love the Lord your God with all your heart, soul, mind, and strength," is the norm for loving one's neighbor and the stranger. Hence, the missional spirit of which we have spoken in this volume is an evangelization and a humanization of individuals and community, which are mutual imperatives. They are integral elements of holistic mission. In 1928, after the Siberia-Manchuria Mission of the Methodist Episcopal Church, South had been closed, four members of the Ladies' Missionary Societies in Harbin, Manchuria wrote to the Woman's Missionary Council of the church. The closing question of that letter provides cause for much reflection and soul searching as the people called Methodists seek to reach out in the CIS or anywhere in the world. They write against the backdrop of the hope of life in and through the Siberia-Manchuria Mission, which has retreated and which they alone can now continue in their own land. They ask:

> Will you accept us among your midst, our dear Sisters, will you teach us what we do not know yet, will you take interest in the worn out soul of a Russian woman, in her sufferings in the recent past and in her joys in the present new life?[41]

EPILOGUE

Sister Anna of Petrograd

It is frustrating indeed to know where to begin and where to end with due homage to the cloud of witnesses across northeastern Europe, Finland, the Baltic states and Russia, who literally gave their lives so fully in the service of Christ and the church. Scores upon scores of names appear in the pages of this book—children, women, and men. God alone knows those who to us are nameless. They were people of many different ethnic, language, and cultural backgrounds, but they shared a common vision—the biblical vision of gospel community, where love molds human relationships in self-giving service to one another imbued with the spirit of Jesus Christ. Such love is the perfect love that casts out fear and makes possible the loving of others in the fullness of their need. It is this love that is redemptive. It is this love that saves. Perhaps this Christ-like love is nowhere better exemplified in the annals of the history of *Methodism in Russia and the Baltic States* than in the person of Sister Anna Eklund, who served as a deaconess of the Methodist Episcopal Church for many years in Petrograd. The following is a tribute to Sister Anna published in 1922 by Roger Prentiss in *The Christian Advocate*.[1]

Sister Anna of Petrograd

Heroic Methodist Deaconess Who Has Remained at Her Post Through Russia's Revolutions

At six o clock one morning last August a man alighted in Petrograd from a train which had just arrived from Viborg, Finland. The church bells were ringing, for it was Sunday. He left the station and made his way afoot—no cabs or tramcars were running—to a church in a distant part of the city, over whose door appeared the words, Tserka Christa Spasityela, which being interpreted, means the Church of Christ the Savior. As he entered he was greeted by a woman in the whitecapped garb of a European Methodist deaconess.

Within he found the congregation on their knees. The service, which had been conducted by the pastor as usual, was over, but the congregation had not left the church to go to their homes. The desperate people were praying in hungry Petrograd for immediate relief. Sister Anna Eklund, who has stayed at her post during these years of isolation and suffering, was the woman who welcomed him. Sister Anna was not only praying but watching, and she saw the man when he appeared at the door. The Rev. Hjalmar Salmi it was who arrived at that critical moment—the district superintendent of the Petrograd District. He had come by permission of the Soviet Government with a consignment of goods from the Methodist European Relief and had found the Petrograd Methodists at prayer in their church.

"I shall never forget," writes Mr. Salmi, "the earnest prayers of thanksgiving that were sent up to Almighty God that morning. It was not so much what I had brought that made them rejoice as that the Mother Church in far-away America had not forgotten them and that now again the connection was established.

"I had accompanied the goods train across the border where every box was opened and the contents inspected. Nothing was taken and the cars were sealed and locked. I was then invited to take a seat in the engine, and so I entered Russia in the company of ten of the most talked of men of our time, with no other feeling than a great satisfaction that at last the long cherished wish was to be realized: to bring the greatly needed supplies to our friends in Petrograd."

A Quarterly Conference was called to arrange for the distribution of the food and clothing, and to this special session were invited the members of the society. Imagine deaconesses, district superintendents, and Quarterly Conferences in Soviet Russia! Think of it: one village Soviet has a Methodist preacher for president. How the imagination creaks at the effort to visualize these Methodist activities in the midst of the life we associate with Russia, and Soviet Russia at that. And ten Soviet leaders have invited a Methodist preacher to ride with them into Petrograd!

But when one thinks of Sister Anna's life during those terrible years, one's imagination, even though it be flexible, stretches to the breaking. To picture her at her insuperable task is beyond one's power. There are no words to express one's admiration. For more than three years she has carried on alone in Petrograd. To her is due the very existence today of the building in which the Methodist congregation meets, and the uninterrupted life of the congregation itself.

Through the Reign of Terror

Isolation, hunger, cold, fatigue, the sight of distress, the sound of the threatening roar of the mob in the street, the frequent death of friends, were her lot in the midst of active ministry and intense labor. This Phoebe, the servant of the Church of Petrograd, has in the days and nights of terror and desolation been a helper to many. She has helped in life and attended in death eighteen who died of starvation.

She has been the friend and stay of those who did not die but only lived and suffered. Among the many who looked to her for strength and succor was a young Finnish woman named Karin Sante, who endured much and that, too, for loyalty to American interests. She was left in charge of the American embassy upon the forced departure of the ambassador. When, in 1919, the embassy was looted, she was thrown into prison, released to a life of hunger and cold, and later arrested again as an American spy and sent to a concentration camp for compulsory labor. Ministry to such as she has been Sister Anna's daily task. Besides she has had the care of the churches.

"I Fought Like a Lion," Says This Gentle Lady

There was the property to be protected and the organization to be conserved. The Soviet Government's policy of confiscation of property was always in the background as a threatening Nemesis. "I have fought like a lion for the Church," Sister Anna says, "and it is safe for the present and I think for the future. I promised to find as much wood as it would yield, if we were allowed to keep it." All the church property is intact because the gentle Sister Anna can fight like a lion. It has never been out of her hands, either the Petrograd church or the chapels in the villages. Only the fence in Petrograd was taken, and probably all danger is now past, since the government is returning all property to private ownership.

But seizure of the church and deaconess home was ever imminent, not for their value for government use, but for the wood they would have yielded. The buildings in Russia's cities are marked all over with spots—like gaping wounds—from which wood has been stripped in the vain attempt to supply their populations with fuel, for as scarce as are food and clothing, fuel is even scarcer. As early as October the bitter cold of winter was upon them; in November the children were freezing in the streets, and in the so-called children's homes, in which children from three to six are brought up by the State, there was no fuel at all.

Sister Anna's promise of wood saved the church and the house; so it was that her parting words to Mr. Salmi, when he left after helping with the distribution of relief, were, "Come again soon, but do not come without fuel." Wood has been sent—several car loads of it—and Sister Anna's contract with the government kept.

Sister Anna writes about the growth of the churches with an optimism like Paul's, and in his style. Her enthusiasm for the Petrograd pastor reminds one of Paul's attitude toward Timothy. "Brother Poeld was quite emaciated during that long period when we were getting no boxes, but he never thought of abandoning his work. You cannot imagine what support I have in this young brother." Again, "The work is increasing daily and the local authorities have promised motor cars for the transportation of the goods needed for social work. My young Timothy is a great help to me and is very suitable for the work."

The Work Goes On

Of two local preachers, brothers, whom she appointed to take the place of ordained men who were forced to leave Russia to save their families from starvation, she writes as follows: "I can give the best report of Sigolowo, the village where they labor. The men out of there are working more than ever and I am sure that trained men could not have done better than these brethren. Our last visit was crowned with rich blessing. After I had made an address, immediately fifty-five persons came forward to be received into full membership, having been recommended by their local preachers. After the reception of members there came the Epworth League with thirty-five members."

"Our work in Petrograd is going forward with great strides," she continues. "Our church now has fifty members, not counting the young people and children. Many have long ago asked to become members and are waiting with longing hearts to be received. I have refrained from receiving them in order to examine them more." A disciple of Paul in her discipline, too.

"The time appears to be ripe to resume relations with Russia," says an editorial in the current number of the *World's Work*. The magazine is speaking of economic and political relations. Lenin has confessed to defeat on his economic front and has advised a change of policy. Whatever may be imminent in the economic realm, it is true that the doors are open for Methodism in Russia. It is the only American Church with continued active operation in Russia under the Soviet regime.

Sharing Food and Clothing with Soviet Children's Homes

Sister Anna's heroism and self-sacrifice have been appreciated by even Soviet leaders. "In the Methodist Church we see what living Christianity means for a community," they say. Food, clothing, and wood from the Methodist European Relief supplies have been shared with the Soviet children's homes.

"We often meet the children who have been clothed by us, and, greeting us in a friendly manner, they swing their caps at us, and their joy—genuine children's joy—radiates from their eyes. They visit us off and on and we are invited to their place. Last Sunday we spent the evening in such an institution. The children rendered a program. They wished to send their greeting to the children of America." They all know Sister Anna, for she personally distributes the food and clothing, and since early autumn she has had the joy of receiving regular shipments.

Recognition of Her Service

On November 6, the thirteenth anniversary of Sister Anna's coming to Saint Petersburg was celebrated. A teacher from one of the Soviet schools, a member of the Methodist Episcopal Church, made an address from which the following extract is taken:

> Sister Anna had a hard time at first in this strange place, not knowing the Russian language, but Sister Anna had another language—the language of love to suffering mankind. The poor, sick and the distressed understood her very well. Who does not know Sister Anna? How many poor has she visited, how many sick has she helped, how many unhappy has she comforted, and how many tears has she dried! Her work was always hard, but God wanted her to do more.
>
> The World War began, then started the Revolution, and Dr. Simons, being an American citizen, was obliged to leave Russia and his beloved work and church. To whom shall he entrust the work? He does not hesitate a moment and hands everything over to Sister Anna.
>
> Here begins the hardest time of all for Sister Anna. All communication with America is broken off. Many of the congregation have to leave. Her money is all gone. How shall she keep up the work, how shall she help the poor, how shall she exist herself? Without hesitation she sacrifices her own things and tries to help others who have less than she.
>
> She could leave Russia. She has a home only a day's ride away. She could live there better than here, but no hardships could make her leave our church and the little group of friends.
>
> Thirteen years of very hard work but very blessed work of this self-denying worker in the vineyard of the Lord.

In the beginning of our story we saw Sister, standing like a sentinel on a city wall, looking for tidings from friends from whom she had been cut off for weary months. We leave her riding through the streets of Petrograd, seated high on her precious boxes of food and clothing, which she will give to her friends, the children, who greet her cheerily from the street as they watch her pass by on her beneficent way.[2]

* * * * * *

Here we have a vision of the spirit of Wesleyan missions wherever they are found: the gospel of love bypasses no human need.

Against the backdrop of the missional spirit and action of the Evangelical and Methodist churches described in this volume, one must ask—Is there no place today for the Sister Annas and Sister Bertas, for the Brother Kuums and Brother Simons in the countries of the Baltic region and the former Soviet Union? Were their lives lived in vain? Was their vision and that of their church anti-ecumenical? They lived out a simple, holistic vision of the gospel of love, which sought to reclaim all that was evil in human beings and the world around them, and to surround them with a world of loving justice. They saw this vision fully expressed in Jesus Christ and dared to articulate the vision with their lives through communities of faith, which were then called "Evangelical" and "Methodist."

Wherever they served it was in a spirit of Christian unity seeking and offering mutual support. Numerous groups and denominations cooperated in a variety of ventures in the Baltic region, such as the building of schools, sharing of food, Bible conferences, and choir festivals, and in Russia, such as Methodist financial support to reopen a Russian Orthodox school of theology, which had been closed by the Bolsheviks. This is no ecumenical romanticizing of history to make it fit a contemporary theology; the facts bear the testimony.

The more we learn from these saints of our past, the more we shall know how to respond to the same needs of human beings and their worlds today, and how to be faithful to the gospel of Christ's love.

Having begun this volume with a chapter by Bishop John L. Nuelsen, it is appropriate to close with his words written in 1925, which could have been written today: "No, religion is not dead in Russia. To the contrary. There is a seeking after God, the living God. . . . Life from God, the work of the Savior, and the powerful evidence of God's spirit are not bound to human-made forms and to historically evolved institutions. The Spirit of God is at work in Russia and many doors are open to the gospel."[3]

TIMELINE

Timeline of Methodism in the Baltic States and Russia, and The Evangelical Church in Latvia

1. Timeline of the Beginnings of Methodism in the Baltic States (Methodist Church of Germany and Methodist Episcopal Church)

1839—Maria Charlotte Hydén begins a Methodist Sunday school in Finland.

1859—Gustav Lervik begins Methodist work in Korsholm, Finland. The first Methodist church in founded in Sweden.

1866—Return of Wilhelm and Gustav Bärnlund to their native Finland (henceforth = F) and the city of Kristinestad (F).

1869—B. A. Carlson is sent to continue Methodist work in Sweden.

1870 & 1874—Gustav Bärnlund travels to Sweden to request of the conference a pastor for Finland; a Swedish lay preacher, Karl Johan Lindborg, goes to Vaasa (F).

1881—Lindborg goes to Vaasa (Nikloaistad); a district is established by Lindborg from Kristinestad (F) to Åbo (F) in the south and to Gamlakarleby (F) in the north; a seaman's mission is established in Kotka by the Lutheran Church. The Methodist Church takes it over in 1901.

1881-82—Lindborg preaches in Saint Petersburg, Russia to a Swedish-speaking group and begins to publish the *Finska Evangelisten (The Finnish Evangelist)*.

1882—The first Methodist church opened in Vaasa, August 30.

1883—Swedish preacher Wagnsson is sent by the conference to Vaasa; a congregation is established at Gamlakarleby, August 19.

1884—B. A. Carlson of Sweden is sent to Helsinki (F).

In the spring Lindborg preaches in Helsinki for the first time.

1885—Finland is made into a special district with three preachers and 174 members; Carlson is forbidden to speak in Helsinki.

1886—A congregation is established in Åbo; B. A. Carlson begins to publish *Nya Budbären (The New Messenger)*.

Nov. 16-18, 1886—The first preaching mission with Finnish preacher, J. W. Häggmann, is held in Vaasa.

1887—K. Lindborg is sent to Björneborg (F).

1888—B.A. Carlson is invited to Russia.

1891—The Methodist Episcopal Church receives the right of cooperation and is officially recognized by the government of Finland. K. U. Strandberg is given charge of the church in St. Petersburg.

1892—A congregation is established in Viborg; Bishop Joyce organizes the "Finland and Saint Petersburg Mission." Roth is made superintendent and Carlson returns to Sweden.

1893—Roth is replaced by N. J. Rosén; Finnish and Swedish youth organizations are established.

1895—A Methodist church is founded in Hangö (F).

1899—A Methodist church is founded in Lovisa (F).

1900—Contact is made between a small, independent congregation in Kaunas, Lithuania and the Methodist Church in Köningsberg, Germany; as a result the independent congregation joins the Methodist Church and a new congregation is begun in Kybartai/Virbalis (Lithuania). The two Lithuanian congregations remain part of the annual conference of Northern Germany until 1907.

1903—A mission conference is organized with two districts: Swedish and Finnish.

Aug. 21, 1904—The congregation in Viborg dedicates its church.

1904—The first conference is held in Hangö (F).

April 17, 1905—Tsar of Russia gives country a constitution that guarantees religious freedom.

1906—The government of Russia officially recognizes the Methodist Episcopal Church in Lithuania (Kaunas).

1907—The congregations at Kuanas and Kybartai/Virbalis are separated from the annual conference of Northern Germany and related to Simons's work.

1908—The first Methodist congregation in Estonia (henceforth = E) is begun in Kuressaare (E).

The Annual Conference in Finland consists of three districts: Finnish, Swedish, and Russian. The Russian district has work in St. Petersburg (R), Khandrovo (R), Kaunas (LI), Virbalis/Kybartai (LI), and Vilnius (LI).

1909—Evangelistic meetings are held on the Island of Ösel (E); congregations are begun in Arensburg (E) and elsewhere on the island and are organized by Martin Prikask. A Methodist chapel is dedicated at Kybartai/Virbalis (LI), the first Methodist house of worship in Tsarist Russia. New Methodist work is established in the Russian district at Lodz and Riga, Latvia (henceforth = LA).

1910—The Kuressaare congregation is recognized as a Methodist Church; Riga, Latvia (henceforth = LA) is listed as a Methodist appointment. New Methodist work in established in the Russian district at Arensburg, Dorpat (E), Marinsk (R, Siberia), and Tallinn (E).

1910—A Methodist Episcopal church is built at Kuanas (LI).

1911—Methodist work is established in Sigolovo (R).

January 14, 1911—The church at Kaunas is dedicated by Bishop William Burt.

1912—A church is built at Kuressaare (E). By 1912 there are eleven pastors working within the Russian district.

1914—Cossacks devastate Kaunas and Virbalis; Methodists flee to Vilnius and establish a refugee congregation on the outskirts of the city; Virbalis is placed under Berlin District by Bishop Nuelsen to protect the property that survived.

1920—The name of the Russian mission appears for the last time in the annual reports of the conference in Finland.

1921—Dr. Wirtanen is assigned to Viborg (F); the organizing session of the Methodist Russian Missionary Conference is held in Khapsalu.

1921–22—Properties are obtained in Riga (LA).

Jan. 21, 1922—A church building is dedicated in Buoksental (F).

1922—The annual meeting of the Russian Missionary Conference is held in Riga (LA).

1923—The annual meeting of the Russian Missionary Conference is held in Kaunas (LI); a place of worship is dedicated in Tammerfors (F).

1924—The Baltic and Russian work is divided into two conferences.

Aug. 24, 1924—The Baltic Slavic and Mission Conference (henceforth BSMC) holds its first meeting in Arensburg.

1924—Bishop Nuelsen reports that there were fifteen pastors working in Estonia, fifteen in Latvia and eight in Lithuania; six are responsible for the work among the Russian-speaking population; General Conference officially divides the one Conference into two mission conferences.

1927—The BSMC reports 50 districts, 160 preaching stations, and 2,122 members.

1939—The BSMC holds last meeting in Tallinn (E).

2. Timeline of Methodism in Russia
(Methodist Episcopal Church)

1868—F. W. Flocken of the Bulgaria Mission baptizes four Russian children and first convert Gabriel Elieff at Schumla; the first Methodist chapel is built at Tultcha on the Danube and is soon abandoned due to opposition.

1888—B. A. Carlson is invited to Russia.

May 1889—B. A. Carlson preaches in Russia; begins monthly evangelizations in Saint Petersburg.

Aug. 1889—Carlson rents meeting Hall, but loses it in 1890 due to lack of funds.

Sept. 17, 1889—Carlson preaches first sermon in a meeting hall.

Nov. 1889—A small Methodist congregation is organized.

Nov. 10, 1889—The sacrament of the Lord's Supper is administered for the first time; H. K. Ridderström, a local preacher, is assigned as pastor.

1891—Carlson returns to Sweden upon the death of his wife.

1902—Carlson returns to Saint Petersburg.

April 1905—The Edict of Toleration granting religious minorities the right to exist becomes law.

1907—Bishop Burt assigns Dr. George A. Simons as pastor to Saint Petersburg; Hjalmar Salmi, who was born in Saint Petersburg and educated in a Methodist school in Finland, obtains the right to speak in Saint Petersburg.

Oct. 10, 1907—Simons arrives in Saint Petersburg and begins work in Swedish, Finnish, and Russian with laypreacher Strandroos and Salmi as assistants.

Nov. 1908—The Bethany Diaconal work is begun in Saint Petersburg with Sister Anna Eklund as director.

Jan, 1908—Simons begins a quarterly newsletter in English, *Methodism in Russia*.

1909—The Methodist Church in Russia is legalized; Simons begins *Khristianski Pobornik*, a Russian version of the *Christian Advocate*, which continues until 1917 in Saint Petersburg and later in Riga (LA).

1911—Work in Saint Petersburg is organized as its own mission; Bishop Burt organizes a separate Russian Mission Conference.

1912—Property is purchased at 58, Bolshoi Prospekt, Saint Petersburg.

Mar. 1, 1915—The building at 58 Bolshoi Prospect is dedicated.

1918—Simons is forced to leave Russia; the work continues under Sister Anna Eklund.

1920—Bishop John Nuelsen proposes to General Conference that the Russian mission be strengthened.

1921—Famine breaks out in Russia and mission relief is established for Saint Petersburg; Simons and Nuelsen request funds for same; somehow the mission and Sister Anna Eklund survive along with Pastor Poeld, a co-worker.

1922—The Peoples' Bible is printed through the efforts of Bishop Nuelsen at the government printshop in Leningrad; Simons moves headquarters from Helsinki (F) to Riga (LA); Bishop Nuelsen and Russian Orthodox

Archbishop Antonin (Living Church) meet in Moscow and Nuelsen is invited to the Sobor of the Federal Council of Churches; tensions increase between the government and churches in Russia and the execution of some Russian Orthodox Church leaders follows.

Aug. 29, 1923—Bishops Nuelsen and Blake attend Sobor; Board of Bishops of the Methodist Episcopal Church denounces Nuelsen and recalls him and Blake after they are already on their way to Moscow; Blake promises to raise $50,000 in the United States between 1924-27 for the reopening of a theological academy to educate Russian Orthodox priests; in the interim Blake helps set up a correspondence course for them.

Nov. 19, 1923—The Board of Foreign Missions refuses to acknowledge Blake's pledge.

Nov. 25, 1923—The Moscow Theological Academy is reopened with fifty students (originally opened in 1913 but was closed by the Bolsheviks).

Mar. 16, 1924—Metropolitan Ryazan opens a second seminary in Leningrad with some funds raised by Blake.

Gen. Con. 1924—Bishop Nuelsen asks for more support for the Russian mission, but by now much of the work has retreated to the Baltics; General Conference refuses further aid to the Russian Orthodox Church and to expand the Methodist work in Russia.

1925—Bishop Nuelsen visits the two Russian Orthodox theological schools in Moscow and Leningrad which have received aid.

1927—The annual meeting of the Russian Mission Conference in Riga was the twenty-fifth anniversary of the Russian Mission (begun 1892), but now apportionments to it were cut by fifty percent.

Gen. Con. 1928—Bishops Nuelsen and Blake complain of the cuts to the Russian Mission, which now retreats largely to Estonia.

1931—Sister Anna Eklund flees.

3. Timeline of Methodism in Siberia-Manchuria (Methodist Episcopal Church, South)

Sept. 1919—Beginnings of the idea: "After the closing of the Korea Annual Conference in Wonsan, Korea, in September, 1919, Bishop Lambuth held the Mission meeting at the Wonsan Beach the next day. At that time he was informed of the great needs and opportunities in Siberia and Manchuria where a great multitude of Koreans have migrated since 1870. He was very much interested in it and ordered Rev. M. B. Stokes and J. S. Ryang to visit Siberia at once in view to opening missionary work for the Koreans in that section. But the party never went, because the State Department at Washington would not issue passport[s] on Siberia at that time."[1]

May 1920—Official authorization: Upon recommendation of Bishop Lambuth to the Board of Missions of the Methodist Episcopal Church, South, in May 1920 at its annual conference the following resolution was approved:

"Resolved: that in view of conditions demanding our ministry in that section, we authorize the bishop in charge of the Oriental fields to open work in Siberia."[2]

Sept. 1920—First missionaries are appointed. During the Korea Annual Conference in September 1920, in Seoul, Korea, Bishop Lambuth appointed the Rev. W. G. Cram as superintendent of the Siberia-Manchuria Mission and the Rev. Chung Chai Duk, a Korean preacher, as a missionary to the new work.

Oct. 1920—First missionary journey: Dr. W. G. Cram, the Rev. Chung Chai Duk, and the Rev. J. S. Ryang depart on first missionary journey to Siberia-Manchuria. The Rev. Chung is assigned to initiate work among Koreans in Kirin and surrounding area. The Rev. Ryang makes visits to Chang Chun, Kirin, and Harbin in Manchuria and Nikolsk and Vladivostok in Siberia.

Nov. 1920—First congregaton in Manchuria: A new Korean congregation of fifteen people was begun in Kirin and another nearby.

Jan. 1921—Further expansion: A Korean congregation is begun in the city of Harbin and in a number of other places.

March 1921—First Korean congregation in Siberia: A Korean congregation of about fifty people is started at Nikolsk, Siberia.

April 1921—Expansion of the work: The office of the superintendent reports addition of some 500 new members in Siberia and Manchuria.

June 1921—Second Missionary journey: Dr. W. G. Cram and the Rev. J. S. Ryang make a second visit to Chang Chun, Kirin, Harbin, Nikolsk, and Vladivostok.

July 1921—Journey to Siberia: Bishop Lambuth, Dr. W. G. Cram, the Rev. J. O. J. Taylor, the Rev. L. C. Brannan, and the Rev. J. S. Ryang travel to Mukden, Chang Chun, Kirin, Harbin in Manchuria, and Nikolsk and Vladivostok in Siberia. Bishop Lambuth assigns Taylor and Ryang to work in these areas.

Aug. 1921—First annual meeting: On August 1, 1921 the first annual meeting of the Mission is held in Nikolsk-Ussuriski in the Methodist Church compound. Summary: three Korean young men licensed to preach; thirty groups had been organized with 1,261 members; a mission office is opened in Vladivostok.

Sept. 1921—Appointment for Russian work: Prof. H. W. Jenkins, appointed by Bishop Lambuth to Harbin, and his family arrive and begin Russian work there.

Nov. 1921—Mission Board member visit: Before his death Bishop Lambuth had requested a visit from the Board of Missions; Dr. F. S. Parker, general secretary of the Epworth League and member of the Board of Missions visits the Siberia-Manchuria Mission.

Dec. 1921—First Training Institute: For the first time a Korean Preachers' Institute is held at the Vladivostok Methodist Church, December 2-9 with the Rev. J. S. Ryang and the Rev. Chung Chai Duk as leaders. Sixteen preachers and one woman attend.

Feb. 1922—Growth Report: As of February 19, 1922: eighty churches and groups with 3,208 members/participants.

May 1922—General Conference definition: "The Siberia Mission shall include Siberia and the work among Koreans and Russians in Manchuria."

1922—Vladivostok falls to the Bolsheviks: Methodist property confiscated, though worship was allowed.

Feb. 1923—Erwin family departs for Harbin, shortly thereafter also the Taylors. By the spring all Russian Methodist work is concentrated in Harbin.

1923–24—The Methodist Institute is opened in the missionary compound at Tilenskaya Street.

1923–25—The mission published a Russian version of the *Methodist Christian Advocate;* this is replaced in August of 1925 with the *Methodist, the Bulletin of the Siberia-Manchuria Mission of the Methodist Episcopal Church, South.*

1925—Enrollment at the Institute is 744.

1927—By this year six churches have been opened in Harbin and along the railway the Jane Brown Evangelistic Center for women is established.

May 1927—Bishop Ainsworth recommends closing of the mission and the Board of Missions votes for closure. Mrs. George Erwin closes the mission and leads an entourage of her three children and twelve Russians across Manchuria to Korea and on to the United States.

4. Timeline of the Evangelical Church in Latvia

1908—A Russian invites the Rev. Baehren of the North Germany Conference to visit Riga.

1909—The North Germany Conference receives a request for a missionary to Riga.

Oct. 1909—Presiding Elder R. Kücklich visits Latvia.

1910—Bishop S. C. Breyfogel and Presiding Elder Max Richter make an exploratory trip to Russia via Kiev to Riga.

Oct. 1910—The Board of Missions of the North Germany Conference appoints Reinhold Barchet, pastor at Wanne, to Riga.

May 11, 1911—Barchet arrives in Riga.

Sept. 12, 1912—The society is given government approval as the "Evangelical Association-White Cross."

Sept. 22, 1912—The first Communion service is held in newly rented quarters.

1913—Mission work opens across the Daugava River at Agenkalns.

1914—World War I begins and Barchet is conscripted; the mission is officially closed.

1914-18—Some meetings continue in private homes; regular meetings continue in Agenkalns.

Nov. 18, 1919—Latvia declares independence.

1919—Barchet makes exploratory visits to Riga.

1920—B. R. Wiener and R. Barchet travel to Riga on behalf of the Board of Missions.

April 1, 1922—The first kindergarten is opened in Riga.

1923—Congregations are begun in Sloka and Sarkan-Daugava; E. Schwenk is appointed to the new work in Kuldiga; the Latvian Mission is placed under the supervision of the Berlin District of the North Germany Conference.

1924—Three young Latvian men are approved to begin study at the seminary in Reutlingen, Germany.

1926—Schwenk is transferred to Liepaja; Sister Berta Engels, who began an independent Latvian Evangelical congregation in Kuldiga, assists Schwenk in the Evangelical Church when the two congregations unite.

Sept. 23, 1928—Property and new buildings are dedicated at Riga.

1930—Sister Berta Engels assumes full responsibility for the work in Kuldiga.

1932—The Seventh Annual Faith Conference is held in Liepaja.

1938—The Board of Missions gives the Latvian Mission its own identity as a separate work; Bishop J. S. Stamm visits Latvia.

1939—The Evangelical Church in American donates $2,250 to the Latvian Mission.

1940—The Soviets take over and after some struggle to survive many of the leaders and the members of the congregations flee.

5. Timeline of the United Methodist Renewal in the CIS and the Russia Initiative of the General Board of Global Ministries[3]

1989-1990—Vladislav Specktorov, native of Samara, Russia, establishes contact with the Russian-speaking congregation of the United Methodist Church in Tallinn, Estonia and begins to distribute literature and organize house meetings in Samara, which result in the formation of a United Methodist church.

June 15, 1990—The Rev. Dea Hee Kim travels to Moscow to conduct the first worship service of a Korean-American UMC which had been organized by diplomat Mr. Schang Sun Kim.

July 1990—The Rev. Dwight Ramsey travels to Sverdlovsk (Ekaterinburg) on peace exchange taking Russian Bibles with him.

Oct. 1990—The UMC is legally registered in Ekaterinburg.

Dec. 28, 1990—The Rev. Cho Young Cheul is assigned to Moscow as a missionary by the New York Annual Conference and Bishop C. Dale White to serve as a pastor in Moscow to the congregation registered as the Moscow-Soviet-American Korean Society of the Methodist Church.

Jan. 1991—Bishop J. Woodrow Hearn (1988–92, president of the General Board of Global Ministries [GBGM] of the UMC) and Dr. Randolph Nugent (general secretary of GBGM) travel to Moscow and meet with leaders of the Russian Orthodox Church, Soviet Peace Fund, and numerous governmental officials, and visit a variety of health care institutions.

Feb. 1991—The Rev. Dwight Ramsey makes a return trip to Ekaterinburg.

April 1991—Bishop Hearn and Dr. Nugent report on their trip to the annual meeting of GBGM with recommendations for developing a Russia Initiative program.

Aug. 1991—Bishops Hans Växby and William B. Oden travel to Russia; in Ekaterinburg they consecrate Lydia Istomina as a local preacher.

Sept. 1991—Bishops Växby and Oden, Dr. Spurgeon Dunham, and educators and physicians primarily from Broadmoor UMC, Shreveport, Louisiana (USA) accompany the Rev. Dwight Ramsey to Ekaterinburg; Dr. R. Bruce Weaver, interim associate general secretary of UMCOR, and the Rev. Dean Hancock, UMCOR staff member, visit the World Council of Churches (WCC) office in Geneva, Switzerland, and UMCOR is assigned as the lead agency of humanitarian aid to the Moscow Region of the WCC Russia 1991 Winter Food Program.

Oct. 1991—Dr. Weaver and Mr. Lloyd Rollins, UMCOR staff member, visit Moscow and negotiate agreement with Moscow ecumenical group to receive and distribute food in the region to the elderly poor, single parents, unemployed and the physically challenged.

Nov. 1991—The Council of Bishops of the UMC assigns Bishop Rüdiger R. Minor to direct the Russian Initiative of the UMC; the Rev. Adam Kuczma, former superintendent of the United Methodist Church in Poland, is recruited by Dr. Bruce Weaver and Dr. Robert Harman, to direct the Russia Winter Food distribution program.

Dec. 1991—From this month through July 1992 over 4 million pounds of boxed staple food items are donated by U.S. United Methodist congregations for the Moscow area.

Jan. 1992—Bishop Minor makes his first episcopal visit to the CIS.

Jan. 22, 1992—The second UMCOR shipment of food arrives in Moscow.

Mar. 1992—Bishop Minor meets with two groups of Christians in Saint Petersburg, and Bishop Växby leads a seminar on Methodism and mission among Russians sponsored by the Estonian UMC; Bishop Minor travels to Riga, Latvia, to explore the return of Methodist Church properties, of which three are returned to The United Methodist Church by the Latvian government.

Mar. 20, 1992—By this date UMCOR has shipped 26,000 boxes of essential foodstuffs to the Moscow region.

April 1992—The First UMC of Moscow is legally registered.

Spring 1992—The First UMC of Saint Petersburg is legally registered.

June 1992—Dr. R. Bruce Weaver is engaged by the World Division of GBGM as Coordinator of New Mission Development in the C.I.S.

Representatives of St. Luke's United Methodist Church (Oklahoma City, OK) and the United Methodist Church (Morristown, NJ) visit Ulyanovsk, Russia and Kerch, Ukraine.

Aug. 1992—The UMC of Sevastopol, Ukraine is organized by the Rev. Dwight Ramsey.

Aug. 16, 1992—The Eurasia Episcopal Area is officially organized.

Fall 1992—Poland Annual Conference makes exploratory visits to Ukraine; Mission Education and Cultivation Department of GBGM begins United Methodist radio broadcast in Moscow.

Oct. 1993—Seven missionaries, recruited and funded by the Korean American Mission to Russia, are commissioned by GBGM.

Nov. 1993—A partner relationship is formed between Methodist Hospital of Indiana, Inc. and Hospital #7 in Moscow, Russia.

Annual meeting with UM partner church representatives. By 1994 thirty-two partnerships are formed with United Methodist churches.

Winter 1993—Through UMCOR United Methodists provide winter coats for Armenia (125,000 coats valued at $1.7 million), a joint effort of UMCOR, the Armenian Apostolic Church, and the North Carolina Annual Conference of the UMC.

Jan. 1993—UMCOR approves "Blagovest 'Good News' Village" appropriation.

Jan. 21-22, 1993—United Methodist leaders attend meeting in Moscow at the invitation of Patriarch of the Russian Orthodox Church.

Spring 1993—UMCOR approves grant of $30,000 for establishment of a Russian Orthodox university in Moscow.

April 1993—Health and Welfare Ministries Program Department begins work in the Semipalatinsk region of Eastern Kazakhstan: outreach to hospitals, orphanages, special schools for physically and mentally challenged children; begins establishing partner relationships between local medical facilities in Russia and the United States.

June 1993—Health and Welfare Ministries program department of GBGM delivers medical supplies.

Aug. 1993—Women's Division of GBGM sends team to explore outreach in Russia.

Sept. 19, 1993—Patriarch Aleksy II of the Russian Orthodox Church is awarded the honorary degree of Doctor of Divinity by Alaska Pacific University, a United Methodist-related institution.

Nov. 13, 1993—The Perovskaya United Methodist Church is established in Moscow.

Nov. 15, 1993—The Chinese United Methodist Church is established in Moscow.

Dec. 1993—At the invitation of Patriarch Aleksy II of The Russian Orthodox Church the general secretary of GBGM, Dr. Randolph Nugent, meets with the Patriarch in his home at Peradelkina.

April 1994—Three nuclear scientists and physicians from Kazhakstan are brought by GBGM to the United States for the first GBGM scientific dialogue with U.S. nuclear scientists and physicians.

Aug. 1, 1994—U.S. scientists and physicians travel to Semipalatinsk (Kazahakstan) for a second dialogue with Kazahakstani scientists and physicians.

Oct. 1994—The second GBGM scientific dialogue is held with Kazahkstan and U.S. scientists.

NOTES

Introduction

1. The *Evangelische Gemeinschaft* is commonly known in the United States as the Evangelical Church. From 1898 to 1926 there was a schism in the Evangelical Church in the United States. One branch was known as the Evangelical Association and the other as the Evangelical Church. After they united in 1926, the denomination became the Evangelical Church. It was during the period of the schism that the mission to Latvia began. While the *Evangelical Missionary Record* of Cleveland, Ohio, carried reports of the work and listed the Latvian mission stations as appointments until 1935, the work was primarily the provenance of the German branch of the church, namely, the *Evangelische Gemeinschaft*. There were occasional appropriations from the United States and visits from bishops and clergy. The primary records of the Latvian mission work of the *Evangelische Gemeinschaft* are housed in the Archives of the Theologisches Seminar of the *Evangelisch-methodistische Kirche* in Reutlingen, Germany. The Evangelical Church later merged with the United Brethren to form the Evangelical United Brethren, which subsequently united with The Methodist Church in 1968 to create The United Methodist Church. In this volume, *Evangelische Gemeinschaft* and Evangelical Church are used interchangeably to refer to the tradition described here.

1. The Methodist Church in Finland, Russia, and the Baltic States

1. Chapter 10 of Part 4, "Geschichte des Methodismus auf dem europäischen Kontinent" [History of Methodism on the European Continent] from *Kurzgefaßte Geschichte des Methodismus*, second edition, by John L. Nuelsen, Theophil Mann, J. J. Sommer (Bremen: Verlagshaus der Methodistenkirche, 1929); English translation by S T Kimbrough, Jr. Copyright of German text 1929 by Christliches Verlagshaus Stuttgart. Used by permission.

2. [In 1839 Maria Charlotte Hydén joined the British Georg Scott's Methodist Church in Stockholm. When she returned to Finland, she started a Sunday School and also held mission talks. In 1859 Firstmate Gustav Lervik returned to his home in Korsholm, outside Vaasa, Finland and began church work there for a time. He became a Methodist in 1858 at the Bethel ship mission in New York harbor. These historical details have been provided by Håkan Eklund in a personal letter, March 30, 1995.]

3. [Hurtig served in Helsinki for thirty-nine years. Nuelsen's account was published in 1929, hence, the discrepancy in the years of service. At that time Hurtig had served for "more than twenty years" there.

4. [Bishop Hans Växby has noted, "The first appointment to Borgå was 1906, but the congregation was organization in 1907." Personal letter, April 1, 1995.]

5. [Translator's footnote: The volume *The World Service of the Methodist Episcopal Church*, edited by Ralph Diffendorfer (Chicago: Methodist Book Concern, 1923), reported that in Finland "there are two orphanages for Finnish children, three for Swedish, a Swedish nursery

and old folks' home and a theological seminary for Finns—the only Methodist school for Finns in the world" (205)].

6. [See chapter 2 of this volume for Donald Malone's discussion of the "Living Church" movement.]

7. [Unquestionably, Bishop Burt's comment reflects a Protestant judgment about the ineffectiveness of Russian Orthodoxy, which itself must be judged by the facts of Russian church history and the full cultural, ethnic, and religious or antireligious complex of nations of the old Russian empire and former Soviet Union.]

8. [The episcopal appointment was never designated Virbalis, rather Kybartai, which was very close to Virbalis (ca. 6 kilometers).

9. [See chapter 9 of this volume regarding Methodist communities in Ukraine.]

2. A Methodist Venture in Bolshevik Russia

1. Donald Carl Malone, "A Methodist Venture in Bolshevik Russia," *Methodist History* 18:4 (1980), 239-261. Published by permission.

2. "All Well!—Simons' Petrograd," *Christian Advocate* 92 (March 22, 1917): 274; "Methodists Have Good News from Petrograd," *Christian Century* 24 (April 5, 1917): 18.

3. John Fletcher Hurst, *The History of Methodism,* (New York: Eaton and Mains, 1899), 209-11.

4. "Progression in Russia," *Daily Christian Advocate* 7 (May 24, 1876): 5.

5. Wade Crawford Barclay, *History of Methodist Missions: The Methodist Episcopal Church, Widening Horizons,* vol. 3 (New York: The Board of Missions of the Methodist Church, 1957), 933ff., 977-80.

6. George A. Simons, "A Rare Opportunity in Russia," *Daily Christian Advocate* 18 (May 28, 1912): 734f.

7. Ibid.; Paul L. Douglass, *The Story of German Methodism: Biography of an Immigrant Soul,* (New York: Methodist Book Concern, 1939), 181.

8. "A Good Word About Our Work in Russia," *Daily Christian Advocate* 18 (May 18, 1916): 286; "Russian Rubles for the Asbury Statue," *Christian Advocate* 92 (January 4, 1917): 2f; "Methodist Christmas in Petrograd," *Christian Advocate* 92 (April 5, 1917), 350.

9. Douglass, *The Story of German Methodism,* 267.

10. George A. Simons, "Russia's Resurrection," *California Christian Advocate* 66 (July 26, 1917): 6f; "From Petrograd," *Christian Advocate* 92 (November 8, 1917): 1166; George A. Simons, "The Little Grandmother of the Russian Revolution," *Christian Advocate* 94 (January 16, 1919): 69f.

11. "Let the Russian People Rule," *Christian Advocate* 92 (March 22, 1917): 274; "The Liberators of Russia," *Christian Advocate* 92 (March 29, 1917): 299. Immediately after the Russian Revolution a group of Russian immigrants meeting at the Church of All Nations in New York City sent a telegram of support to the Provisional Government in Russia. The one dissenting vote came from a Bolshevik, Lev Bronstein (later Leon Tolstoy). Cf. John R. Henry, "Fighting New York's Bolshevism," *Christian Advocate* 93 (January 10, 1918): 47f.

12. "Simons Petrograd," *Christian Advocate* 92 (November 29, 1917): 1264.

13. "Sister Anna of Petrograd," *Christian Advocate* 95 (January 15, 1920): 91f.

14. Roger Prentiss, "Sister Anna of Petrograd," *Christian Advocate* 97 (March 16, 1922): 328f.

15. "Proceedings of the General Conference," *Daily Christian Advocate* 19 (May 8, 1920): 193-47; John L. Nuelsen, "The Work of Europe During the Quadrennium," *Daily Christian Advocate* 19 (May 6, 1920): 106-10.

16. Walter Duranty, *Duranty Reports Russia,* (New York: Viking Press, 1934), 15-36. Duranty's book is a collection of his news articles concerning Russia taken from the *New York Times:* "Millions Starving in Lenin's Paradise of Atheism," *Literary Digest* 70 (August 6, 1921): 32f; "The Third Horseman Rides in Russia," *Literary Digest* 70 (August 13, 1921): 7-10; "Bolshevism's Harvest of Famine," *Literary Digest* 70 (August 20, 1921): 18.

17. "The Third Horseman Rides in Russia," 7-10; Alva Taylor, "Save Russia!" *Christian Century* 38 (November 3, 1921): 18f; "Famine in Russia," *Christian Advocate* 96 (July 28, 1921): 956; "Famine and Death in Russia," *Christian Advocate* 96 (August 25, 1921): 1668; "Saving the Children of Russia," *Christian Advocate* 97 (January 26, 1922): 103f; "Bishop Endorses Plan to Send Fish to Russia," *Christian Century* 38 (October 27, 1921): 24; "Will Aid the Unfortunate Russian Clergy," *Christian Century* 38 (December 8, 1921): 26; "Government Votes Supplemental Gift to Russian Relief," *Christian Century* 39 (March 2, 1922): 281; "Cannibalism Breaks Out in Russia," *Christian Century* 39 (March 9, 1922): 291; "Chicago Leader Will Go to Russia," *Christian Century* 39 (April 20, 1922): 505f; "Disciples Aid in Russia," *Christian Century* 39 (December 28, 1922): 1634; "To Cure Russia by 'Absent Treatment,' " *Literary Digest* 67 (August 3. 1918): 40. Herbert Hoover regarded famine relief to Russia as a better alternative to counteracting the Bolshevik threat than the British proposal of an Allied invasion of Russia, since famine was being used by the Bolsheviki for political purposes. Had relief been sooner in coming, the Bolshevik seizure of the government might have been averted. Cf. Eugene Lyons, *Herbert Hoover: A Biography* (Garden City: Doubleday, 1964), 130f.

18. Henry Clay Foster, "A Centenary Cargo for the Baltic Republics," *Christian Advocate* 95 (February 12, 1920): 225. Simons supported the Provisional Government, as did most Americans, for it promised a government patterned after European constitutionalism. However, from the beginning of the Russian revolution the Soviet Workers and Soldier's Deputies were in unofficial control. A faction of the Soviet called the Bolsheviki, later the Communist Party, eventually seized control. Therefore, Simons's support of the revolution, but not of the Bolsheviki, is not inconsistent.

19. George A. Simons, "The Agony of the Metropolis," *Christian Advocate* 96 (January 13, 1922): 39; "Methodist Relief in Petrograd," *Christian Advocate* 96 (September 15, 1921): 1161.

20. Anton Bast, "Campaigning for Christ on the Russian Border," *California Christian Advocate* 70 (January 19, 1922): 7; "Personal," *Christian Advocate* 97 (October 12, 1922): 1282; "Methodist Headquarters in Riga," *Christian Advocate* 97 (October 26, 1922), 1349.

21. Prentiss, "Sister Anna of Petrograd," 328; "Methodist Russian Worker Has Large Responsibility," *Christian Advocate* 39 (December 21, 1922): 1526.

22. "Bishop Nuelsen Out of Russia," *Christian Advocate* 97 (November 23, 1922): 1467.

23. Paul Miliukov, *Religion and the Church*. Part I of *Outlines of Russian Culture*, ed. Michael Karpovich, trans. Valentine Ughet and Eleanor Davis, three parts (New York: A. S. Barnes and Co., 1942), 151f.

24. Miliukov, *Religion and the Church*, 153ff.; Paul B. Anderson, *People, Church and State in Modern Russia* (New York: Macmillan Co., 1944), 45ff; Matthew Spinka, *The Church and the Russian Revolution* (New York: Macmillan Co., 1927), 69-83.

25. Ibid.

26. Miliukov, *Religion and the Church*, 154f.; John Shelton Curtiss, *The Russian Church and the Soviet State: 1917-1950* (Boston: Little, Brown and Co., 1953), 129f.

27. Curtiss, *The Russian Church and the Soviet State*, 129ff.; Miliukov, *Religion and the Church*, 154ff., 168; Spinka, *The Church and the Russian Revolution*, 69-83.

28. Curtiss, *The Russian Church and the Soviet State*, 27f.

29. "Bishops Turned Out in Russia," *Christian Century* 34 (July 26, 1917): 14.

30. The patriarchate was abolished by Peter the Great in 1702 and was replaced by the Holy Synod.

31. Miliukov, *Religion and the Church*, 155ff.; Spinka, *The Church and the Russian Revolution*, 88-93; Julius F. Hecker, *Religion Under the Soviets* (New York: Vanguard, 1927), 54f.

32. "Bishops Turned Out in Russia," 14; Miliukov, *Religion and the Church*, 157ff., 166ff., 169-72.

33. Curtiss, *The Russian Church and the Soviet State*, 129f.; Miliukov, *Religion and the Church*, 171f., 178.

34. Duranty, *Duranty Reports Russia*, 61ff.; Miliukov, *Religion and the Church*, 171, 177; Spinka, *The Church and the Russian Revolution*, 190-96.

35. Miliukov, *Religion and the Church*, 158-64; Spinka, *The Church and the Russian Revolution*, 104-15; Hecker, *Religion Under the Soviets*, 67-70; "The Bolsheviki Antagonizing Religion," *Literary Digest*, 56 (March 2, 1918): 35f. An interesting development during this period was

that Bolshevism began to replace the church as a religion, taking over the ritual functions including baptism. Cf. Duranty, 70-74, 76-81; "Bolshevism as a Religion," *Literary Digest*, 56 (February 2, 1918): 28f.; "Russia's New Gods," *Literary Digest* 57 (April 6, 1918): 41.

36. Duranty, *Duranty Reports* Russia, 57-61; Miliukov, *Religion and the Church*, 167f.; Spinka, *The Church and the Russian Revolution*, 175-77.

37. Miliukov, *Religion and the Church*, 163f., 171.

38. Duranty, *Duranty Reports* Russia, 61-67; Hecker, *Religion Under the Soviets*, 82ff.; Miliukov, *Religion and the Church*, 171ff.; Spinka, *The Church and the Russian Revolution*, 198-208.

39. Anderson, *People, Church and State in Modern Russia*, 78ff.; Miliukov, *Religion and the Church*, 175ff.; Spinka, *The Church and the Russian Revolution*, 203-8.

40. Anderson, *People, Church and State in Modern Russia*, 82; Miliukov, *Religion and the Church*, 177; Spinka, *The Church and the Russian Revolution*, 236; Paxton Hibben, "The Church in Russia," *Christian Century* 39 (December 28, 1922): 1590-92.

41. Miliukov, *Religion and the Church*, 177ff.; Spinka, *The Church and the Russian Revolution*, 236; Louis O. Hartman, "The Religious Situation in Russia," *Missionary Review of the World* 46 (August 1923): 611-19.

42. Hartman, "The Religious Situation in Russia," 611-19; Miliukov, *Religion and the Church*, 176-81; Spinka, *The Church and the Russian Revolution*, 240-45.

43. Duranty, *Duranty Reports* Russia, 67f.; Hecker, *Religion Under the Soviets*, 99f.; Miliukov, *Religion and the Church*, 176, 180; Spinka, *The Church and the Russian Revolution*, 240-45.

44. Miliukov, *Religion and the Church*, 180f.; Louis O. Hartman, "The Russian Church Reformation," *California Christian Advocate* 71 (June 14, 1923): 7, 14f.; Louis O. Hartman, "The Methodists and Red Orthodoxy," *Outlook* 134 (January 2, 1924): 36.

45. Anderson, *People, Church and State in Modern Russia* 182f.; Miliukov, *Religion and the Church*, 182f.; Matthew Spinka, *The Church in Soviet Russia* (New York: Oxford University Press, 1956), 45f.; news article in the *New York Times*, September 15, 1923, 6.

46. Hecker, *Religion Under the Soviets*, 114, 119; Miliukov, *Religion and the Church*, 182f.; Spinka, *The Church in Soviet Russia*, 45f.; news article in the *New York Times*, June 27, 1923, 3; "Blood Curdling Story of Tikhon's Torture a Myth," *Christian Century* 40 (September 20, 1923): 1187f.

47. Duranty, *Duranty Reports* Russia, 74-81; Miliukov, *Religion and the Church*, 183.

48. Hecker, *Religion Under the Soviets*, 107-9; Miliukov, *Religion and the Church*, 182-85; news article in the *New York Times*, July 3, 1924, 867.

49. Miliukov, *Religion and the Church*, 85f.; news article in the *New York Times*, July 3, 1924, 867.

50. [It is interesting that on the day Patriarch Tikhon died Methodist Bishop John L. Nuelsen was scheduled to meet with him. The archbishop of the Russian Orthodox Church invited Bishop Nuelsen to the funeral of the patriarch and reserved a seat for him in the area of the high altar with the bishops of the church. See *Der Christliche Apologete* (1925), 465. With the closure of this chapter of the "Living Church" movement in Russian Orthodox history, this was a strong symbolical statement on the part of the archbishop.]

51. Hecker, *Religion Under the Soviets*, 110-16; Miliukov, *Religion and the Church*, 187; Spinka, *The Church in Soviet Russia*, 42f.; Spinka, *The Church and the Russian Revolution*, 209f., 292f.

52. Spinka, *The Church in Soviet Russia*, ix.f.

53. "Plans to Evangelize Russia," *Literary Digest* 57 (June 22, 1918): 30; "To Evangelize Russia," *Literary Digest* 58 (August 3, 1918): 40; "Religion in Russia is not Dead," *Christian Century* 35 (July 11, 1918); 4f.; "Report of the Russian Conference Held in Chicago," *Christian Century* 35 (July 11, 1918): 19.

54. "All Faiths United by the Red Assault on Religion," *Literary Digest* 77 (April 21, 1923): 33-35; "The Eastward Outreach of the Roman Church," *Christian Advocate* 97 (February 23, 1922): 222; *infra.*, 21.

55. "What Is the Future of the Russian Church?" *Christian Century* 34 (April 5, 1917): 6; "Democracy in the Russian Church," *Christian Century* 34 (July 26, 1917): 7; "Episcopalians and Orthodoxy Friendly," *Christian Century* 34 (September 20, 1917): 14; "Will Exchange Pulpits with Russian Orthodox," *Christian Century* 37 (November 25, 1920): 23; "Changes in Church Life in Russia," *Christian Century* 37 (December 9, 1920): 30f.

56. "Bishop Endorses Plan to Send Fish to Russia," *Christian Century* 38 (October 27, 1921): 24; "Will Aid the Unfortunate Russian Clergy," *Christian Century* 39 (December 8, 1921): 26.

57. Ralph Lord Roy, *Communism and the Churches* (New York: Harcourt, Brace and Co., 1960), 381-86; news article in the *New York Times*, November 9, 1923, 19; news article in the *New York Times*, November 14, 1923, 6; news article in the *New York Times*, December 31, 1923, 5; Louis O. Hartman, "The Methodists and Red Orthodoxy," *Outlook* 136 (January 2, 1924): 36f.; "Democracy in the Russian Church," Christian Century 34 (July 26, 1917): 7; "Carry Russian Church Case Higher," *Christian Century* 53 (January 7, 1926): 24; "Soviet Controlled Church Wins Court Decision," *Christian Century* 54 (March 17, 1927): 324; Louis O. Hartman, "The Russian Church Reformation," *California Christian Advocate* 71 (June 14, 1923): 7, 14f.; Louis O. Hartman, "The Methodists and Red Orthodoxy," *California Christian Advocate* 72 (January 24, 1924): 2.

58. "Bishop Nuelsen Reports on Russia," *Christian Century* 40 (January 4, 1923): 22f.; "Bishop Nuelsen out of Russia," *Christian Advocate* 97 (November 23, 1922): 1467; John L. Nuelsen, "Soviet Russia Opens to Religion," *Christian Advocate* 97 (November 30, 1922): 1507f.

59. Nuelsen, "Soviet Russia Opens to Religion," 1507f.; Paxton Hibben, "The Church in Russia," *Christian Century* 19 (December 28, 1922): 1590-92; Paxton Hibben, "The View Over Russia and the Living Church Reform Movement," *Christian Century* 40 (February 14, 1923): 196.

60. Nuelsen, "Soviet Russia Opens to Religion," 1507f.; Hecker, *Religion Under the Soviets*, 95.

61. "The New Church in Russia," *Christian Advocate* 97 (December 21, 1922): 1610.

62. "Unparalleled invitation from the Russian Church," *California Christian Advocate* 70 (December 21, 1922): 6, 23; the "Eighth Hill of Rome" is Monte Mario, which Methodists bought and occupied between 1920 and 1922. Methodists boast about that the school on Monte Mario overlooking the Vatican was a source of irritation to the Roman Catholic Church. Cf. Bertrand M. Tipple, "Rome 1872-1922," *Christian Advocate* 97 (June 15, 1922): 743-45; Bertrand M. Tipple, "The Protestants in Rome," *Christian Advocate* 96 (July 21, 1921): 939f.

63. "The Expedition to Moscow," *Christian Advocate* 98 (January 4, 1923): 4f.

64. Richard J. Cooke, "Methodism and the Religious Situation in Russia," *Christian Advocate* 98 (January 4, 1923): 15, 23.

65. Louis O. Hartman, "The Russian Church Reformation," *California Christian Advocate* 71 (June 14, 1923): 7, 14f.

66. "Representatives to Russia," *Christian Advocate* 97 (November 30, 1922): 1514.

67. Paul L. Douglass, *The Story of German Methodism: Biography of an Immigrant Soul*, (New York: Methodist Book Concern, 1939), 194; "President L. H. Murlin, Who Was in St. Petersburg," *Christian Advocate* 92 (February 15, 1917): 149; Louis O. Hartman, "The Sunday School and the Youth of Europe," *Christian Advocate* 95 (July 8, 1920): 931; "The Expedition to Moscow," *Christian Advocate* 98 (January 4, 1923): 4f.

68. "Moscow Meeting Postponed," *Christian Advocate* 98 (January 25, 1923): 115.

69. Edgar Blake, "The Methodist Mission in Russia," *Christian Advocate* 40 (July 19, 1923): 905-8.

70. News article in the *New York Times*, March 23, 1923, 2; News article in the *New York Times*, March 26, 1923, 8.

71. News article in the *New York Times*, March 27, 1923, 1, 6.

72. News article in the *New York Times*, April 5, 1923, 1,3.

73. News article in the *New York Times*, March 31, 1923, 1f; news article in the *New York Times*, May 15, 1923, 3; "Archbishop Cieplak Dead," *Christian Century* 43 (March 4, 1926): 301f.

74. 1,766,188 people were executed by the Bolsheviki before 1922. Of these, 1,243 were Orthodox priests. Cf. "The Red Church of Russia," *Literary Digest* 75 (October 14, 1922): 39f.

75. News article in the *New York Times*, March 28, 1923, 1, 4; News article in the *New York Times*, March 30, 1923, 1, 3.

76. News article in the *New York Times*, March 31, 1923, 1, 2.

77. News article in the *New York Times*, March 31, 1923, 19; "Europe Astir Over the Red Killings," *Literary Digest* 77 (April 28, 1923): 12f.

78. " 'On the Holy Front' in Russia," *Literary Digest* 77 (May 19, 1923): 19; News article in the New York Times, April 19, 1923, 3.

79. "All Faiths United by the Red Assault on Religion," *Literary Digest* 77 (April 21, 1923): 33-35; "The Methodist Split on Russia's New Church," *Literary Digest* 77 (June 28, 1923): 30f.; "Russia and Religion," *Christian Century* 40 (May 10, 1923): 581; "The Martyrs of Moscow," *Christian Advocate* 98 (April 12, 1923): 452f.

80. News article in the *New York Times,* March 26, 1923, 13; news article in the *New York Times,* March 27, 1923, 2; news article in the *New York Times,* March 31, 1923, 1, 2; news article in the *New York Times,* April 11, 1923, 1f.

81. "The Methodist Split on Russia's New Church," 30f.; "The Martyrs of Moscow," 452f.

82. "Bolshevism's 'Public Challenge to God,' " *Literary Digest* 77 (April 14, 1923): 7-9.

83. John B. Ascham, "Interview with Captain McCullagh," *Christian Advocate* 98 (September 27, 1923): 1182.

84. Ascham, "Interview with Captain McCullagh," 1182; "The Martyrs of Moscow," 452f.; Edgar Blake, "The Methodist Mission to Russia," *Christian Century* 40 (July 19, 1923): 905-8.

85. "Bolshevism's 'Public Challenge to God,' " 7-9.

86. "All Faiths United by the Red Assault on Religion," 33-35; "The Invisible Empire," *Christian Advocate* 98 (April 5, 1923): 421.

87. "All Faiths United by the Red Assault on Religion," 33-35; Isabel Hapgood, "Life of Russia's Patriarch Now Hangs in Soviet Scale," *New York Times,* April 8, 1923, sec. 9, 3; "The Methodist Split on Russia's New Church," *Literary Digest* 78 (June 28, 1923): 30f.; "A Shot Heard Round the World," *Christian Advocate* 98 (April 12, 1923): 453.

88. News article in the *New York Times,* April 12, 1923, 4.

89. Blake, "The Methodist Mission in Russia," 905-8.

90. "The Bishop's Cold Feet," *Christian Century* 40 (May 17, 1923): 613; "Bishop Blake Was in Moscow," *California Christian Advocate* 71 (May 19, 1923): 5.

91. Blake, "The Methodist Mission in Russia," 905-8; Louis O. Hartman, "The Russian Church Reformation," *California Christian Advocate* 71 (June 14, 1923): 7, 14f.

92. Louis O. Hartman, "The Russian Church Reformation," 7, 14f.

93. Edgar Blake, "Bishop Blake's Address at Moscow," *Christian Century* 40 (June 21, 1923): 791, 198; "The All-Russian Council of the Orthodox Church in Moscow," *California Christian Advocate* 71 (June 14, 1923): 6f.

94. Ibid.

95. Hartman, "The Russian Church Reformation," 7, 14f.

96. News article in the *New York Times,* November 20, 1923, 10.

97. Hartman, "The Methodists and Red Orthodoxy," 36f.; "Let's Help Put the Top on This Christian Pyramid," *Christian Century* 40 (January 3, 1924): 3f.; "Religion in Russia," *Christian Advocate* 67 (January 10, 1924): 4.

98. Hartman, "The Methodists and Red Orthodoxy," 36f.

99. Julius F. Hecker, "Russian Church Reopens Theological Academy," *Christian Century* 40 (January 3, 1924): 22; Julius F. Hecker, "The Reopening of the Moscow Theological Academy," *California Christian Advocate* 77 (January 3, 1924): 2; "Curriculum at New Russian Theological Seminary," *Christian Century* 41 (April 10, 1924): 44.

100. "Second Theological Seminary Opened in Russia," *Christian Century* 41 (May 1, 1924): 673.

101. "Launch Progressive Paper for Russia," *Christian Century* 41 (August 14, 1924): 1055. The report of indebtedness of Russian theological education to American Protestantism is confirmed by Edgar Blake, "Religion in Russia," *Northwest Christian Advocate* 74 (September 23, 1926): 897.

102. John L. Nuelsen, "A Letter from Russia," *California Christian Advocate* 75 (May 20, 1926): 2f.; "Reports Russian Theological Schools Flourishing," *Christian Century* 62 (April 30, 1925): 582.

103. "The Soviet Living Church," *California Christian Advocate* 72 (February 7, 1924): 5.

104. "Russian Church Thanks Methodists for Aid," *Christian Century* 62 (May 23, 1925): 709.

105. Edgar Blake, "A Letter from Bishop Blake on the Bishop's Recall," *California Christian Advocate* 71 (July 5, 1923): 14; news article in the *New York Times*, May 6, 1923, 3.

106. "The Religious Melee in Russia," *Literary Digest* 77 (May 26, 1923): 32f.; "The Methodist Split on Russia's New Church," *Literary Digest* 78 (July 28, 1923): 30f.: Edgar Blake, "The Methodist Mission in Russia," *Christian Century* 40 (July 19, 1923): 905-8; "Bishop Blake and the Russian Church," *California Christian Advocate* 71 (June 7, 1923): 4; "Bishop Blake's Own Story," *California Christian Advocate* 71 (June 7, 1923): 8; "A Thrilling Message on the Russian Mission," *California Christian Advocate* 71 (August 2, 1923): 4.

107. "Methodist Bishops Meet in New York," *Christian Century* 40 (December 6, 1923): 1592f.

108. John Nuelsen, "Report of the Zurich Area," *Daily Christian Advocate* 20 (May 3, 1924): 66-70; John Witt, "Methodism in Russia and the Baltic States," *California Christian Advocate* 72 (August 21, 1924): 19; John Witt, "Methodism in a Lithuanian Catholic Stronghold," *California Christian Advocate* 74 (April 9, 1925): 3.

109. Ibid.

110. John L. Nuelsen, "Bishop Nuelsen Describes Conditions in Germany," *California Christian Advocate* 72 (February 21, 1924): 6f.; John L. Nuelsen, "A Letter from Russia," *California Christian Advocate* 75 (May 20, 1926): 2f.

111. Jaan Puskay, "Twenty Years of Russian and Baltic Methodism," *Northwest Christian Advocate* 75 (March 24, 1927): 1119.

112. "Our Methodist Soviet," *Northwest Christian Advocate* 75 (December 1, 1927): 1132.

113. "Proceedings of the General Conference," *Daily Christian Advocate* 21 (May 8, 1928): 210-21.

114. John L. Nuelsen, "Report of the Zurich Area," *Daily Christian Advocate* 21 (May 5, 1928): 130-33.

115. Walter Kolarz, *Religion in the Soviet Union* (London: Macmillan and Co., Ltd., 1961), 34f., 241.

116. "Methodist Church in Russia," *Together* 7 (July 1963): 1f.

117. News article in *Christian Century* 95 (September 20, 1978): 849; Trevor Beeson, "Metropolitan Nikodim, 1929—1978," *Christian Century* 95 (October 18, 1978): 985f.

3. George A. Simons and the *Khristianski Pobornik*

1. "George A. Simons and the *Khristianksi Pobonik*," by John Dunstan, *Methodist History* 19:1 (1980): 21-40. Published by permission. Dunstan's charts are not included.

2. P. P. Pirogov, *Vasil'evskii ostrov* (Leningrad: Lenizdat, 1966), 8.

3. Pirogov, *Vasil'evskii ostrov*, 10.

4. Pirogov, *Vasil'evskii ostrov*, 12-13. See also Christopher Marsden, *Palmyra of the North*, (London: Faber and Faber, 1942), 52-53, 62-63.

5. Pirogov, *Vasil'evskii ostrov*, 17-18.

6. Marsden, *Palmyra of the North*, 77.

7. Pirogov, *Vasil'evskii ostrov*, 23. The mixture of translated and untranslated street names, admittedly inconsistent, follows the usage of the Saint Petersburg Methodist leadership.

8. James H. Bater, *St. Petersburg: Industrialization and Change* (London: Arnold, 1976), 213, 248-49, 372-75.

9. Bater, *St. Petersburg: Industrialization and Change*, 318, 324-25; Pirogov, *Vasil'evskii ostrov*, 28-29.

10. Ibid.

11. B. A. Carlson, "The Beginnings of Methodism in Finland," *The Gospel in All Lands* (hereafter *GAL*) (November 1896): 505-8, at 505-6; B. A. Carlson, "Religion in Finland," *GAL* (March 1898): 109-13, at 111. For an overview of the early history of Methodism in Finland, see Wade Crawford Barclay, ed., *History of Methodist Missions*, vol. III (New York: Board of Missions of the Methodist Church, 1957), 976-81.

12. John L. Nuelsen et al., *Kurzgeschichte des Methodismus von seinen Anfangen bis zur Gegenwart*, 2nd ed. (Bremen: Verlagshaus der Methodistenkirche, 1929), 760.

13. Manfred Hurtig, "Carlson," in Nolan B. Harmon, ed., *The Encyclopedia of World Methodism*, vol. 1 (Nashville: The United Methodist Publishing House, 1974), 412-13.

14. For 1888: B.A. Carlson, *Minnen ur mitt liv: Sjalvbiografi*, (Stockholm: Nya Bokforlags Aktiebolaget, 1921), 140-41. (The writer is grateful to Jean Morgan and Eva Holmquist for thier help in translating this source.) For 1889: Carlson, "The Beginnings of Methodism in Finland," (1896); Nuelson et al., *Kurzgeschichte des Methodismus*, 767.

15. "Our Missionaries and Missions," *GAL* (June 1888): 287.

16. S. Thomoff, "Annual Meeting of the Bulgaria Mission," *GAL* (November 1888): 508.

17. Carlson, *Minnen ur mitt liv: Sjalvbiografi* (1921), 141-42.

18. Ibid. Carlson, "The Beginnings of Methodism in Finland," (1896). The numbers cited in Barclay, *History of Methodist Missions*, vol. III, 979, differ slightly.

19. According to Nuelsen, *Kurzgeschichte des Methodismus*, this was H. K. Ridderstrom. Oddly enough, Carlson does not mention him in his autobiography but refers with appreciation to K. U. Strandroos, who recurs in the story later.

20. "Boundaries of Foreign and Mission Conferences and Missions," *GAL* (July 1892): 337.

21. J. Tremayne Copplestone, *History of Methodist Missions*, vol. IV (New York: Board of Global Ministries of The United Methodist Church, 1973), 366-72, at 367. Copplestone's useful study is the most complete account in English of the history of Methodism in the Russian Empire known to the writer and the fullest on Saint Petersburg before the present essay.

22. Carlson, *Minnen ur mitt liv: Sjalvbiografi* (1921), 143.

23. Ibid. Adherents included, the total was probably about forty (*GAL* [January 1891]: 29; *Khristianski Pobornik*, 1/8 [August 1909]: 64).

24. *GAL* (March 1898): 129.

25. *GAL* (January 1899): 22.

26. Nuelsen et al., *Kurzgeschichte des Methodismus*. It was later claimed that in recent years the returns had been falsified to present a more satisfactory picture (George Albert Simons, "Report of the Superintendent" [1910], 8: ms. in Burt Collection, Archives Division, United Methodist Church, Lake Junaluska).

27. *GAL* (March 1896): 116; (February 1897): 123; (March 1898): 115; (January 1899): 7. A society had been founded in Viborg, then in Finland, in 1892. There, six years later, things were much more buoyant, with forty-nine members, twenty-one probationers, and a Sunday school of 180.

28. Carlson, *Minnen ur mitt liv: Sjalvbiografi* (1921), 144.

29. Nuelsen et al., *Kurzgeschichte des Methodismus*, 762-63; Copplestone, *History of Methodist Missions*, 14:366-72.

30. Nuelsen et al., *Kurzgeschichte des Methodismus*, 762-63; Copplestone, *History of Methodist Missions*, 14:366-72; *Methodism in Russia* 1/1 (January-March 1908): 15-16 and outside cover.

31. Simons died unmarried in Glendale, New York, in 1952. The author would be pleased to hear from any reader who knew this interesting man.

32. Leslie A. Marshall, *The Romance of a Tract and Its Sequel* (Riga: Jubilee Fund Commission of the Baltic and Slavic Mission Conference of the Methodist Episcopal Church, 1928), 16-21, 43. We owe this source to Manfred Hurtig, "Simons," in Nolan B. Harmon, ed., *The Encyclopedia of World Methodism*, vol. II, 2157-58.

33. Simons, "Report of the Superintendent" (see note 26); *Annual Report of the Board of Foreign Missions of the Methodist Episcopal Church* (hereafter *AR*) *for the Year 1910* (New York: The Board of Foreign Missions of the Methodist Episcopal Church, 1911), 478.

34. This is where Simons preached his first sermon after arriving in Russia and escaped a drunken murder attempt. He afterwards liked to suggest that his epitaph might have been, "Here lies a Metodistski pastor, killed by vodka."

35. *Methodism in Russia* 1/1 (January-March 1908): inside front cover and 15-16. The first issue is held at Lake Junaluska. There appears to have been a set in the New York Public Library, but this set cannot be traced now. The author would be interested to learn of any other surviving copies. Professor Wilhelm Kahle (Marburg) is thanked for his comments on the Protestant background at this point.

36. *AR* (1910): 51, 482; *AR* (1910): 477; Nuelsen et al., *Kurzgeschichte des Methodismus*, 769.

37. Simons "Report of the Superintendent," 19.

38. It is also unknown whether any copies have survived in the West, though such Methodist librarians and archivists whom we have consulted in Britain, Germany, Switzerland, and the U.S.A. think not. But since the journal was sent out of the country, the possibility cannot be ruled out.

[On Feb. 10, 1995, S T Kimbrough, Jr. discovered two copies of *Khristianski Pobornik*, published in July 1925 and October 1926, in the Lithuanian State Archives in Vilnius, Lithuania. Hence, it is now a known fact that the periodical was published after 1917; however, it is clear from the content of these two newly discovered issues that the orientation had shifted from Saint Petersburg to interests of the Baltic and Slavic Mission Conference and the place of publication is designated as Riga, Latvia, which is where Dr. George A. Simons was living. The headquarters of the Methodist Episcopal Church in the Baltic States was located in Riga at the seminary building on Elizabeth Street.]

39. *Khristianski Porbornik* (hereafter *KP*) 2/2 (February 1911): 12-14.

40. *KP* 12(48) [*sic*] (December 1914): 9, 11. The serialization is erratic.

41. The Methodist Church apparently became known as the American Church (George F. Kennan, *Soviet-American Relations, 1917-1920: Russia Leaves the War* [London: Faber and Faber, 1956], 111-12).

42. *KP* 7/2 (February 1915): 11-12.

43. *KP* 7/82 [*sic*] (October 1915): 11-13.

44. September 1914 to May 1915; this was the preacher killed at the front, for the editor's Christian names given in the Saint Petersburg directory for 1915 (*Ves' Peterburg na 1915 god*) match those in his obituary (*KP* 7/4 [April 1915]: 8-11), but it is odd that his name was retained after the news of his death. Certainly his successor continued to be listed as editor after being drafted about June 1916 (*KP* 8/91 [July 1916]: 11).

45. Respectively *KP* 7/80 (August 1915): 5; 8/85 (January 1916): 10; 8/90 (June 1916): 3.

46. Photograph in *KP* 2/22 (October 1912): 83.

47. *Ves' Peterburg na 1909 god* (Saint Petersburg: Izdanie A. S. Suvorina, no date), col. 212.

48. *KP* 1/1 January 1909): 8.

49. *KP* 1/20 (August 1910): 63; supplemented from Simons, "Report of the Superintendent," 6-8, 23. On the Chinese school see also *KP* 1/13 (January 1910): 3. There is also mention of a further day school in Korea (*AR*, 1912, 414; *AR*, 1913, 412). For further details of the Sunday school, see *KP* 1/17 (May 1910): 41-42.

50. For the Karelian episode see Copplestone, *History of Methodist Missions*, 4:369-70. Mariinsk is now in the Kemerovo Region, 350 km. east of Novosibirsk.

51. *KP* 1/20 (August 1910): 65. Karlson's defection evidently did nothing to mar the excellent relations between the Methodist leadership and the Bible Society in Saint Petersburg.

52. *KP* 7/2 (February 1915): 6; 7/82 (October 1915): 4.

53. Three years later they moved to apartment 4 at 34 Ninth Line, and by 1915 they were based in apartment 6 at 21 Twelfth Line.

54. *KP* 1/1 (January 1909): 4-5; George A. Simons, "Die ersten methodistischen Diakonissen in St. Petersburg, Rußland," *Der Evangelist* 59/48 (October 1908): 2; *AR*, (1908): 117.

55. *KP* 2/9 (September 1911): 74.

56. *KP* 2/11 (November 1911): 96.

57. See note 34.

58. *AR*, (1913): 411; *KP* 12(48) (December 1914): 14; Copplestone, *History of Methodist Missions*, 4:372.

59. *KP* 8/86 (February 1916): 24; 8/94 (October 1916): 4; 9/98 (February 1917): 28. Two of these were directed at the English-speaking community.

60. *KP* 1/20 (August 1910): 67.

61. Ralph E. Diffendorfer, ed., *The World Service of the Methodist Church* (Chicago: Methodist Episcopal Church, Council of Boards of Benevolence, Committee on Conservation and Advance, 1923), 220. One of the very few Soviet writers to refer to Methodism. K. Smolin, "Metodizm i metodisti. Proshloe i nastoyashchee," *Ateisticheskie chteniya*, 8 (Moscow: Politizidat, 1976), 115, also seems to think that Methodism in Saint Petersburg began in 1907.

62. *KP* 1/20 (August 1910): 63

63. *KP* 1/16 (April 1910): 28-29

64. Simons, "Report of the Superintendent," (1910), 8.

65. Ibid., 22; Copplestone, *History of Methodist Missions*, 4:372.

66. *KP* 2/24 (December 1912): 124; 5/25 (January 1913): 8; *AR* (1912): 415.

67. *KP* 7/4 (April 1915): 19.

68. Ibid.

69. The question of Sunday schools is considered below, *vis-a-vis* relations with the secular power.

70. *KP* 2/22 (October 1912): 90.

71. *KP* 7/1 (January 1915): 12.

72. John L. Nuelsen, "Report on Russia to the Executive Committee of the Board of Foreign Missions of the Methodist Episcopal Church," (1923), 23; ms., Russia Conference, Archives Division, The United Methodist Church, Lake Junaluska.

73. *KP* 7/81 (September 1915): 16; 8/86 (February 1916): 11, 24; 8/96 (December 1916): 16; 9/100-101 (April-May 1917): 52. The classes had started in 1912.

74. Copplestone, *History of Methodist Missions*, 4:369.

75. Marshall, *The Romance of a Tract*, 27.

76. *KP* 1/1 (January 1909): 2; 1/4 (April 1909): 28; *AR* (1912): 415; *AR* (1913): 411.

77. *KP* 1/2 (February 1909): 9-11, 14-16; 1/4 (April 1909): 25-27, 32; 1/7 (July 1909): 49-51, 1/8 (August 1909): 57-58, 63; 1/14 (February 1910): 9-11; 1/15 (March 1910): 17-19, 22-23.

78. *KP* 1/10 (October 1909): 75-77, 80; 1/11 (November 1909): 83-85; 1/12 (December 1909): 92-93.

79. *KP* 1/16 (April 1910): 26-27; 1/17 (May 1910); 38-39; 1/18 (June 1910): 45-47.

80. *KP* 7/79 (July 1915): 3-6.

81. *KP* 8/90 (June 1916): 1-2.

82. *KP* 2/24 (December 1912): 117-19. There was also fairly frequent reporting of international Christian news (World's Sunday School Association, World Week of Prayer, Y.M.C.A., etc.).

83. *KP* 5/33 (September 1913): 5; 6/37 (January 1914): 8.

84. Not Cornish, but English: said to have been based on "the honest yeomanry about Ipswich [in Suffolk], where he was stationed from 1867-9" (Mrs. George Unwin and John Telford, *Mark Guy Pearse: Preacher, Author, Artist* [London: Epworth Press, 1930], 112). Serialized in *KP* from 1/13 (January 1910) to 2/3-4 (March-April 1911).

85. See Bishops Hurst's remarks in *GAL* (December 1892): 592.

86. Gerhard Simon, "Church, State and Society," in George Katkov et al., eds., *Russia Enters the Twentieth Century* (London: Methuen, 1973), 229.

87. Copplestone, *History of Methodist Missions*, 4:369.

88. This is clear from his reports to the Board. But he was always scrupulously careful not to give offense in the *Pobornik*, at least until the fall of the empire. The Methodists' real feelings about Orthodoxy can perhaps be better glimpsed at the end of 1917, when the magazine prints a miscellany of news of the church, nearly all of it bad (*KP* 9/107-108 [November-December 1917]: 4-5).

89. Simon, "Church, State and Society," 234-35.

90. *KP* 2/1 (January 1911): 8.

91. *AR* (1912): 415; *KP* 5/25 (January 1913): 8.

92. *KP* 7/1 (January 1915): 12; similarly in 8/85 (January 1916): 6.

93. *KP* 9/97 (January 1917): 12.

94. George F. Kennan, *Russia and the West under Lenin and Stalin* (New York: New American Library, 1960), 23.

95. Simons subsequently set this to music and published it under the title, "Brotherhood, Love and Freedom" (Marshall, *The Romance of a Tract*, 26-27).

96. K. S. Aksakov (1817-1960), eminent publicist, critic, and historian.

97. *KP* 9/100-101 (April-May 1917): 37, 42-45, 47, 49-50, 51-52.

98. *KP* 9/102 (June 1917): 53.

99. *KP* 9/100-101 (April-May 1917): 49-50.

100. Methodist Episcopal Church, *The Centenary Survey of the Board of Foreign Missions* (New York: Joint Centenary Committee, Methodist Episcopal Church, 1918), 25-29.

101. *Minutes of the Annual Conference*, Methodist Episcopal Church, 1918, 1108-9. On page 662 there is a list of twenty-eight places and circuits, of which five are held by Methodists, and ten by others; the remainder are to be supplied.

102. Manfred Hurtig, "Russia," in Nolan B. Harmon, éd., *The Encyclopedia of World Methodism*, vol. II, 2057.

4. The Methodist Episcopal Church, South, in Siberia/Manchuria

1. "The Methodist Episcopal Church, South, Mission to Russians in Manchuria, 1920-1927," by Dana L. Robert, *Methodist History* 26:2(1988): 67-83. Published by permission.

2. Elmer T. Clark, *The Church and the World Parish* (Nashville: Methodist Episcopal Church, South, Board of Missions, 1929), 85.

3. J. S. Ryang, "Annual Report of Korean Department, Siberia Mission, 1925," *The Missionary Voice* (June 1926): 173.

4. Elmer T. Clark, ed., *Missionary Yearbook of the Methodist Episcopal Church, South, 1927* (Nashville: Board of Missions, Methodist Episcopal Church, South, 1927), 259-61.

5. Interview with George F. Erwin, Hiawassee, Georgia, December 30, 1978.

6. A. F. Gavrelovchuk, "Russia and Religion," *The Missionary Voice* (September 1928): 357.

7. Unfortunately, much missionary correspondence and other sources of the Methodist Episcopal Church, South, have been missing for a number of years. The Methodist Archives at Drew University in Madison, New Jersey, contain printed *Minutes* of the annual meetings of the Russian Department of the Siberia-Manchuria Mission (1922-25). The major mission sources are in the possession of Mrs. Eunice Erwin Brown of Macon, Georgia. Mrs. Brown is the daughter of two of the original missionaries appointed to the field, George and Vada Erwin. Mrs. Brown owns scrapbooks and correspondence related to the mission. She also holds copies of the Russian version of the *Methodist Christian Advocate: Metodistski Chrestanski Pobornik*, and of the *Metodist: Byulletin Sib.-Manch. Misii Met. Ep. Tserkvi, Yug. (The Methodist, the Bulletin*, published by the Siberia-Manchuria Mission).

Dr. Gergory I. Yasinitsky, formerly of San Francisco, California and now deceased, was one of the first Russian pastors related to the mission. He owned scrapbooks and ephemeral material such as songbooks and several copies of his publication, *Myech Gidiona* (The Sword of Gideon) which was distributed to Russian Protestants in twenty-two countries in the late 1920s and 1930s.

The Methodist and *The Sword of Gideon* contain information not only about Methodists in Manchuria, but about other Protestant groups as well.

8. James Cannon, III, *History of Southern Methodist Missions* (Nashville: Cokesbury Press, 1926), 169-70; J. S. Ryang, "Koreans in Siberia and Manchuria," *The Missionary Voice* (January 1922): 12.

9. Cannon, *History of Southern Methodist Missions*, 172. Bishop Lambuth appointed the Rev. J. S. Ryang as a missionary to the Manchurian Koreans. Ryang became supervisor of the mission to Koreans in Manchuria and years later became the first Korean bishop of the Methodist Church.

10. Ethnic Byelorussians, or "White Russians," were a different group from the political "White Russians" who fought against the Bolsheviks, or "Red Russians."

11. In a comity agreement over post-World War I Europe reached with the Methodist Episcopal Church in 1919, the Methodist Episcopal Church, South, received Southern Russia, Poland, Czechoslovakia, and Belgium. The Northern Methodist church maintained work in Estonia, Finland, and Northern Russia. For background to how the comity agreement evolved, see W. W. Pinson, *Walter Russell Lambuth: Prophet and Pioneer* (Nashville: Cokesbury Press, 1924), 181-86. For a brief history of Methodist Episcopal Church efforts in Russia during the

revolutionary period, see Donald Carl Malone, "A Methodist Venture in Bolshevik Russia," *Methodist History* 19 (July 1980): 239-61 [published in this volume].

12. Pinson, *Walter Russell Lambuth: Prophet and Pioneer*, 190.

13. Robert Watson Sledge, *Hands on the Ark, The Struggle for Change in the Methodist Episcopal Church, South, 1914-1939* (Lake Junaluska, North Carolina: Commission on Archives and History, The United Methodist Church, 1975), 77.

14. Sledge, *Hands on the Ark*, 77.

15. Cannon, *Southern Methodist Missions*, 70.

16. John C. Hawk, "New Mission to Chinese in Manchuria," *The Missionary Voice* (March 1925): 79.

17. For background to the political turmoil in Manchuria during the early twentieth century, see George Kennan, *Soviet-American Relations, 1917-1920*, vols. I and II (Princeton: Princeton University Press, 1956): Sherwood Eddy, *The World's Danger Zone* (New York: Farrar and Rinehart, 1932); Aitchen K. Wu, *China and the Soviet Union* (New York: John Day Co., 1950).

18. See the small but interesting collection of the J. O. J. Taylor letters to his mother and sister (1918-1922) held by the Pitts Theology Library, Candler School of Theology, Atlanta, Georgia. Although Taylor stayed only briefly in Vladivostok, he opened the mission and his correspondence reflects his work among the Koreans. See also his letters in *The Missionary Voice*, e.g., "Siberia and Manchuria" (January 1922): 8.

19. George F. Erwin, "My First Missionary Experience," *The Missionary Voice* (August 1922): 233.

20. Mabel K. Howell, "The City of Vladivostok," *The Missionary Voice* (February 1923): 53; Hiram A. Boaz, "Vladivostok," *The Missionary Voice* (March 1923): 69; W. W. Pinson, "A Mayflower of the Far East," *The Missionary Voice* (March 1923): 75.

21. George Erwin interview.

22. A. J. Weeks, ed., *78th Annual Report, Board of Missions, Methodist Episcopal Church, South, 1924* (Nashville: Methodist Episcopal Church, South, 1924), 170.

23. Hiram A. Boaz, "Our Siberia Mission," *The Missionary Voice* (October 1925): 295.

24. "Institute," *Byulletin, Sib.-Manch. Misii Metodistkoy Episkopalnoy Tserkvi, Yug.* (Sentyabr 1925): 9-10. ("Institute," *Bulletin of the Siberia-Manchuria Mission, Methodist Episcopal Church, South* [September 1925]: 9-10).

25. H. W. Jenkins, "Annual Report of Russian Department, Siberia Mission, 1925," *The Missionary Voice* (April 1926): 105.

26. Interview with Dr. Gregory Yasinitsky, San Francisco, California, June 3, 1985.

27. *Missionary Yearbook*, 1927, 260. Interview with Ludmilla Skaredoff, Leningrad, USSR, July 24, 1986. Mrs. Skaredoff graduated from the Methodist High School in Harbin. Even though her parents were not religious, they enrolled her in the Methodist school because of its high academic standards. After the mission withdrew in 1927, the high school was taken over by Russians and continued as a non-Methodist school. Mrs. Skaredoff reported that the best two high schools in Harbin in the 1930s were the former Methodist school and one run by the Y.W.C.A.

28. "Zaboti o Dyetak," *Byulletin* (Sentyabr 1925): 10 ("Concern for Children," *Bulletin* [September 1925]: 10); A. J. Weeks, ed., *80th Annual Report, Board of Missions, Methodist Episcopal Church, South, 1926* (Nashville: Methodist Episcopal Church, South, 1926): 151.

29. A. J. Weeks, ed., *79th Annual Report, Board of Missions, Methodist Episcopal Church, South, 1925* (Nashville: Methodist Episcopal Church, South, 1925), 184; B. N. Bradovitch, "Liga Zaschiti Dyete," *Metodist Byulletin . . .*, (Fevral 1926): 14 ("League for the Protection of Children," *Methodist Bulletin* [February 1926]: 14).

30. *79th Annual Report*, 184; *80th Annual Report*, 149.

31. Sunday schools were a prominent part of the Methodist work. Frequent articles on them appeared in the *Metodist Byulletin* (*Methodist Bulletin*). Sunday schools were a major responsibility of the missionaries from the Woman's Board.

32. One of the first Russian workers, Mr. B. Venogradoff, died while in Methodist service. Born in Saint Petersburg of Orthodox parents, Venogradoff had moved to Vladivostok where he attended the university and began to work for the Y.M.C.A. He fled to Harbin, entered the Methodist theological school, and gave his life to Methodist work.

33. Gregory Yasinitsky interview. Gregory Yasinitsky letter to Dana Robert, July 15, 1985. "Harbinski Bibleski Institute," *Byelletin* (Noyabr 1925): 7 ("Harbin Biblical Institute," *Bulletin* [November 1925]: 7).

34. Yasinitsky interview and letter to Dana Robert; "Harbinski Bibleski Institute," 7.

35. Telephone interview with Dr. Alexis Shelekoff, November 11, 1985.

36. George F. Erwin, "The First in the World," *The Missionary Voice* (June 1926): 175.

37. Originally, Lillian Wahl of Paris, Arkansas, accompanied Constance Rumbough to Manchuria, but Wahl died of spinal meningitis in 1926. Sallie Browne replaced her. Constance Rumbough, of the Virginia Annual Conference, had been trained at Scarritt Bible and Training College.

38. On woman's work at the mission, see *The Missionary Voice* (May 1923): 151; *79th Annual Report*, 186-87; *Minutes of the Third Annual Meeting of the Siberia-Manchuria Mission (Russian Department)* of the MECS, held in Harbin, China, September 27, 1924, 22-24; *Minutes of the Fourth Annual Session of the Siberia-Manchuria Mission (Russian Department)* of the MECS, Harbin, China, September 17, 1925, 23-29.

39. George Erwin, "Thumb-Nail Sketches from Manchuria," *The Missionary Voice* (January 1927): 202-3.

40. *Missionary Yearbook*, 1927, 98.

41. Interview with Mrs. Vada Erwin, Hiawassee, Georgia, December 20, 1978.

42. "After many experiences and much suffering, the first fruits of Methodism were beginning to show when the news came that the Board of Missions would have to close the Mission because of lack of funds. This order came upon us like a storm. The blow was too hard." A. F. Gavrelovchuk in Elmer T. Clark, ed., *Missionary Yearbook of the Methodist Episcopal Church, South 1928* (Nashville: Board of Missions, MECS, 1928), 333. George and Vada Erwin believed that the reason the mission was closed was because the Board of Missions went broke.

43. Clark, *Church and the World Parish*, 85.

44. Esther Case, "Miss Case Visits Poland," *The Missionary Voice* (November 1928): 426-27.

45. Noreen Dunn Tatum, *A Crown of Service* (Nashville: Parthenon Press, 1960), 219.

46. *Missionary Yearbook*, 1927, 20.

47. "Bishop Ainsworth did not realize the potential of our mission. He did not know that when our converts leave Manchuria they carry with them a witness of Christ. Mr. Ponkin, who left for the Soviet Union wrote: 'In a short time I am able to organize a group of believers more than a hundred in number . . .' This kind of report was coming to us from Poland, Australia, Canada, and even from New Zealand." Gregory Yasinitsky letter to Dana Robert, July 15, 1985.

48. Vada Erwin interview; Eunice Erwin Brown letter to Dana Robert, August 1, 1985.

49. Ainsworth was elected bishop from the South Georgia Conference in 1918. (*Daily Christian Advocate, Methodist Episcopal Church, South, General Conference of 1918*, Atlanta, Georgia, 94.) Historian Albert Outler, who grew up in the South Georgia Conference, believes that Ainsworth was a highly authoritarian, "imperial bishop." Conversation with Albert Outler, Fort Worth, Texas, April 3, 1986.

50. Tatum, *Crown of Service*, 217.

51. See for example, the scrapbook of Constantin Egoroff, now in the possession of Dana Robert. Egoroff and his wife continued their church work in Manchuria through the 1930s, despite the fact they had no support from the Methodists and that Egoroff was blinded by glaucoma. Finally, in 1959 the Methodist Committee on Relief brought the Egoroffs to San Francisco. For the Egoroff story, see "The Long Dark Road," *Inasmuch (25 Years of Service through MCOR)*, clipping in the Eunice Erwin Brown collection, Macon Georgia.

Gregory and Irene Yasinitsky also continued their church work after the withdrawal of the Methodists. Yasinitsky published the evangelistic magazine *The Sword of Gideon* to support his Bible distribution and youth work. After arrest by the Japanese as a possible American spy, Yasinitsky and his family excaped to San Francisco in December of 1940. See Yasinitsky correspondence to Dana Robert; Susan Lyon, "Gregory Yasinitsky: Profile of an Alumnus," clipping from the alumni magazine of the Pacific School of Religion.

Alex and Panya Gavrelovchuk traveled with Vada Erwin in 1927 to the United States, where they received college educations. The Gavrelovchuks then returned to Harbin. During World

War II, they assisted Methodist missionaries who were interned in Shanghai by the Japanese. Eunice Erwin Brown letter to Dana Robert, August 1, 1985.

52. See Vless Halaimov materials, Eunice Erwin Brown collection, Macon, Georgia.

53. John F. Burns, "Russian Legacy Fades in North China," *New York Times*, 11 August 1985, 16.

5. The Evangelical Church in Latvia

1. Karl Steckel, C. Ernst Sommer et al., eds., *Geschichte der Evangelisch-methodisten Kirche* (Stuttgart: Christliches Verlagshaus, 1982), 172.

2. Paul Himmel Eller, *History of Evangelical Missions* (Harrisburg: The Evangelical Press, 1942), 185.

3. Brother Linz's wife was Russian. Both had been converted in Essen and joined the *Evangelischer Gemeinschaft* in that city.

4. A copy of the text of the letter is in the unpublished collection *Dokumente/Berichte über die Arbeit der evangelischen Gemeinschaft hinter Oder and Neisse 1885-1945*, compiled by Wilhelm Wecke, 160-64. The manuscript is located in the archives of the library at the Theologisches Seminar der Evangelisch-methodistischen Kirche in Reutlingen, Germany.

5. Steckel and Sommer, *Geschichte der Evangelisch-methodisten Kirche*, 172.

6. G. E. Epp, "Evangelical Advance on the Baltic," *Evangelical Missionary World* 4(1926): 470.

7. *Konferenzverhandlung [Nord]* (1914): 48.

8. This is not entirely accurate, as many did not perish but remained in exile; personal correspondence to the author/editor from Wilhelm Volskis, May 16, 1994.

9. Eller, *History of Evangelical Missions*, 187.

10. W. Mohr, "Latvia as a Mission Field," *Evangelical Missionary World* 9(1931): 341.

11. Waldemar Steinert, "Aus Riga, Lettland" [From Riga, Latvia], *Evangelischer Missionsbote* (January 1923): 3.

12. Brother Linz was eventually banned to Siberia. Whether this was during World War I or after is not known.

13. Otto Michaelis, *Evangelischer Botschafter* (1939). The 1939 issues of the *Evangelischer Botschafter* were available to this author/editor only in the unpublished compilation of articles by Wilhelm Wecke. They are not in the Methodist archives at Drew University (USA) or in the archives of the library of the Theologisches Seminar in Reutlingen, Germany.

14. "Vom Königsberger Distrikt," *Konferenzverhandlung [Nord]* (1918): 50.

15. This was through the efforts of Nadeschda Brüggemann.

16. Eller, *History of Evangelical Missions*, 188.

17. "Eye Witnesses in Latvia," *Evangelical Missionary World* 2(1924): 335. The article includes portions from 1921 reports of Bishop G. Heinmiller and the Rev. B. R. Weiner, edited by the latter.

18. *Konferenzverhandlung [Nord]* (1921): 54.

19. Reinhold Barchet, "News from Riga," *Evangelical Missionary World* 1(1923): 168.

20. The 1922 report of the Mission Society of the North Germany Annual Conference states that the Evangelical Church had eighty members and forty-three probationary members in the Latvian work. *Konferenzverhandlung [Nord]* (1922): 45.

21. Reinhold Barchet, "News from Riga, Latvia," *Evangelical Missionary World* 1(1923): 168.

22. Waldemar Steinert, "The Evangelical Church in Latvia," *Evangelical Missionary World* 2(1924): 333.

23. *Konferenzverhandlung [Nord]* (1925): 49-50.

24. A local preacher, Brother Arnack, assisted him in Kuldiga.

25. *Konferenzverhandlung [Nord]* (1923): 43.

26. George Edward Epp, "Our Mission in Riga," *Evangelical Missionary World* 2(1924): 334.

27. Ibid.

28. Ibid. When the Board of Missions learned the two young women were in Berlin studying for mission work in Latvia, it appropriated funds for the purchase of a parsonage

and church building and in 1925 appropriate property was purchased. See Eller, *History of Evangelical Missions.*

29. G. E. Epp, "Evangelical Advance on the Baltic," 470.

30. S. J. Umbreit, "Von meiner Reise nach Lettland" [From My Trip to Latvia], *Evangelischer Botschafter* (1927): 332-33.

31. Wilhelm Mohr, "Aus Lettland" [From Latvia], *Evangelischer Botschafter* (1926): 45.

32. *Konferenzverhandlung [Nord]* (1925): 50.

33. E. Schwenk, "Gruß aus Libau, Lettland" [Greetings from Libau, Latvia], *Evangelischer Botschafter* (1927): 19. Libau is the German equivalent for Liepaja.

34. Wilhelm Mohr, "Unser Werk in Polen und Lettland" [Our Work in Poland and Latvia], *Evangelischer Botschafter* (November 11, 1928): 365-66.

35. S. J. Umbreit, "Von meiner Reise nach Lettland" [From my trip to Latvia], 333.

36. Eller, *History of Evangelical Missions,* 189.

37. *Konferenzverhandlung [Nord]* (1929): 72.

38. *Konferenzverhandlung [Nord]* (1931): 79.

39. Goldingen is the German equivalent for Kuldiga.

40. Mohr, "Latvia as a Mission Field," 341-42.

41. "Aus Riga" [From Riga], *Evangelischer Botschafter* (1934).

42. See Eller, *History of Evangelical Missions,* 190.

43. Schkobe later became a Methodist pastor.

44. Steckel and Sommer, *Geschichte der Evangelisch-methodisten Kirche,* 202.

45. From the unpublished notes of Wilhelm Wecke (1885–1945), English translation by S T Kimbrough, Jr. The manuscript is dated: "Pinneberg, April 1989."

6. The Rise and Fall of Methodism in Lithuania and Latvia

1. Wade Crawford Barclay, *Widening Horizons 1845-1939,* vol. 3 in *History of Methodist Missions* (New York: Board of Missions, 1957), see particularly part 2, "The Methodist Episcopal Church," 976-81; J. Tremayne Copplestone, *Twentieth Century Perspectives,* vol. 4 in *History of Methodist Missions* (New York: Board of Global Ministires of The United Methodist Church, 1973), 366-72, 509-18; see especially the section, "The Methodist Episcopal Church, 1896-1939."

2. Heigo Ritsbek, "Estonian Methodism during the First Year under the Plague of the Red Commissars," *Methodist History* 31:4 (1993): 248-55.

3. Mark Elliott, "Methodism in the Soviet Union Since World War II," *The Asbury Theological Journal* 46:1 (1991): 5-47.

4. [Some pastors and congregations did survive until 1944, but with grave difficulty.]

5. Ritsbek, "Estonian Methodism," 253. However, Wilhelm Volskis, a United Methodist clergyman now serving in Virginia and a native-born Latvian and son of a Latvian Methodist minister, notes (personal correspondence, May 16, 1994): "Many, if not all, Methodist congregations continued to meet for preaching, prayer, and Bible study. The dissolution of the church came in 1944, not in 1940."

6. Methodism survived in Lithuania and Latvia until the second Soviet takeover in 1944. This is discussed later in the chapter. According to Wilhelm Volskis, "In Latvia, at least, Methodists fared almost as well as in the 1930s." (Personal correspondence, May 16, 1994.)

7. Most of the information and photographs concerning the life of the Methodist Episcopal Church in Kaunas during its first twenty-five years of existence which appeared in the anniversary *Program* are included in an article, "Jubilejaus svente," by Dr. George A. Simons published in *Krikščionvstes Sargas* (the Lithuanian *Christian Advocate*), 7:3 (1925) 5-8.

8. Šanciai = Schanzen in German. This is the name of the section of the city of Kaunas in which the Methodist Episcopal Church was built.

9. The author of the text for the program is not given. The portion of the text printed here is published in English for the first time.

10. The city name appears as Kaunas, Kowno, and Kauen as per various language adaptations of the spelling.

11. Wilhelm Volskis notes, "Hitler's 'call to come home' issued to Germans scattered throughout Eastern Europe came in 1939; 1941 would have been too late for many of them." (Personal correspondence, May 6, 1994.)

12. The internal headings and division of the text have been added for clarity by the editor of this volume, who translated the manuscript.

13. Emma Robbert's account of the origin of the early contact of the independent congregation in Kaunas with the German Methodist Church differs from that of the program booklet for the twenty-fifth anniversary of the Methodist Episcopal Church in Kaunas. Her story of Mr. Pieper's trip to Königsberg and his encounter with the Methodists may be a valid part of the whole story. Nevertheless, the account in the program booklet should be regarded as an accurate description of the first connection between the independent congregation in Kaunas and the German Methodist Church.

14. The *Program for the Twenty-Fifth Anniversary of the Methodist Episcopal Congregation in Kaunas* maintains that the first congregational celebration as Methodists was held in the Durcholz apartment on October 29, 1901 and that "This day was regarded as the birthday of the congregation and of Methodism in Kaunas and Russia," (6).

15. It was dedicated on January 14, 1911 by Bishop William Burt.

16. "The cause is yours, Lord Jesus Christ, / the cause on which we stand; / trusting in you we shall persist, / for all is in your hand."

17. According to Kostas Burbulys, retired Lithuanian Methodist pastor, Methodist work in the Lithuanian language began in 1923 in the cities of Birzai and Siauliai. In the latter city, where Burbulys later served as Methodist pastor, services were held in Lithuanian and German. Letter of Kostas Burbulys to Bishop Hans Växby, July 7, 1993.

18. Hitler required their return when the Germans reoccupied the Baltic states.

19. The church was last converted by the Soviets into a sport center for table tennis for which it is still used today (1995). The original two parsonages of the church remain adjacent to the church but are in bad condition.

20. Copplestone, *Twentieth Century Perspectives*, 368.

21. Oswald Olechnowitsky, "Die Methodistenkirche in Litauen," *Heimatrgruß, Jahrbuch der Deutschen aus Litauen 1967* (Leer: Landsmannschaft der Deutschen aus Litauen, 1967).

22. New York, 1909, pp. 116-17.

23. The pressures on Lithuanian Protestants differed greatly from those in Latvia and Estonia, for Lithuania's Christian population was largely Roman Catholic. In Latvia it was primarily Protestant and Estonia was no more Roman Catholic than Finland. Latvia had been touched by the Reformation already by 1522 and the influence of John Calvin and Gustavus Adolphus was clearly evident.

24. In 1938 Vilnius became once again a part of Lithuania. In the interim years of Polish annexation the Methodist work was continued by a number of Polish Methodist pastors.

25. The Methodist Episcopal Church building in Pilviskiai, which functioned as a parsonage and place of worship, still exists, but is used only as a dwelling and is in poor condition.

26. S T Kimbrough, Jr. interview with Pastor Arthur Leifert, September 27, 1994. Leifert, a baptized Lutheran, joined the Methodist congregation in Taurage and served it as a lay worker before entering theological studies at the Frankfurt seminary in Germany. He later received Methodist ordination in Germany and served Methodist parishes there until his retirement in 1977.

27. On the site where this church once stood there is now a funeral home, however, the parsonage of the Methodist Episcopal Church in Taurage, located on Presidento Street No. 28 immediately adjacent to the site of the former church, is still in good condition and has been preserved essentially as it was built with some minor alterations.

28. Pastor Lupp was a member of the Methodist Episcopal Church in Taurage and later became a Methodist clergyman and served a number of appointments in Lithuania including his home church of Taurage. He was the last pastor to serve the Methodist Episcopal Church in Taurage before the Soviet takeover. Lupp endured extreme hardships due to the world wars and imprisonment by the Russians but he survived and became a Methodist minister in Germany where he served churches until his retirement. S T Kimbrough, Jr. interview with Pastor Richard Lupp, September 28, 1994 in Utarp, Germany.

29. The congregation in Biržai never had the means to purchase property or build its own church and it rented space in a two story building on Kestucio Street No. 3, which today is a local court building.

30. Olechnowitsch, 103.

31. The house is still standing, in good condition, and is now owned by the Baptist Church.

32. Olechnowitsch, 106.

33. The author, S T Kimbrough, Jr., visited Tauragė, Lithuania on Nov. 8, 1994 and found one surviving member of the Methodist Episcopal Church in Tauragė, Else Bendikiene, who has a copy of this hymn book from which she still reads the texts of the hymns from time to time with joyous memories of the days when she attended the Methodist Episcopal Church in Tauragė and sang them. On Nov. 9, 1994 he visited Algimantes Serafinaficius in Siauliai, who was baptized in the Methodist Episcopal Church as a boy by the minister of the church there the Rev. Kostas Burbulys. He also owns a copy of the hymn book which was passed on to him from his mother. The hymn book included an introduction by Dr. George A. Simons and the place and date of publication are Kaunas, 1923.

34. Kaunas, n.d. "Methodists, who are they and what do they want?"

35. Biržai, 1927. "Catechism of the Methodist Episcopal Church."

36. The Lituanian *Christian Advocate*. The following issues are to be found in the State Library of Vilnius, Lithuania: 1923; No. 2 Aug., 1924; No. 3 March, No. 5 May; 1925: No. 3 April & May, No. 4 July, No. 5 Aug. & Sept. No. 6 Oct. & Nov., No. 7 Dec.; 1926: No. 1 Jan.; 1929: No. 1 Jan., No. 2 Feb.; 1930: Nos 4 & 5 April & May [one issue]; 1931: Nos. 1-11, Jan.-Nov.; 1932: No. 2 Feb., No. 7, July.

37. Copplestone, *Twentieth Century Perspectives*, 510.

38. Manuscript, "The Beginning of Lettish Methodism," by George A. Simons (1921); six pages, located at the Methodist Archives, Drew University, Madison, N.J. Used by permission.

39. Raymond J. Wade, *Reunion, Baltic and Slavic Refugee Pastors of the Methodist Church in the United States, July 1-5, 1962* (Bay View, Mich.: np, nd), 10; henceforth cited as *Reunion*.

40. When Simons was forced to leave Saint Petersburg, he moved his headquarters to Riga, Latvia. Much of his activity has already been related in preceding chapters.

41. April, May, June, 1924 issue, 12.

42. It is interesting to note that Simons includes the work of the Methodist Episcopal Church, South, in Siberia. He was an ardent advocate of union of the Methodist Churches.

43. S T Kimbrough, Jr. interview with Pastor Richard Lupp, September 28, 1994.

44. Sister Anna Eklund worked closely with government children's institutions, supplying them with food, medicine, and clothing as regularly as possible.

45. Page 22.

46. S T Kimbrough, Jr. interview with Pastor Richard Lupp, September 28, 1994.

47. Burbulys states that Kvedaravicius was deported to Siberia when the Communists occupied Lithuania and he died there. Letter of Kostas Burbulys to Bishop Hans Växby, July 7, 1993.

48. Letter of Kostas Burbulys to Bishop Hans Växby, July 7, 1993.

49. Wade, *Reunion.*

50. Wade, *Reunion.*

51. Ralph Diffendorfer, ed., *The World Service of the Methodist Episcopal Church* (Chicago: Methodist Book Concern, 1923): 224.

52. George A. Simons, "Die Baltische und Slavische Missions-Konferenz," *Der Evangelist* (1926): 680.

53. Page 13.

54. Leslie A. Marshall, *The Romance of a Tract and Its Sequel* (Riga: The Jubilee Fund Commission of the Baltic and Slavic Mission Conference, 1928): 28.

55. In an article entitled, "Russian Open to the Gospel!" Bishop Walter R. Lambuth of the Methodist Episcopal Church, South, and initiator of much of the mission work in Siberia and Manchuria stated that he found the Orthodox Church nearer the evangelical ideals and standards of Protestantism than Roman Catholicism. See *The Missionary Voice* (January, 1922): 7.

56. Karl Steckel, C. Ernst Sommer, et al., *Geschichte der Evangelisch-methodisten Kirche*, (Stuttgart: Christliches Verlagshaus, 1982): 104.

57. Wade, *Reunion*, 4.

58. See Mark Elliott's discussion in "Methodism in the Soviet Union Since World War II" *The Asbury Theological Journal* 46:1(1991): 1-21.

59. S T Kimbrough, Jr. interview Pastor Rev. Richard Lupp, September 28, 1994.

60. Paul Ernst Hammer, *Die Nordotdeutsche Konferenz der Bischöflichen Methodistenkirche 1927-1945* (Stuttgart: Chrisliches Verlagshaus, 1986), 17.

61. Mosienko, whose father was Russian, later served as a pastor in Detroit, Michigan.

62. This is the Polish city of Lodz.

63. Hammer, *Die Nordotdeutsche Konferenz der Bischöflichen Methodistenkirche*, 17-18.

64. Ibid., 22.

65. Here is perhaps the reason for Emma Robbert's return to Kaunas in 1943.

66. Hammer, *Die Nordotdeutsche Konferenz der Bischöflichen Methodistenkirche*, 23.

67. Ibid., 28.

68. Ibid., 29.

69. Ibid., 62.

70. Wade, *Reunion*, 12.

71. Ibid.

7. The Development of Estonian Methodism

1. S. Klaos, *Metodisti kogudused Eestis, nende tekkimine ja areng* (Tartu, Estonia: mag. theol. dissertation, 1924), 127.

2. Leslie A. Marshall, *The Romance of a Tract and Its Sequel* (Riga, Latvia: Jubilee Fund Commission of the Baltic and Slavic Mission Conference of the Methodist Episcopal Church, 1928), 24.

3. Martin Prikask, "Eesti Methodistic Kiriku arenemine ja aastakonverentsid," *Kristlik Kaitsja* 14 (1933): 120-23.

4. K. Oja, "Religioon ja kirik," in G. Naan, ed., *Nôukogude Eesti* (Tallinn, Estonia: Valgus, 1978), 228-29.

5. Prikask, "Eesti Methodistic Kiriku arenemine ja aastakonverentsid," 120.

6. Aleksander Kuum, "Metodismi jôuallikad," *Kristlik Kaitsja* 14 (1933): 123.

7. Aleksander Kuum, "Eesti metodistide sotsiaaltööst," *Kristlik Kaitsja* 14 (1933): 132-34.

8. Prikask, "Eesti Methodistic Kiriku arenemine ja aastakonverentsid," 120-23.

9. [The first Methodist church built on the soil of the old Russian Empire was in Kybartai, Lithuania.]

10. Jaan Puskay, "Mõnda ükfikkoguduste ajalooft," *Kristlik Kaitsja* 14 (1933): 127-32.

8. Estonian Methodism During the First Year Under the Plague of the Red Commissars 1940–1941

1. "Estonian Methodism During the First Year Under the Plague of the Red Commissars," by Heigo Ritsbek, *Methodist History* 31:4(July 1993): 248-55. Published by permission.

2. Aarand Roos, ed., *A Nation Unconquered* (Baltimore: Estonian World Council, Inc., 1985): 37.

3. Roos, *A Nation Unconquered*, 41.

4. Heigo Ritsbek, *Settsekümmend viis aastat Eesti Metodisti Kirikut 1907-1982* [Seventy-five years of the Methodist Church in Estonia] (Tallin: 1982), 3. (Unpublished manuscript.)

5. On June 18, 1990, Mr. Arvi Lindmäe, the chairman of the board of Kuressaare United Methodist Church (this was the first Methodist congregation in Estonia and the place from where the Rev. Martin Prikask led the Methodism activities in Estonia) very boldly visited the local KGB office and asked for information concerning the death of Martin Prikask. He was

told that the file of Martin Prikask was in Tallinn and that they would try to locate it. After some time Arvi Lindmäe returned to the Kuressaare office of the KGB, and he was allowed to see Martin Prikask's file (!!!). Arvi Lindmäe asked for permission to take the photo of Martin Prikask from the file and to make some copies of it. The KGB officer then made a phone call to Tallinn and asked what to do. After some explanations the KGB chief at Kuressaare, Valeri Tootsman, gave this photo of the Rev. Martin Prikask to Arvi Lindmäe so he could make some copies of it. When Arvi Lindmäe later asked permission to take the whole file home and copy it, he was refused ("this time may come in future"), but at the same time the KGB officers allowed him to copy the text from the file on the spot. He managed to copy some parts of it. There were according to him "some 28-30 sheets" in the file. (Arvi Lindmäe to the author, May 15, 1991), 1-2.

6. The exact time of the arrest of the Rev. Martin Prikask is not very clear from the file. As it happened on the night of July 1, 1941, then in some places it is mentioned July 1, 1941, in some other places June 30, 1941. Also it is not known exactly when his wife was freed, because we know that "Prikask was arrested with his wife" (Lindmäe to the author, December 18, 1990, 1). We know that his wife was not imprisoned or taken to the Gulag. We know that the Rev. Martin Prikask was advised to hide, but he refused (The Rev. Tiit Henno to the author, July 12, 1988).

7. Lindmäe, May 15, 1991, 2.

8. Lindmäe once spelled his name "Kikas" (Lindmäe to the author, December 18, 1990).

9. Of course, we do not know the actual testimony of Martin Prikask during these interrogations. As the torture and the fabrications of KGB are well known, all these "documented" interrogations do not represent the actual happenings.

10. This term, *nationalized*, meant actually that Soviets robbed the best apartments and houses for themselves; in many cases the families who lived in these places were simply thrown into the street. I know personally several people who had to endure such suffering. Officially they were told that some "representatives of the working class" *needed* these places much more than the real working people who lived there.

11. Lindmäe, May 15, 1991, 3.

12. It is interesting to mention that this person had two brothers—one of them was in the Nazi army, and later was shot to death by the Soviets. The third brother was not involved in politics at all and "still lives in Kuressaare" (Lindmäe, May 15, 1991, 4).

13. It is interesting to see the basic accusation model from this "testimony": Methodists are called "sectarians"; the only motivation for pastoral activities is money; clergy are always connected with "reactionary" or "against the people" movements. The only details that are missing here are accusations of sexual immorality.

14. For example, there is a protocol from January 5, 1942. Someone by the name of B. Osikin, a tractorist from Russia, witnessed that Martin Prikask "showed his anti-Soviet attitude [during their trip to the concentration camp] and had said that they would never reach Siberia, because the Germans are so strong" (Lindmäe, May 15, 1991, 5-6).

The protocol dated March 14, 1942: **Q.** "When did you begin to do anti-Soviet propaganda?" **A.** "I began to do the anti-Soviet propaganda immediately after the Soviets took the power. I do not remember all, but I told to my neighbour Markus Kõdar, that the food products will be taken out from Estonia and Estonia will suffer the hunger. During the elections to the Supreme Soviet of the Estonian Soviet Socialist Republic I said that there is a need to tell to the people that none of the Estonians will vote for the candidates to the Supreme Soviet. Also during our trip to Irkutsk, I stated in the wagon that the German army is non-defeatable and they will conquer the whole Europe and the Soviet Union will lose the war. At the end of August, when we reached one railway station and the German airplanes came to bomb, then I said that they cannot take us to the place they want, because the German government will require us all back soon. I do not remember that I had done the anti-Soviet propaganda more." **Q.** "Have you been at the National Guard?" **A.** "No." **Interrogator:** "Now you have totally exposed yourself that you are hostile to the Soviet power and in the midst of your acquaintances you did the anti-Soviet agitation, discriminated the Soviet activities and glorified the German technology. Do you consider yourself guilty in this?" **Prikask:** "Yes, I consider myself guilty in all of this" (Lindmäe, May 15, 1991, 7-8).

15. Lindmäe, May 15, 1991, 4.

16. We have such testimonies from the brother of the Rev. Konstantin Mägi, who was together with Martin Prikask in Siberia (Lindmäe, May 15, 1991, 5). But at the same time we have several stories, which are more like legends, from the people who came back from the Soviet concentration camps. The officials of Estonian Methodism tried to control some of these stories, and they were not true (people were not actually in the same concentration camp as Martin Prikask; in the midst of torture someone who preached the gospel seemed to them as Martin Prikask, etc.). So we need to do some more research to find these people who actually were together with Martin Prikask in the concentration camps or in the prisons.

17. Lindmäe, May 15, 1991, 8.

18. Lindmäe, May 15, 1991, 9.

19. Lindmäe, December 18, 1990, 1.

20. Lindmäe, May 15, 1991, 10.

21. Henno, 1.

22. Henno, 1.

23. Rev. Ewald Leps was interviewed by the author, August 8, 1991. At the time the Rev. Jaagupsoo was killed he was a Moravian lay preacher near Haapsalu, Estonia. In 1944 he escaped to the West and later became a United Methodist pastor in the United States. He died January 3, 1992.

24. Vello Salo, *Riik ja kirikud, 1940-1974* (State and the churches 1940-1941) (Rooma: Maarjamaa, 1974), 14. It is one of the best surveys of the church life in Estonia after World War II. The author is an Estonian Roman Catholic priest.

25. The report by the Rev. Jaan Puskay to the Board of the Methodist Church in Estonia. The manuscript is in the possession of the author.

9. Methodism in the Soviet Union Since World War II

1. "Methodism in the Soviet Union Since World War II," by Mark Elliott, *The Asbury Theological Journal* 46:1(1991): 5-47; pages 5-21 appear here. Edited and published by permission.

2. [This date is inaccurate. The earliest date for Methodism in Lithuania is 1900. The evangelical awakening or movement that spawned the independent congregation of baptized Lutherans, which joined the Methodist Church and became the first Methodist congregation in Lithuania (Kaunas or Kowno), did begin in the 1890s, but there was neither direct Methodist influence nor an official connection with Methodism until 1900/1901.]

3. J. Tremayne Copplestone, *History of Methodist Missions* (New York: Board of Global Ministries of The United Methodist Church, 1973), 4:366-72; Mark Elliott, "Methodism in Russia and the Soviet Union," *Modern Encyclopedia of Russian and Soviet History*, vol. 22 (Academic Press International, 1981); John Dunstan, "George A. Simons and *The Khristianski Pobornik*, A Neglected Source on St. Petersburg Methodism," *Methodist History* 19 (October 1980): 21-40.

4. K. Smolin, "Proshloe i nastoiashchee metodisma," *Nauka i religiia* no. 12(1974): 61; Dunstan, "Simons and Pobornik," 32; Heigo Ritsbek, "The Beginning of Methodism in Tsarist Russia (1859-1909)," unpublished paper, Asbury Theological Seminary (Spring 1990): 9, 11.

5. Ritsbek, "Beginning of Methodism," 17-18.

6. Ritsbek, "Beginning of Methodism," 18; *Eesti Metodisti Kiriku Kalender 1989* (Tallinn: Eesti Metodisti Kiriku, 1988), 13; Peter Stephens, *Methodism in Europe* (Cincinnati: The United Methodist Church, General Board of Global Ministries, 1981), 27.

7. Lorna and Michael Bourdeaux, *Ten Growing Soviet Churches* (Bromley, Kent: MARC Europe, 1987), 25-26; Elliott, "Methodism in Russia," 17; Heigo Ritsbek, "God at Work in Estonia," *Challenge to Evangelism Today* 23(Spring 1990): 8; "Report from Estonia, U.S.S.R.," *World Parish*, publication of the World Methodist Council 24 (September 1984): 3.

8. "Report from Estonia," *World Parish*, 3; *Eesti Metodisti Kalender*, 13; H. Eddie Fox, "The People of God in Estonia," *New World Outlook* 71 (October 1981): 28; Rauli Lehtonen, "Meth-

odists in the Soviet Union—Bridge Between East and West," unpublished paper delivered in Rome at Vatican Conference on Religious Liberty, March 1988, 1; author's interview with Heigo Ritsbek, July 15, 1990.

9. Arthur Võõbus, *The Martyrs of Estonia: The Suffering, Ordeal and Annihilation of the Churches Under the Russian Occupation* (Stockholm: Estonian Evangelical Lutheran Church, 1984), 41; *Eesti Metodisti Kalendar,* 13; Ritsbek, "God at Work," 8; Ritsbek, "The Methodist Church in Estonia Today," Wheaton Conference on Glasnost and the Church, June 14, 1990.

10. Philip Walters, *World Christianity: Eastern Europe* (Monrovia, Calif.: Missions Advanced Research Communication Center, 1988), 88.

11. Leonard Perryman, *United Methodist Information Service,* 15 March 1971; V. Voina, "Tysiasha granei odnoi problemy," *Nauka i religiia* No. 2 (1971): 22; Ritsbek interview, July 16, 1990. Letter from David Bridge to author, July 30, 1990. Harpenden Methodist Church with some 750 members has been for some years the largest British congregation.

12. Toivo U. Raun, *Estonia and the Estonians* (Stanford, Calif.: Hoover Institution Press, 1987), 168; Ole Borgen interview, January 28, 1970; Olav Pärnamets interview, April 8, 1990; Ritsbek interview, January 27, 1990.

13. "Reunion, Baltic and Slavic Refugee Pastors of the Methodist Church in the United States, Bay View, Mich., July 1-5, 1962," unpublished paper in author's possession.

14. Ritsbek interview, July 16, 1990.

15. "Reunion."

16. Pärnamets interview, March 4, 1989.

17. Ibid.

18. Leonard Perryman, World Methodist Conference press release, August 25, 1971.

19. Edward L. Tullis, *Shaping the Church from the Mind of Christ* (Nashville: The Upper Room, 1984): 48-49; David Bridge, "Estonian Diary," *Methodist Recorder* (January 24, 1985): 10-12; Bridge, "Obituary [Alexander Kuum]," *Methodist Recorder* (June 15, 1989): 18; Elliott, "Rõõmsad Teated! Good News in Estonia," *Good News* 15 (September/October 1981): 8, 11; Elliott, unpublished Soviet trip report, April 7, 1989; Steven O'Malley, unpublished Soviet trip report, 1988, 3; Pärnamets interview, March 4, 1989.

20. Alexander Kuum, "Superintendent's Circular Letter No. 75," Tallinn, Estonia, March 1979, 1; Bourdeaux, *Ten Growing Churches,* 27-28; Borgen interview, January 28, 1990; Ritsbek interviews, January 27 and July 16, 1990; Ritsbek, "God at Work," 8.

21. C. V. Elliott, "MWS&E Preaches in Soviet Estonia," *The Explorer* 21 (Winter 1989): 1; Bourdeaux, *Ten Growing Churches,* 34-35; Fox, "People of God," 29; Olav Pärnamets, "Superintendent's Circular Letter No. 76," Tallinn, Estonia, May 1979; Borgen interview, January 28, 1990.

22. "O missionerskoi i propovednicheskoi deiatel'nosti Estonskoi metodistskoi tserkvi," *Voprosy nauchnogo ateizma* 24 (Moscow: Mysl', 1979): 175; see also "Metodisty," *Slovar' ateizma,* (Moscow: 1964), 159-60. Western accounts following this Soviet lead include Bourdeaux, *Ten Growing Churches,* 29-30; Lehtonen, "Methodists in the Soviet Union," 2; "Looting from Churches Goes Unpunished," *The Guardian of Liberty* 24 (March-April, 1980). For an earlier Soviet commentary anxious over Estonian free church growth, including Methodists, see Vallo Salo, "The Struggle Between the State and the Churches" in Elmar Järvesoo and Tõnu Parming, eds., *A Case Study of a Soviet Republic: the Estonian SSR* (Boulder, Colo.: Westview Press, 1978): 210, quoting from a major atheist serial, *Nauka i religia.*

23. Borgen interview, January 28, 1990; Pärnamets interview, April 8, 1990; Ritsbek interview, January 27, 1990.

24. Bourdeaux, *Ten Growing Churches,* 22.

25. Borgen interview, January 28, 1990; Lehtonen, "Methodists," 4.

26. Borgen interview, January 28, 1990. See also Lehtonen, "Methodists in the Soviet Union," 4.

27. Borgen interview, January 28, 1990. See also Lehtonen, "Methodists in the Soviet Union," 3.

28. Ritsbek interview, January 27, 1990.

29. Borgen interview, January 28, 1990.

30. Ritsbek, "God at Work," 8; see also "The Chairman Interviews Leo and Ida Mondschein," *Euroflame* (January 1976): 6-7.

31. Michael Bourdeaux, "Letter to the Editor," *New Christian* (December 1, 1966): 17; Bourdeaux, *Ten Growing Churches*, 28.

32. Conversation with author, July 1981.

33. "Report from Estonia," *World Parish*, 3; see also Ritsbek, "God at Work," 18. Walter Sawatsky reports similar waves of growth in Baptist churches following the return of pastors from prison: *Soviet Evangelicals Since World War II* (Scottdale, Penn.: Herald Press, 1981), 64-65.

34. *Eesti Metodisti Kalendar*, 13.

35. Lehtonen, "Methodists in the Soviet Union," 2.

36. "O missionerski i propovendnicheskoi deiatel'nosti," 174, 172-73.

37. Lehtonen, "Methodists in the Soviet Union," 2; Peter Stephens, "The Methodist Church of Eastern Europe," *Religion in Communists Lands* 5 (Spring 1977): 17; Ritsbek, "God at Work," 8; Borgen interview, January 28, 1990.

38. Bourdeaux, "Letter to the Editor," 17.

39. Borgen interview, January 28, 1990.

40. Scott Wesley Brown interview, February 7, 1990; Ritsbek interview, July 13, 1990.

41. Brown interview, February 7, 1990; Bourdeaux, *Ten Growing Churches*, 22, 31, 40. (Selah is a designation in the Psalms for a musical interlude.)

42. Ritsbek, "God at Work," 8.

43. "O missionerskoi i propovendnicheskoi deiatel'nosti," 177; Stephens, "Methodist Church," 16.

44. On Herbert Murd see Bourdeaux, *Ten Growing Churches*, 22; Keston News Service 137 (November 19, 1981): 1-2; "Estonian Methodist Arrested," *Religion in Communist Lands* 8 (Winter 1980): 329; "Music and Ministry: Estonian Methodists," *Frontier* 1 (January-February 1987): 14. On Heigo Ritsbek see Douglas Ens, "Restrictions Force Estonian Pastor to Emigrate," *News Network International* (March 20, 1989): 16-17; Ritsbek, "God at Work," 8-9; Lehtonen, "Methodists in the Soviet Union," 3; Ritsbek interview, January 27, 1990.

45. Letter from Herman Will, United Methodist Division of World Peace, to Walter Sawatsky, October 30, 1973, "Methodist, U.S.S.R." file, Keston College Archives, Keston, England.

46. Moscow Patriarchate, *Conference in Defense of Peace of All Churches and Religious Associations in the U.S.S.R. Held in Troitse-Sergiyeva Monastery, Zagorsk on May 9-12, 1952* (Moscow: Moscow Patriarchate, n.d.), 16, 179-81. See also Bourdeaux, *Ten Growing Churches*, 26.

47. Letter from Heigo Ritsbek to Robert McClean, director of the Department of Peace and World Order, United Methodist Office for the United Nations, February 5, 1990. Copy in author's possession.

48. "Methodist Church in Russia," *Together* 7 (July 1963): 1; Ritsbek interview, July 19, 1990.

49. Pärnamets interview, March 4, 1989; Borgen interview, January 28, 1990; Ritsbek interview, July 16, 1990.

50. Perryman, *United Methodist Information Service*; Ritsbek interview, July 16, 1990. Heigo Ritsbek (January 27, 1990, interview) noted that Estonian emigrés purchased two cars for Kuum for Methodist work with Estonia.

51. Elliott, "Methodism in Russia," 18.

52. Kuum, "Circular Letter No. 75," 1-2.

53. Avril Bottoms, "Estonian Methodists Support Alcohol Fight," *Methodist Recorder* (August 15, 1985): 1, 13; Fox, "People of God," 30.

54. Borgen interview, January 38, 1990; Ritsbek interview, January 27, 1990.

55. A number of Scandinavian East European ministries are listed in Mark Elliott, ed., *East European Missions Directory* (Wheaton, Ill.: Institute for the Study of Christianity and Marxism, 1989). See also Mark Elliott, "In the Household of Faith," *Eternity* 37 (July/August 1986): 24-29.

56. Elliott, "Rõõmstad Teated," 8-12. Former Northern European Conference Bishop Ole Borgen began teaching at Asbury Theological Seminary in 1988.

57. M. Robert Mulholland, Jr., unpublished Soviet trip report, 1986; J. Steven O'Malley, unpublished Soviet trip report, 1988; David Seamands, unpublished Soviet trip report, fall 1989.

58. Hazel Carmalt-Jones, "A Warm Welcome in Uzhgorod," *Frontier* 6 (November-December 1988): 4-6. Services are in Russian for a mixed congregation of Russians, Ukrainians, Slovaks, and Hungarians (Ritsbek interview, July 19, 1990).

59. Pärnamets interview, March 4, 1989; Ritsbek interview, January 27, 1990. For critical discussions of the political orientation of U.S. United Methodist leadership see: Steven Beard, "Our Embarrassing Leftward Tilt," *Good News* 23 (January-February 1990): 18-20; Roy Howard Beck, *On Thin Ice: A Religion Reporter's Memoir* (Wilmore, Ky.: Bristol Books, 1988); James Heidinger II, "The United Methodist Church," in Ronald Nash, ed., *Evangelical Renewal in the Mainline Churches* (Westchester, Ill.: Crossway Books, 1987), 15-39; Edmund W. and Julia Robb, *The Betrayal of the Church: Apostasy and Renewal in the Mainline Denominations* (Westchester, Ill.: Crossway Books, 1986); George Weigel, *Must Walls Confuse?* (Washington D.C.: Institute on Religion and Democracy, 1981); and Robert L. Wilson, *Biases and Blind Spots: Methodism and Foreign Policy Since World War II* (Wilmore Ky.: Bristol Books, 1988). Supportive of the church's postwar political orientation are Peggy Billings, *Paradox and Promise in Human Rights* (New York: Friendship Press, 1979) and James E. Will, *Must Walls Divide? The Creative Witness of the Churches in Europe* (New York: Friendship Press, 1981).

60. Perryman, World Methodist Conference Press Release, August 25, 1971; Perryman, *United Methodist Information Service*, March 16, 1971; Heigo Ritsbek, "The Number of Organized Churches and Full Membership in the Methodist Churches in the U.S.S.R.," unpublished report, May 1990; Ritsbek interview, July 16, 1990. The Kärsa Methodist Church, registered in February 1990 with approximately thirty-five members, needs to be added to the tally in the Ritsbek report. Adding the single West Ukranian and single Komi A.S.S.R. churches, the total 1990 Methodist membership in the U.S.S.R. was 1,838.

61. Bottoms, "Estonian Methodists," 3. On several occasions the Rev. Pärnamets has asked visitors from Wilmore, Kentucky, to share with his people concerning the historic 1970 spontaneous revival at Asbury College: Mark Elliott in 1985 and David Seamands, professor of pastoral ministry, Asbury Theological Seminary, in 1989. In 1985 the Rev. Pärnamets commented with some feeling that of the various books given to him by the present writer, the one he most appreciated was Robert Coleman's account of the 1970 Asbury Revival, *One Divine Moment*.

62. Author's personal observations based on visits in 1981, 1985, and two in 1989; Lehtonen, "Methodists in the Soviet Union," 1; letters from David Bridge to Mark Elliott, February 1 and May 5, 1990; Borgen interview, January 28, 1990. See also Ritsbek, "God at Work," 8.

63. Letter from Bridge to Elliott, February 1, 1990; Ritsbek interviews, January 27 and July 16, 1990.

64. Ritsbek interview, January 27, 1990; Borgen interview, January 28, 1990. "Healthy competition from other churches," which Lorna and Michael Bourdeaux cite as a factor in Methodist growth, would apply generally for Estonia as a whole, but not for Tallinn in the 1970s, a decade that saw many youth move from the Methodist to the Baptist Church (see *Ten Growing Churches*, 39).

65. Ens, "Restrictions," 16-17; Toomas Pajusoo interview, July 9, 1989; Pärnamets interview, April 8, 1990; Ritsbek interviews, January 27 and July 19, 1990; Christine McLain, "Estonian Christian Views U.S.," *The Explorer* 22 (July/August 1990): 2.

66. Antonia Barbosa da Silva, "The 'Theology of Success' Movement: A Comment," *Themelios: An International Journal for Theological Students* 11 (April 1986): 91. More than thirty books by Kenneth Hagin have been translated into Estonian (Ritsbek interview, July 19, 1990).

67. World Without War Council, *Neformalniye: A Guide to Independent Organizations and Contacts in the Soviet Union*, (Seattle, Wash.: WWWC, 1990), 35; "A Singing Revolution," *Frontier* (November-December 1989): 21; Keston News Service 293, March 31, 1988, 9. Marite Sapiets has provided helpful treatment of the group's political orientation, except that it should not be described as a specifically Baptist movement ("The Baltic Churches and the National Revival," *Religion in Communist Lands* 18 [Summer 1990]: 162-63).

68. Pärnamets interview, March 4, 1989; Ritsbek interview, July 19, 1990; Endel Meiusi interview, February 1, 1990; Scott Wesley Brown interview, February 7, 1990.

69. Letter from Bishop Hans Växby to Elliott, February 6, 1990.

70. Ritsbek interview, January 27, 1990. A letter from Robert McClean to the author, January 26, 1990, expressed the same sentiment. The year referred to with five hundred guests was 1985.

71. Letter from Bridge to Elliott, February 1, 1990.

72. Ritsbek interview, January 27, 1990.

73. Ibid.

74. Donn Ziebell, Slavic Gospel Association, unpublished trip report, August 1987.

75. Fox, "People of God," 29.

76. "O missionerskoi i propovednicheskoi deiatel'nosti," 177.

77. Bourdeaux, *Ten Growing Churches*, 31.

78. Douglas Ens, "Estonians Receive Record Number of Bibles," *News Network International* (March 20, 1989): 15; Üllas Tankler, "Estland," unpublished report, November 1989. The author saw boxes of these Bibles in the Methodist headquarters building in Tallinn in March 1989.

79. Ritsbek, "Methodist Church," June 14, 1990. Rauli Lehtonen ("Methodists in the Soviet Union," 3) estimates the total number of Estonian Bibles published from 1945 to 1988 was 6,400. Even with the majority of these Bibles making their way into Estonia by unofficial means, the dramatic nature of 1988-1900 deliveries still obtains.

80. Glen Larum, "Estonian UMs Credit Growth to 'Hero of Faith,'" *United Methodist Reporter*, March 17, 1989, 1.

81. Urve Pärnamets, "The Role of Women in the Church in Estonia," Wheaton College Brown Bag Seminar, April 16, 1990. Heigo Ritsbek (July 19, 1990, interview) suggests that the "targeted mission activity" in child and youth evangelism fostered by Olav and Urve Pärnamets has been that family's "most wonderful contribution to Tallinn Methodists."

82. Tankler, "Estland," 13.

83. Rauli Lehtonen interview, March 10, 1989.

84. Ritsbek, "God at Work," 8; Ritsbek, "Methodist Church," June 14, 1990. This author attended a youth choir rehearsal on March 3, 1989, with twenty persons in attendance, ages fourteen to twenty-five.

85. Lehtonen interview, March 10, 1989.

86. Toomas Pajusoo interview, July 9, 1989.

87. Tankler, "Esland," 13.

88. David Seamands, unpublished Soviet trip report, August 1989, 5; Rick Bailey, "Young People of Estonia Hungry for Christianity," *Lexington Herald-Leader*, September 2, 1989, 32; Tankler, "Estland," 10; Ritsbek, "God at Work," 8.

89. Christine McLain, "Estonian Christian Views U.S.," 1-2.

90. Letter from Växby to Elliott, February 6, 1990; unpublished Pärnu building appeal letter signed by the Rev. Olav Pärnamets, September 9, 1989; letter from Bridge to Elliott, May 3, 1990; Ritsbek interview, January 27, 1990; Ritsbek, "God at Work," 8; C. V. Elliott, unpublished Soviet trip report, August 1988, 4.

91. United Methodist General Advance Special for Eastern Europe (01-09006-4A-N) may be used with funds designated for the Tallinn Church. In April 1990 the United Methodist General Board of Global Ministries approved forty-one fund-raising projects ("Advance Specials") for Eastern Europe totaling $2.6 million. George Cornell, "Local Missions Entering E. Europe," *Wheaton Daily Journal*, June 4, 1990, 5.

92. Urve Pärnamets, "Role of Women."

93. Fedor I. Federenko, *Sekty, ikh vera i dela* (Moscow: Izdatel'stvo Politicheskoi Literatury, 1965), 157.

10. Methodism Renewed but Never Abandoned

1. Near the time that the Methodist Episcopal Church and the Methodist Episcopal Church, South were beginning missions in Finland, Russia, and Manchuria, the Evangelical Church began missions to Latvia with goals closely related to those of Methodists.

2. See chapter 6 of this volume.

3. Ibid.

4. Ralph Diffendorfer, ed., *The World Service of the Methodist Episcopal Church* (Chicago: Methodist Book Concern, 1923), 220.

5. *The Missionary Voice* (September 1923): 260.

6. Some of aspects of the "ecumenical beginnings" have been discussed previously in chapter 6.

7. "Russian Church Thanks Methodists for Aid," *Christian Century* LXII (May 23, 1925): 709.

8. Report of the World Division Task Force on Developing Mission with European Central Conferences: "Church Development: Russia and Former Soviet Republics," (March 3, 1992): 1; henceforth cited as "Church Development: Russia."

9. The Rev. Kim is president of the Korean-American Mission Association to Russia. The association has cooperated with GBGM in the support, training, and sending of missionaries to countries of the CIS. The association also works with Korean-American United Methodist churches and the Korean Methodist Church in missionary assignments in the CIS.

10. The official registration by the Russian government took place on July 30, 1991.

11. The church has already extended its ministry through forming congregations in Moscow and Nabershnije Tschelny (Tartaria), Saint Petersburg, and Sevastopol (Crimea), and plans extension in Zlatoust (Ural); "Church Development: Russia."

12. See the "Proposal—European College of Bishops of The United Methodist Church and the United Methodist Council of Bishops in cooperation with the General Board of Global Ministries," October 5, 1991; revised October 14 and 18, 1991.

13. Text of letter provided by Dr. R. Bruce Weaver.

14. No. 250372-4. Later an Advance Special with the title "Russia Food/Medical Crisis" was established with the No. 250375-A.

15. "Church Development: Russia," 1.

16. Bishop Rüdiger Minor, "Report on My First Trip," (Moscow/Dresden) January 23, 1992: 3.

17. "Church Development: Russia."

18. Ibid., 3-4

19. *General Board of Global Ministries 1991 Annual Report*, 6.

20. It has been reported that seven congregations of the "Methodist tradition" have been established in Saint Petersburg due, in part, to evangelist Bruce Ingles, "who formerly worked with the Mission Society for United Methodists in Latin America. A representative of the Overseas Division of the Methodist Church in the United Kingdom has been contacted to assist with leadership training, and a local Russian organizing pastor/supervisor has been identified." "Church Development: Russia."

21. Letter from W. James White, March 14, 1994.

22. The "Connecting Congregations" from other countries are listed within the parentheses.

23. On the beginning of the work of GBGM's Health and Welfare Ministries Program Department in Kazahkstan during April 1993, see the section, "Outreach in Kazahkstan."

24. UMCOR program department document "Special Grant Request, January 1993."

25. Personal communiqué to S T Kimbrough, Jr., April 6, 1994.

26. Ibid.

27. Text supplied by Dr. F. Thomas Trotter, personal correspondence of June 8, 1994.

28. *Contact* [Published for Alumni and Friends of Alaska Pacific University], 5:4 (Winter 1994): 1.

29. According to Bishop Minor's "Third Report: trip to Estonia, Russia, and Poland, March 19-26, 1992," the congregation consisted of about nineteen members at the time.

30. "The Story of Fritz Hervarth," from the newsletter of the United Methodist Church of South Yarmouth, Massachusetts, (p.3) provided through a letter from the church's pastor, the Rev. Roger A. Davis, to Dr. W. James White, area secretary for Europe of GBGM.

31. Report of February 3, 1994.

32. Ibid., 2-3.

33. Cathie Lyons, "Come by Here, Lord—Healing Ministries in the Commonwealth of Independent States," unpublished manuscript (October 1993): 9. As of April 1994, UMCOR and Health and Welfare Ministries cooperatively have secured and delivered some $5.5 million worth of medicines, general hospital supplies, and equipment to countries of the former Soviet Union.

34. Konrad Reiser, *Ecumenism in Transition: A Paradigm Shift in the Ecumenical Movement?* (Geneva: World Council of Churches, 1991).

35. Lesslie Newbigin, "Ecumenical Amnesia," *International Bulletin of Missionary Research* 18:1 (January 1994): 4.

36. *Methodist History* 18:4 (1980): 239-61.

37. Bishop Rüdiger R. Minor, "Report to the United Methodist Council of Bishops presented at its fall meeting 1992, Epworth by the Sea, St. Simon's Island, October 31-November 5, 1992," 4.

38. Ibid., 7-8.

39. "A Farther Appeal to Men of Reason and Religion," Part One, in Gerald B. Cragg, ed., Oxford Edition of *The Works of John Wesley*, vol. 2, 106.

40. *Short Hymns on Select Passages of the Holy Scriptures* (Bristol: Farley, 1762): 1:57, No. 283, stanza 2.

41. Noreen Dunn Tatum, *A Crown of Service* (Nashville: Parthenon Press, 1960), 217.

Epilogue

1. "Sister Anna of Petrograd," by Roger Prentiss, *The Christian Advocate* (March 16, 1922): 328-39.

2. End of the article.

3. *Christlicher Apologete* (1925): 465.

Timeline

1. See the anonymous article, "The Historical Facts of the Siberia-Manchuria Mission," *The Missionary Voice* (August 1922): 231.

2. Ibid.

3. Abbreviated throughout as UMC.

INDEX

Printed in the United States
138106LV00002B/79/P

9 780687 006007